Applied Design Patterns in Software Development

Applied Design Patterns in Software Development

Willem Forcucci

KNOWLEDGE
BAKERS

KNOWLEDGE BAKERS

Cataloging in Publication Data--DK
Courtesy: D.K. Agencies (P) Ltd. <docinfo@dkagencies.com>

Forcucci, Willem, author.
Applied design patterns in software development / Willem Forcucci.
pages cm
Includes bibliographical references and index.
ISBN 9788194483021

1. Software patterns. 2. Computer software--Development. I. Title.

LCC QA76.76.P37F67 2020 | DDC 005.1 23

ISBN 978-81-944830-2-1

9 788194 483021

Published by : **Knowledge Bakers**
Pune, India

Digitally Printed at : **Replika Press Pvt. Ltd.**

Preface

The notion of 'pattern' originates in the work of Christopher Alexander and, in recent years, patterns have become a popular part of software development. A pattern is defined as a 'three-part rule': a relationship between a given context, a recurring system of forces peculiar to that context, and a specific spatial configuration that permits the resolution of these forces. In essence, the 'context' of a pattern is the whole system under construction and its state in the construction process at the point at which the pattern is being applied. The nature of the context, therefore, changes at every step of the process and this has significant implications for how patterns should be used. Specifically, applying each pattern changes the context by changing the state of the system under construction and creates both a new design problem and a new context for the next pattern to be applied. The next picked pattern must have certain criteria for it to be applied successfully and this is will be determined by the characteristics of the new context just created. The issue of composing pattern sequences is, therefore, more temporal than it is static and structural (as provided currently via pattern maps). The decision as to which one to use is temporally constrained in the sense that the choice is made only at a particular point in the construction process of some specific system, and may well be determined, or at least further constrained, by the current state of that system.

The fundamental research question that is addressed here is: how is this dynamically changing context to be presented to guide pattern applications?

In this book, a framework is presented to provide a systematic analysis of the composition of pattern applications in terms of the properties of their context. Such an approach will reveal the ordering of patterns in space and time dimensions. Examples of composition of pattern applications include: One pattern contains or generalizes another smaller-scale pattern (this will be called in book refinement); Two patterns are complementary, i.e., one pattern needs the other to be applied before (Sequential Order); Two patterns solve different problems that overlap and coexist on the same level (Parallel Order), and Two patterns solve the same problem in alternative, but equally valid ways (Choice in Order).

At the design phase, the framework provides mechanisms for analysing the choice of composition to ensure the correctness of a design or to compare two different designs or to modify an existing design.

This framework describes a pattern's context via a pair of constraints, known as Assumption and Commitment. In general, the Assumption is a constraint placed on the context and the Commitment is what the solution provided by the pattern commits to after the pattern's application. In addition, the book provides a set of composition rules that can be applied to aid in the analysis of the application of pattern sequences.

Finally, I, the author is grateful to the publisher and its staff for their kind co-operation and for bringing the book through publications.

It is hoped that this effort will help the readers in their endeavours. All the suggestions in making the book further information are always welcome.

Willem Forcucci

Contents

CHAPTER 1

Introduction

1.1 General Background

The notion of 'pattern' and 'pattern language' originates in the work of Christopher Alexander [1, 2], an architect who proposed the use of collections of architectural patterns to address deficiencies in modern building design. In later works, Alexander expanded the scope of his rather interesting concept of patterns to a broader design context [30].

In recent years, patterns have become popular in software development [3, 18, 23, 40, 42, 44, 65, 78]. From an original concern with generic design patterns, the systems-building communities have subsequently evolved analysis patterns [18, 40, 53], process patterns [8, 9], organisational patterns [27, 28, 29, 48], architectural patterns [1] and web usability patterns [44, 45], to name but a few. Patterns have increasingly been referred to as open standards, most recently, in The Open Group Architecture Framework, edition 9, for example [85].

A pattern is defined as a 'three-part rule': a relationship between a given context, a recurring system of forces peculiar to that context, and a specific spatial configuration that permits resolution of these forces. In his most recent work, Alexander [4, 5, 6, 7], says very little about patterns *per se*. Rather he talks about the quality of 'wholeness' in successful natural organisms and formations and in 'good design'. Wholeness comes from the organization of mutually-related centres in harmony with each other, [63]. This raises the question as to whether this shift in emphasis in Alexander's thinking requires a change in the Pattern movement's understanding of the definition of a pattern. If Kavanagh, [63] is right, there certainly seems to be a shift in emphasis from a pattern implying a structure to implying the process by which the structure is constructed. In retrospect, however, this might not be such a big shift after all. Coplien has, in the past, already argued that a pattern is both a 'thing' and the set of instructions by which that thing can be created [25]. It is, therefore, reasonable from the point of view of this study to consider the three-part rule to be the established definition of a pattern and it is therefore the one that will be used for the purpose of the research. Having said that, it is interesting to note an evolution of the definition in which the notion of 'context' has become more and more important. Software patterns originated as a two-part rule in which context was ignored (at least as part of the *definition* of a pattern), and was subsequently replaced by the three- part definition. In essence, the 'context' of a pattern is the whole system under construction and its state in the construction process at the point at which the pattern is being applied. A pattern is thus a phenomenon, a rule creating that phenomenon and the specification of the time at which that phenomenon must occur. "It is both a process and a thing; both a description of a thing which is alive, and a description of the process which will generate that thing" [26]. The description of the "thing" lies in the realm of problem specification, whilst the process of "generating the thing" is the concern of its derivation or implementation. The nature of the context changes at every step of the process and this has significant implications for how patterns should be used.

Specifically, applying each pattern changes the context by changing the state of the system under construction and creates both a new design problem and a new context for the next pattern to be applied. The next picked pattern must fulfil certain criteria in order for it to be applied successfully and this will be determined by the characteristics of the new context just created. The difficult question is: how is this dynamically changing 'context information' to be represented to guide the developer/builder? This is indeed the fundamental research question that this book is addressing.

In which order to apply patterns, plus adjacent patterns, is important to the right use of a pattern language: but this is mostly determined by the specific context supplied by the current state of the system in the building process. This is mainly why the key problem of composing pattern is more temporal and dynamic than it is static and structural. In so far as pattern languages particular sequences are suggested, for example through a patterns map, they can only refer to these structural relations, those that can be inferred in advance independently of any specific system or context. For example, a large pattern and a smaller pattern can be shown to be reliant on each other in the sense that the smaller pattern always, or at nearly always, refines the larger pattern. This sort of dependency implies that the use of a smaller pattern should not come before the larger pattern. However, current representations of patterns have no way of capturing or presenting the detailed contextualization required for the actual construction of a specific system. Very often, even in current maps a pattern at one 'level' may be connected to two or more patterns at the next lower level. The decision as to which one to use is temporally constrained in the sense that the choice is made only at a particular point in the construction process of some specific system, and may well be determined, or at least further constrained, by the current state of that system. Add to this the further complication of multiple variants for the implementation of any given pattern, and it can be seen that something considered as a set of instructions to build something *specific,* then the current forms of Pattern Languages are inadequate. They leave out entirely these dynamic aspects. This will need more investigation because, as mentioned earlier, the key problem of composing pattern languages is more temporal than structural. Pattern sequences present one way of making logic of the popular notion of compound patterns [77, 90]. From the perspective of pattern sequences, compound patterns can be considered as an identifiable and general sequence of patterns that can be considered as a whole with reference to the problem it concentrates on and the design it accomplishes [54].

1.2 Research Questions

The book research context is the design of software engineering systems using patterns. The scope of the research is in the analysis, verification and modification of software system design. The research facilitates for the software system designer the use and application of patterns.

The main aim of this research is:

To provide a framework for pattern applicability, within which the patterns' applicability can be analysed compositionally. In particular:

Q1. How to facilitate the applicability of patterns?

Q2. How can designers be aided in the construction of pattern sequences?

Q3. How can the applicability relationships between patterns be described more rigorously?

1.3 Research and Validation Methods

The research methodology follows a typical software engineering approach [43, 46, 55]. The approach has the following phases:

Phase 1: Critical Review of Literature

This has been achieved and given in chapter 2. The review concentrated on patterns, pattern catalogues, pattern languages and sequences. This results in the identification and articulation of the research questions 1.2 which are considered by this work.

Phase 2: Establish Assumption/Commitment Framework

A framework is introduced to facilitate the applicability of patterns. The framework is initially evaluated using some small case studies. The framework is fully described in chapter 3.

Phase 3: Establishment of Pattern Connectors

The framework requires a set of operators that are used during the application process of patterns. These operations are Sequence, Choice and Parallel. These operators and their role in the framework are discussed in chapters 4.

Phase 4: Evaluation

To investigate the usefulness of the framework two case studies are conducted that use a set of patterns from Ian Graham's Web Usability (WU) pattern bank and Welie's User Interface (UI) pattern bank.

1.4 Success Criteria

So how does one know whether the framework facilitates the applicability of patterns during the system design? What are key elements in a particular design?

The key design elements should include the following:

- The ability of the designer to apply patterns to solve a particular problem.
- The ability of the designer to detect design errors.
- The ability of the designer to modify an existing design to enhance the functionality of a system.

The case studies will be used to check whether the framework provide these three elements to the designer.

1.5 Book Structure

The following describes the structure of the rest of the book:

Chapter 2: Patterns and Their Applicability

This chapter provides a critical review of the literature relevant to patterns, catalogues, pattern languages, pattern sequences and the challenges posed by the state of this literature.

Chapter 3: Compositional Framework for Pattern Applicability

This chapter gives an overview of the framework for the analysis of pattern applicability. It introduces the constraints (via Assumption/ Commitment) that are imposed on the solution and its context. Furthermore it discusses how these constraints influence the applicability of patterns. The Assumption/Commitment informs/constrains the applicability of the next pattern.

Chapter 4: Operators

The framework requires a set of operations that are used during the pattern application process. This chapter will introduce them and their role in the framework.

Chapter 5: Case studies

In this chapter two case studies are conducted using two set of patterns (WU and UI). These case studies will be used to investigate the usefulness of the framework, i.e., whether it provides the three key design elements to the designer.

Chapter 6: Conclusions

This chapter summarises the present work's research. It highlights the potential applicability of the contributions that have been made. Furthermore a critical review of the contribution is given. Finally, the possible research and development directions that are based on the presented results are discussed.

CHAPTER

2

Patterns and their Applicability

2.1 Introduction

The chapter begins with a brief explanation of the notion of a pattern and its background, showing why people currently use patterns and what these patterns consist of. This chapter will also explore some of the essential aspects of pattern catalogues, pattern languages and pattern sequences, in order to highlight some unclarities in current understanding and to draw out the unfolding importance of the idea of 'context'.

In particular this chapter explores the concepts of:

- Patterns
- Architecture, Design and Code Patterns
- Pattern Catalogues
- Pattern Languages
- Patterns Description Format
- Pattern Formalisation

2.2 Pattern Based Software Development

Patterns have - in the course of less than fifteen years - risen from being the concern of a minority group within the object-oriented programming community to a mainstream concern of a number of domains within information sciences and software engineering. From an original concern with generic design patterns, the systems-building communities have subsequently evolved analysis patterns [18, 40, 53], process patterns [8, 9], organisational patterns [27, 28, 29, 48], architectural patterns [1] and web usability patterns [44, 45], to name but a few. Patterns have increasingly been referred to as open standards, most recently, in The Open Group Architecture Framework, edition 9, for example [85]. All of this is testimony that patterns are increasingly a 'mainstream' rather than peripheral concern of the computer systems-building world.

Nevertheless this growth of interest has been uneven across domains and, perhaps inevitably given its rapidity, resulted in an uneveness in understanding as well. It is worth reviewing a brief history of 'software patterns' (the book will use this as an umbrella term covering all related domains, and to distinguish them from patterns of the built environment) movement.

Patterns do not originate in software. Christopher Alexander, widely acknowledged as one of the foremost building and urban planning architects of the previous century [37], first introduced the concept of patterns. He studied mathematics and architecture at Cambridge University and later obtained a Ph.D. in architecture from Harvard. His published corpus, of more than one hundred articles and monographs, encapsulate the development for which he is best known. He wrote several books on patterns in urban planning and architecture [1, 2] in which he was the first to note that certain types of problem call for the same types of solution, types which he called 'patterns' which, when combined (connected), form 'pattern languages'. He made this observation regarding the creation of towns and neighbourhoods, houses, gardens and rooms' in his own field of architecture [1]. The characteristic of patterns is the idea "that *you can use this solution a million times over, without ever doing it the same way twice*" [1].

Since the mid-1990s (i.e., some twenty years after Alexander first published his ideas on patterns), patterns and pattern languages have spawned from architecture and building into the realm of computer technology.

The first introduction to patterns for the software development community came via a paper presented by Kent Beck and Ward Cunningham in the ACM Object-Oriented Programming Systems, Languages and Applications (OOPSLA) conference in 1987 [13]. In that paper, they demonstrated the utility of patterns in designing applications implemented in the Smalltalk programming language.

It was, however, another five years before the penetration of Alexander's ideas took a qualitative step forward. The OOPSLA conferences of 1992 and 1993 both held workshops on the creation of a handbook of software architecture, hosted by Bruce Anderson and Peter Coad. Coad reintroduced Alexander's ideas for discussion, and at the second of these workshops managed to spark the interest of four people who became widely known in the object-oriented community as 'The Gang of Four' - an affectionate collective name for the authors (Erich Gamma, Richard Helm, Ralph Johnson and John Vlissides) of the highly influential book, Design Patterns - elements of reusable object-oriented software [42] which was first published on the web in 1994 and in print the following year.

The Gang of Four (GoF) published some twenty three patterns in three categories ('creational', 'structural' and 'behavioural') that they had found in a number of successful object-oriented frameworks and which seemed therefore to be characteristic of good design. Their book was published in what might be considered the embryonic period of object-oriented development (1997 is generally identified as its year of 'breakthrough' into the computer systems industry) when the computer programming community in particular was looking for evidence of best practice on which it could construct a knowledge-base for the disciplines of object- oriented design and construction.

The GOF book remains a best-seller fourteen years after its first print, but the OOPSLA workshops triggered parallel developments of equal, or perhaps even greater significance. A mountain retreat sponsored by Kent Beck and Grady Booch in August 1993 in Colorado [9, 13], turned out to be the first meeting of what became known as the Hillside Group. The Hillside Group was formed from attendees at those OOPSLA workshops. It was so-named because a dozen or so of them met on a hillside to experiment with Alexander's techniques to design a building. Many became pattern authors who worked to lay down the foundations for the format and use of design patterns in software, and to become the facilitating organization of the worldwide Patterns Movement. The group built on the work by Gamma and his colleagues, and on the patterns of Alexander, and held the first Pattern Languages of Programming (PLoP) conference in 1994. The proceedings of this conference were published in the same year as Pattern Languages of Program Design (PLoPD), and may be regarded as the starting point for a body of literature that is considered to be 'owned' by the Patterns Movement. There have been five volumes of PLoPD published in subsequent years by Addison Wesley [23, 52, 68, 69, 89] and the Hillside Group uses the royalties to fund, amongst other things, the conferences of the Patterns Movement world-wide, notably PLoP [60] and EuroPLoP [61].

The format of these broadly follows the lines of the original PLoP. The proceedings are not the text of papers which have been submitted to the conference, but are the output of the conference after each pattern has been through a Pattern Writers' Workshop. In a format suggested by Richard Gabriel, a leading member of the original Hillside Group, and borrowed from the widespread practice of poetry circles, pattern papers were peer- reviewed by other pattern authors, and the strengths and weaknesses of the patterns discussed with suggestions for change being made to the paper's author. Patterns' papers which have gone through this process have a reputation for undergoing one of the most stringent peer-reviews known in either the academic or industrial worlds.

The Communications of the ACM's special issue on software patterns was symptomatic of the object-oriented community's increasing espousal of pattern languages in the early 1990s [82]. This community has used them in the production and re-use of high quality programming constructs, to the extent that there are now annual conferences, mailing lists, websites [10, 51, 56, 57, 58, 59, 60, 61] and books [23, 42, 44, 52, 78] whose focus is on the use of patterns in object-oriented software design. Since then, literally hundreds of patterns have been published through the PLoP conferences and thousands more (probably only a minority of which, it should be said, have gone through the Pattern Writers' Workshops) have been published in academic papers, professional series' books and on websites.

The following extract, taken from the website of the software Patterns Movement [57] which is hosted by Hillside, summarises what appears to be the current consensus about patterns amongst software developers:

> *"Patterns are the recurring solutions to the problems of design. People learn patterns by seeing them and recall them when need be without a lot of effort. Patterns link together in the mind so that one pattern leads to*

another and another until familiar problems are solved. That is, patterns form languages, not unlike natural languages, within which the human mind can assemble correct and infinitely varied statements from a small number of elements"[57].

An important challenge that the book concern with here is the process by which one pattern is chosen to follow another until the problem is resolved. The choice of a pattern depends on the context (or environment) of the problem. The application of the pattern will result in a new context which dictates the choice and selection of other patterns. The changes in context represent dynamisms that characterises the choices and applicability of patterns to solve a given problem. Such dynamism needs to be studied and analyse so as to increase the successful choices and applications of patterns.

However, it seems that the computing industry has still not completely grasped Alexander's intentions. In a keynote speech to the 1996 OOPSLA convention in San Jose, California that might have been anticipated as the final fusion of the visions of architectural and software design Alexander himself simultaneously praised the then infant Patterns Movement for its creative use of the pattern form, but also criticized it for 'missing the point' [3]. Mary Lynn Manns in her doctoral book has drawn attention to the fact that patterns and pattern languages have not been incorporated into software development, as was expected even by the Patterns Movement let alone by Alexander [66]. She does acknowledge that although the use of patterns is often encouraged by managements, it is only to the extent of supporting individuals to acquire private pattern knowledge, the domain of advanced programmers or developers, rather than being accepted as a universal culture of design. There seems, therefore, despite the widespread adoption of patterns, to be some confusion about the essential idea of what a pattern is that contributes in some way to a less than effective usage of them in practice.

Software patterns have been described in a number of ways by figures in the Patterns Movement. From a programming perspective, the GoF state that *"Patterns identify and specify abstractions that are above the level of single classes and instances, or of components."* [42]. Fowler, in his book on analysis patterns [40] talks more generally of an *"an idea that has been useful in one practical context and will probably be useful in others."* While both these statements are true, neither quite adds up to what might be an acceptable definition of a pattern.

GoF quote selectively from Alexander, including the following

"Each pattern describes a problem which occurs over and over again in our environment, and then describes the core of the solution to that problem, in such a way that you can use this solution a million times over, without ever doing it the same way twice"[42].

This has led to a widespread acceptance of the idea that a pattern is a general solution to a recurring problem, in other words, it is a problem- solution pair. However, this is too wide a definition to be useful, and the second part of the quotation highlights the issue. In the GoF book, for example, a number of variations of implementation are suggested for most of the patterns, and the choice is not an arbitrary one. In most cases, the choice depends upon the existing state of the system. The pattern gives a general design approach to a problem, but more design work needs to be done for this 'solution' to be fit for purpose. This contrasts with, for example, the notion of a software component which might also be seen to fit the problem-solution couplet definition. Daniels defines a component as an independent unit of deployment and reuse [21]. In other words, it is context-free. A pattern's use, on the other hand, is context-specific. This is not a theological difference, it has practical implications. In one widely known example template collaborations in UML (i.e., visual design 'components') have been explicitly confused with patterns [14]. The problem is that while template collaborations or indeed anything that could rightfully be described as a component can be 'plugged in' as-is to an emerging solution a pattern clearly cannot. This understanding appears to be crucial to the proper and productive use of patterns in design.

In fact, the Patterns Movement itself has been at pains to make the distinction. Gabriel has reminded the Movement that for Alexander, "*Each pattern is a three-part rule, which expresses a relation between a certain context, a problem, and a solution*" [2]. For Alexander, in his publications in the 'seventies at least, the phenomenon 'pattern' is a relationship between a given context, a recurring system of forces peculiar to that context, and a specific spatial configuration that permits resolution of these forces. More recently, a study of his work by Maria Kavanagh claims to find an evolution of this idea [63]. In his most recent work, The Nature of Order [4,5,6,7], Alexander says very little about patterns *per se*. Rather he talks about the quality of 'wholeness' in successful natural organisms and formations and in 'good design'. Wholeness comes from the organization of mutually-related centres in harmony with each other, and Kavanagh argues that the very strong implication of this is that patterns are "rules for creating [these] centres" [63]. This raises the question as to whether this shift in emphasis in Alexander's thinking requires a change in the Pattern Movement's understanding of the definition of a pattern. If Kavanagh is right, there certainly seems to be a shift in emphasis from a pattern implying a structure to implying the process by which the structure is constructed. In retrospect, however, this might not be such a big shift after all. Coplien has, in the past, already argued that a pattern is both a 'thing' and the set of instructions by which that thing can be created [25]. Certainly, in the four years since the Kavanagh book was published, no discernible shift in the thinking of the Patterns Movement is noticeable. It is, therefore, reasonable from the point of view of this study to consider the three-part rule to be the established definition of a pattern and it is therefore the one that will be used for the purpose of the research.

Having said that, it is interesting to note an evolution of the definition in which the notion of 'context' has become more and more important. Software patterns originated as a two-part rule in which context was ignored (at least as part of the *definition* of a pattern), and was subsequently replaced, after some debate it must be said, by Gabriel's three-part definition. Kavanagh - and by inference, Alexander - is now giving even greater importance to context. Without going into the details of her book the nub is that the 'context' of a pattern is the "whole" system under construction and its state in the construction process at the point at which the pattern is being applied. It is important to make it clear that designing a system should not be taken in isolation.

A pattern is thus a phenomenon, a rule creating that phenomenon and the specification of the time at which that phenomenon must occur. "It is both a process and a thing; both a description of a thing which is alive, and a description of the process which will generate that thing" [26]. The description of the "thing" lies in the realm of problem specification, whilst the process of "generating the thing" is the concern of its derivation or implementation. Therefore the book do not need to change the basic, three-part definition of a pattern but it should be noted, especially from the perspective of this research, the enlarged importance of 'context' within that definition (i.e. The nature of the context changes at ever step of the process): as it will be notice in the following sections of this chapter, and in subsequent chapters, this has significant implications for how patterns should be used.

2.3 Architecture, Design and Code Patterns

Because design patterns provide common solutions to recurring design problems, they feature heavily in the design of complex systems using object-oriented methods. Patterns enable designers to break a system down into groups of cooperating objects without needing to find the relationships between those objects. In fact, the unconscious employment of pattern in the form of the reuse of class relationships and object collaborations in design is extremely common. Such patterns have existed for some time; the first, and probably still the best, pattern collection for common design problems, the GoF's *Design Patterns: Elements of Reusable Object- Oriented Software*, was published in 1995.

Design patterns make it much easier for designers to share their designs by providing them with a common language, so that they can simply refer to a particular design (e.g. Bridge Pattern) without having to explain the elements of the class relationships involved. *Design Patterns* set out the requirements: when a particular problem recurs in object- oriented systems, a design pattern names a design that deals with this problem, describes the circumstances which give rise to it, and explains it, as well as describing the problem and its solution, when that solution should be used, and the results when it is. It also provides programmers with hints and tips as well as illustrations as to how to implement the solution, which is a general arrangement of objects and classes that solve the problem. Design patterns are tailored for a particular problem in its context [42].

The GoF's book defines design patterns as "descriptions of communicating objects and classes that are customised to solve a general design problem in a particular context." It goes on:

> *A design pattern names, abstracts, and identifies the key aspects of a common design structure that make it useful for creating a reusable object-oriented design. The design pattern identifies the participating classes and their instances, their roles and collaborations, and the distribution of responsibilities. Each design pattern focuses on a particular object-oriented design problem or issue. It describes when it applies, whether or not in can be applied in view of other design constraints, and the consequences and trade-offs of its use. Since we must eventually*

implement our designs, a design pattern also provides sample ... code to illustrate an implementation. Although design patterns describe object-oriented designs, they are based on practical solutions that have been implemented in mainstream object-oriented programming languages...[42].

Despite the fact that this description was intended to apply to object- oriented design, with some slight modifications it could be used to describe any software pattern. Because of the book's primacy in the software development community, the term "design pattern" is more widely used for any pattern that deals with matters relating to software architecture, design or programming implementation. These conceptual levels are sometimes classified into architectural patterns, design patterns and idioms (or coding patterns). *Pattern-oriented Software Architecture – A System of Patterns (POSA1)* [18] defines these thus:

1. Architectural Patterns

These define the basic organisational principles or schema for software systems. They consist of a set of predefined subsystems and indicate what functions these must perform, as well as providing rules and guidelines regulating their interrelationships.

2. Design Patterns

These are mid-level, and consist of designs for refining a software system's subsystems or components. They exemplify the concept of pattern elaborated above, describing recurring structures common to the interrelating components described in 1. These structures can be used to solve design problems with reference to their contexts.

3. Idioms (or coding patterns)

Operating at the lowest level of programming languages, idioms use the features of particular languages to describe the means by which specific elements of components and their relationships are implemented.

These three types of pattern operate at different levels of abstraction and detail. The first type deals with large scale components and a system's general properties and procedures. Their implementation would affect a software system's structure and organisation. Design patterns have no effect on system structure; rather, they define micro-architectures inherent in subsystems, their constituent elements and the interrelationships between them. Idioms are specific to certain paradigms and languages, and complete the lowest level of a component's structure and behaviour.

Design patterns initially attracted the attention of the software community. Gamma et al [42], describe the object-oriented type of design pattern. These are not the only kinds of pattern in software, however; they appear in every aspect of software, including:

1. development organisation
2. software process
3. project planning
4. requirements engineering
5. software configuration

Organisational and other types of pattern are gaining in popularity over design patterns. The following are just some of the possible categories into which software patterns can fall [12]:

1. Design patterns: patterns in software engineering
2. Analysis patterns: patterns that describe recurring and reusable analysis models
3. Organisation patterns: patterns that describe software process design
4. Other domain-specific patterns

A conceptual pattern, tailored to a specific application domain, uses concepts from that domain in its description. Design patterns use software design constructs such as objects, classes, inheritance, aggregation and reuse relationships, and programming patterns use programming language constructs.

In [77] Reihle and Zullighoven give a somewhat different classification of software patterns. They identify three types of software pattern: conceptual, design and programming patterns. These are similar to the types introduced by the authors of *Pattern-oriented Software Architecture – A System of Patterns (POSA1)* [18].

These types deal with successively greater levels of detail. The first type is based upon metaphors in specified application domains, the second implements elements of the first, and the third deals with the last level of detail using a stipulated implementation language.

Comparing the POSA1 and Reihle and Zullighoven definitions, some similarities become apparent. What the latter calls programming patterns, the former calls idioms. The POSA1 authors identify patterns by their architectural scope, while the other two decide on the origin of their language, from the problem or from the solution.

2.4 Pattern Catalogues and Pattern Languages

The GoF book contained, as mentioned previously, a collection of 23 discrete patterns which could, largely, be used stand alone. Many papers published at the PLoP conferences contain just a single pattern. In fact, the GoF book contained a graphic called a pattern map which joined some of the patterns together with arrowed vectors and labelled the relationships. Quite separately, they also produced a categorization of the 23 patterns which classified them in two dimensions. Each pattern was classified as either a 'Creational', 'Structural' or 'Behavioral' pattern and then also as a 'Class' pattern or as an 'Object' pattern (The Adapter pattern, for example, had variants of each of these last two divisions). Buschman et al., in a taxonomy that has gained wide acceptance in the Patterns have classified different kinds of pattern collections that acquire varying degrees of structure and relations into pattern catalogues, pattern systems, and pattern languages [18, 80]. The GoF book [42] is an example of a Pattern Catalogue according to this classification which is described as follows:

A *Pattern Catalogue* is a collection of correlated patterns. They are possibly only informally or loosely related or part of a group. It usually subdivides the patterns into a small number of wide categories or groups and may include some amount of cross referencing between patterns [18, 12]. As was just stated, the Design Patterns book is an example of a patterns catalogue [42].

A *System of Patterns* is an interrelated set of associated patterns which work together to maintain the creation and evolution of whole architectures. Not only is it arranged into associated groups and subgroups at various levels of granularity, it describes the many interdependencies between the patterns and their groupings and how they may be used together solve more compound problems. The patterns in a pattern system should all be described in a dependable and standardized style and need to cover a suitably broad base of problems and solutions to allow considerable portions of whole finished architectures to be constructed [18]. The next section of this chapter will discuss the significance of 'standardized styles'.

According to Buschman *et al.*, a pattern catalogue shows a degree of arrangement and association to a pattern collection, but does not generally go very much further than showing only the most apparently noticeable relationships and structure. A pattern system adds loaded pattern relations, profound structure, and uniformity to a pattern catalogue. A pattern system can be considered as a coherent collection of patterns about a topic that is usually, but not necessarily, very broad. The so-called POSA (Patterns of Software Architecture) patterns of Buschman and his colleagues would seem to fall in this category [18].

The final category to be discussed here is that of a Pattern Language. In many ways it is the most challenging of these categories. Christopher Alexander first presented patterns in a book called *A Pattern Language* which contained 253 patterns for the built environment [1]. In a companion volume, *The Timeless Way of Building* he makes it clear that, from his perspective, a pattern can only exist in the context of a Pattern Language [2]. It is clear then, that there is a big difference in the conception of software patterns as held by the Patterns Movement and that of Alexander himself, in that for Alexander' only one kind of pattern collection exists - the Pattern Language. In contrast, the Patterns Movement tolerates standalone patterns, pattern catalogues and pattern systems as well. This may be part of the reason why Alexander claimed in 1996 that the software Patterns Movement had missed the point. A deeper examination of the notion of Pattern Languages may give greater insights as to the challenges posed in the Introduction to this book can be addressed.

Pattern Languages are not formed all at once and this is may be the most important difference between pattern languages and pattern systems. They may develop from pattern systems through the process of piecemeal growth (and a pattern system may, in turn, develop from a pattern catalogue in a similar way). So just as pattern languages help to increasingly grow complete architectures, pattern systems may serve to increasingly grow into complete pattern languages.

Patterns may be designed to operate on their own or in a pattern group. They can also be part of the next step, a pattern language. DeLano [32], says that patterns are grouped by subject, and that because the groupings are open, new patterns can be added to them. Incidentally, Kavanagh creates a parallel concept of 'focus' in her guidance as to how to use patterns in construction [63]. More formalised pattern languages develop from such groupings to become contextualised within specific domains and wider subject areas. "Every pattern makes the most sense in the context of the patterns it precedes and completes" [17, 18].

A deeper understanding of pattern languages can be obtained by examining language as a general phenomenon. One definition of language is *"the communication of ideas by articulate sounds or words of agreed meaning; the vocabulary peculiar to a nation, tribe or people; the vocabulary appropriate to a particular science, profession etc"* [20]. Natural languages are built up of words whose order, tense and number is determined by grammar, which also decides punctuation and other such matters. Far more complex, and therefore more productive, are the syntactical principles that underlie those grammatical rules.

Syntax and the grammatical rules which apply to it differ greatly from language to language. English, for example, differs from Mandarin Chinese, not only in the grammar and syntax that determine the order of its signifiers (words), but in its semiotic construction. Both languages have their written signs denoting the signifiers (signs governed in turn by their own rules), but in Mandarin, unlike English, this written notation also determines the intonation with which the words are spoken, as does their context.

Both, however, have the property common to all languages: the principles and the rules to which they give rise can yield a theoretically infinite number of statements of thought, called sentences [21]. The expressive potential of a language thus comes from the way and the context in which these signifiers are arranged in strings (sentences). *"It is, in other words, a generative system* [emphasis added- HH] *which allows us to generate sentences that are appropriate to any given situation"* [2].

Complex as this may be, a pattern language is even more so, according to Alexander. Rather than words, the individual elements are patterns, each of which has a structure detailing how it is itself composed of lesser patterns, and all of which are governed by embedded rules determining how they are created and their position relative to other patterns [2]. A language is complete only when every individual pattern in that language is also complete, and therefore new patterns must be invented, whenever necessary, to fill out each pattern which is not complete. The structure of a pattern language is created by the fact that individual patterns are not isolated. A pattern language contains useful connective information that helps to validate the patterns, and to apply them [62]. This important topic of 'connective information' will examine in the next section. Indeed it turns out to be central to the whole argument of this book.

Generally, a pattern language is not a programming language; rather it is a procedural document, with the purpose of guiding and informing the designer. A pattern language includes rules and guidelines that explain how and when to apply its patterns to solve a problem, insoluble by an individual pattern. These rules and guidelines suggest the order and granularity for applying each pattern in the language. A pattern language could also be viewed both as a lexicon of patterns and a grammar. The grammar defines how to weave patterns from a lexicon together into valid software equivalents of sentences. Ideally, good pattern languages should be generative, and capable of producing all possible sentences from a rich and expressive pattern vocabulary.

There are many collections of software patterns that claim to be languages. The following can be count Ward Cunnigham's *CHECKS* [31], Meszaros and Doble's *Pattern Language for Pattern Writing* [70] and *GAMA – A Pattern Language for Computer Supported Dynamic Collaboration* by Schümmer [83], but none of these three at least declares itself to be generative in the sense described above. Meszaros and Doble offer this definition of a pattern language, and it seems to be one that fits many languages that cover software patterns [70]:

> *"A pattern language defines a collection of patterns and the rules to combine them into an architectural style. Pattern languages describe software frameworks or families of related systems"* [56].

Coplien, however, offers a definition with a different emphasis and one that appears closer to Alexander's thinking [26]. The difference appears to be a stronger implication of generativity together with an implication about the completeness and comprehensiveness of the language:

> *"A pattern language is a structured collection of patterns that build on each other to transform needs and constraints into an architecture"* [26].

The purpose of such languages is to capture patterns in their contexts, and to establish the means of realising the wider implications of design decisions. Applying each pattern changes the context by changing the state of the system under construction and creates both a new design problem and a new context for the next pattern to be applied. The next picked pattern must have a certain criteria in order for it to be applied successfully and this is will be determined by the characteristics of the new context just created. The difficult question is: how is this dynamically changing 'connective information' to be presented to guide the developer/builder?

This is indeed the fundamental research question that this book is addressing.

2.5 Pattern Description Formats

As been seen, the software community has collected patterns and 'pattern languages' in order to improve its utilisation of those practices which it uses repeatedly, an endeavour based on the seminal work of Christopher Alexander, who developed the concept in order to codify best practice in the building industry in order to help create high quality structures.

To be useful, patterns have to be accurate technically, but also accessible by all the stakeholders in a project. Alexander makes clear that pattern languages are shared by everyone with an interest in a design, not merely its specialist 'architects'. The descriptions of patterns are pieces of literature, and it is no accident that the publication process used by the Patterns Movement draws so heavily on the experience of writers' and poets' circles.

The GoF put across a collection of constructs that at the very least should be there when describing a pattern; therefore the following can be consider as notions that must be available in the form in any pattern description:

- **Pattern name** - a common denominator of both GoF and Alexander. Both of them bring up the importance, and the difficulty of finding an evocative name for a pattern.
- **Problem** - an explanation of when to apply the pattern. There are two parts to this explanation, namely the problem itself and the context in which the given pattern applies. Both Alexander and GoF acknowledge this essential difference.

- **Solution -** context, in software, is a description of the artefacts that form the solution, context, in object-oriented, is describes the composition of the solution through the interfaces, classes, packages, etc. that may be play a part in resolving the given problem and context. Still, the solution is not idiom or concrete - it describes the solution in an abstract manner. The implementation may vary dependant on the technical stage or variants of the context.
- **Consequences -** express the costs and compromises that accrue while applying the pattern - and are the most important factors to be taking in consideration when choosing different design solutions. Basically they describe how that specified pattern may affect the non-functional requirements of the system; e.g. portability, extendibility, flexibility, complexity, performance.

While the GoF claim, probably correctly, that these elements are common both to their own pattern descriptions and to Alexander's the actual form (or template) used is very different. The Design Patterns book describes 23 patterns in about 320 pages and for each has a heading with twelve separate clauses: Name, Intent, Motivation, Applicability, Structure, Participants, Collaborations, Consequences, Implementation, Sample Code, Known Uses and Related Patterns. Allowing for discussion in the front and end chapters, the average description is over ten pages long. Alexander adopts a much more accessible, narrative style with each pattern taking no more than a few pages to describe, occupying on average less than half the column inches of a GoF pattern.

Historically, the software Patterns Movement has refused to mandate any single format, recognising that different formats will suit different audiences. Gamma [42] points out that it is of greater importance to explore the space of design patterns than to formalise their description, but much of the preparation of the PLoP conferences involves pattern authors being 'shepherded' by experienced authors to help them find an appropriate format.

Currently, standard shepherding advice suggests that as well as the essential components of problem and solution, a pattern template should contain information on the oppositional factors (forces) involved in causing the design problem, the context in which the pattern may be employed, the reasoning behind the solution and the consequences of its application. In particular, the description of the solution should demonstrate how the forces previously described will be resolved in a way favourable to the overall design. One popular format is the Coplien form [24, 30], which typically fits on one page with the headings,

- Pattern Name
- Problem
- Context
- Forces
- Solution
- Resulting Context
- Rationale
- Related Patterns

While some commentators advance clear segmentation of the pattern, so that users can find key components [70], others advocate a more liberal procedure more akin to Alexander's prototype (e.g. Olson [74], Harrison [49, 50, 51, 52]). A multiplicity of formats for software patterns has been advocated in order to find the most advantageous one for each set of circumstances [16], and during this investigation it has been discovered that patterns have provided a means of capturing abstract concepts that are otherwise difficult if not impossible to formulate [41].

One interesting insight is that while the Coplien form is considered the easiest to write, the Alexandrian form is recognized as the easiest to read and so there has been a recent trend towards narrative styles - the first POSA patterns have been rewritten, for example [19]. It also appears to be the case that shorter forms are enabled by systems of patterns and pattern languages with much of the requirement for explanation being amortized across the collection of patterns, while stand alone patterns seem to demand lengthier templates.

A single recurring problem can be solved using a single pattern. There is far greater potential, however, in developing the relationships between them into pattern languages that provide the means of solving problems of complexity a degree of magnitude greater [44, 72]. In order to illustrate this, Alexander lists a sequence of ten patterns from *A Pattern Language,* by which a farmhouse in the Bernese Oberland was built, and another eight used to construct stone houses in the south of Italy [1, 2].

To enable this accumulation of patterns into languages that realise their potential, individual patterns in a language need to document their relationships with each other. The structure created by the sum of these relationships demonstrates the order (the 'syntax') in which patterns can be applied in a variety of sequences to construct any number of complete forms.

According to Alexander, *"every pattern we define must be formulated in the form of a rule which establishes a relationship between a context, a system of forces which arises in that context, and a configuration, which allows these forces to resolve themselves in that context"* [2].

He recommends visual representation as illustrations. This is relatively easy for the three-dimensional world of buildings, but as Fred Brooks Jr. pointed out, software is intangible and difficult to visualize [16]. Many patterns address the issue of the illustration of software patterns with UML class and sequence diagrams (with the possible unwanted side effect of their being confused with UML template collaborations as described above). While for Alexander a sketch can show an incremental shift in the design through the application of a pattern, no such option exists for software developers. As part of the presentation of their pattern language, many pattern authors include an overview of the patterns in the language, often referred to as 'roadmaps'. Such maps illustrate the relationships between the patterns in the language.

Figure 2.1 is an example map for *Small Memory Pattern Relationships* by Noble and Weir [71], arrows indicate that if a pattern at the plain end is used, the other pattern at the arrow end should also be considered to be used next. They also show specialisations (triangles) and conflicts (crosses on dotted arrows).

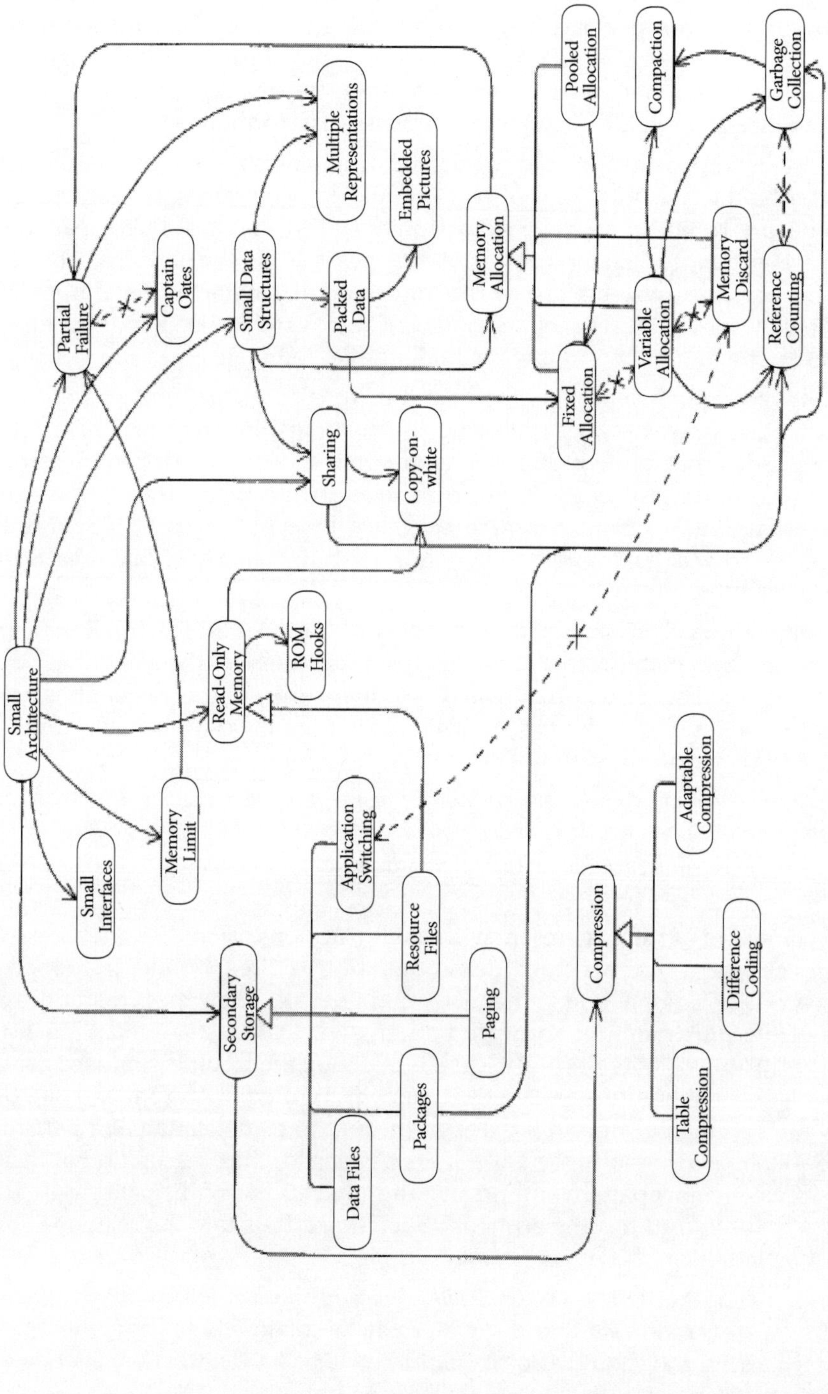

Figure 2.1: Pattern map for 'Small Memory Pattern Relationships' [71]

Another example from other roadmap styles, this map included the type of relationships between the patterns in the language. Figure 2.2 illustrate a pattern map for A Presentation Pattern Language [76], Reiβing used different arrows on the pattern map to indicate whether one pattern 'may use' or 'does use' another. As in many other software pattern languages, this examples shows that the arrows on the pattern map effectively contain the rules of the language and the grammar.

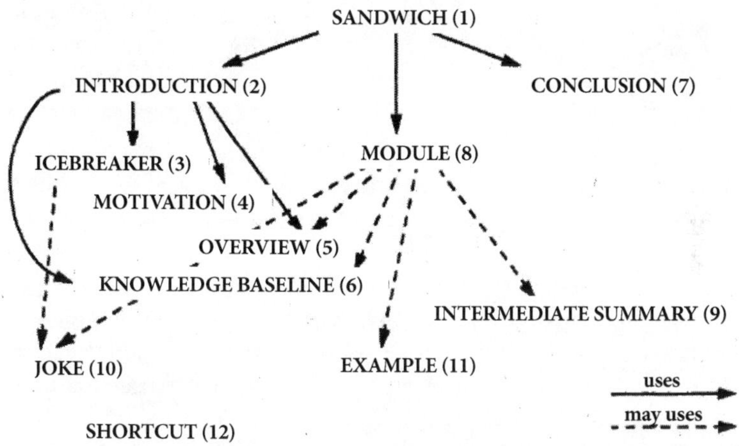

Figure 2.2: Pattern map for 'A Presentation Pattern Language' [76]

Pattern maps seem to be a common feature of software pattern languages and there is strong anecdotal evidence that in Patterns Writers' workshops they are favoured by reviewers [73].

However, Kavanagh has clearly demonstrated problems with such an approach. She argues coherently that they present an overly static view of the relationships between patterns which, when applied, are actually dynamic. Simplistically, the overall process of building using a pattern language can be characterize like this: problem 1 is addressed by pattern A which, as a resulting context, creates problem 2 which can be addressed by Pattern B which creates a new context and so on. Remembering that, theoretically, a pattern can be implemented a million different ways depending on context, and that context is essentially the current state of the system being constructed, it is clear that pattern maps cannot give the necessary guidance for the order of application of patterns. In fact both Kavanagh [63] and Manns [66, 65, 64] before her have shown that the centre of gravity for the Patterns Movement has so far been the production of patterns (i.e., mining the expertise for the knowledge base that is required) rather than their consumption (i.e., their use). The point they make is easily illustrated by the fact that for all the PLoP conferences that have taken place across the world, only one - in 1997 [11] - was focussed on how patterns are used. The issues become clear when looking at pattern sequences and how they might be put together.

2.6 Pattern Application Process

The writing of patterns is an issue which has been addressed more or less successfully by the Patterns Movement over the last decade and a half, but composing them into meaningful design sequences is a problem that has drawn far less attention in the literature.

Pattern sequences can be seen to have always been an implicit part of the concept of both pattern systems and pattern languages. Nevertheless a rigorous and understandable notion of pattern sequences has been omitted as an explicit part of the majority of pattern concept, and has only lately been given this consideration. Pattern languages do not give a clear strong notion of the order and sequences in which patterns should be applied during the construction process.

Christopher Alexander's used the word sequence in his original pattern writing A Pattern Language [1] and The Timeless Way of Building [2] but its meaning is ambiguous regarding its role within the pattern idiom and is not at all times obvious.

In A Pattern Language (APL) Alexander discusses the use of sequences within a pattern language [1]. Instead of using a pattern map to present the patterns in the pattern language, he uses a hierarchical sequence of patterns as the grammar rules and the language is a sequence of operators, where each pattern is an operator which changes space. Each pattern in the sequence is affected by the pattern before it, and itself has an overall change effect on the design as a whole. Also, those patterns which come later in the sequence will fit into the design which has evolved so far.

In The Timeless Way of Building [2], Alexander uses sequences with the network of application patterns as his pattern language as authoritative way of using patterns to generate a design. In fact, Alexander seems to use sequences in two ways. Firstly, sequences are used as a way of introducing the patterns in the language, where patterns sequence is a summary of the language and also an index to the patterns. Secondly, sequences are used as a means of building a system, where the patterns have the structure of a network when it is used, and are always used as a sequence, i.e., one pattern subsequent to another in a particular order.

In APL the strict style of sequences state that the patterns can only be used in the order in which they appear in the catalogue, which tend to limit the flow that should be apparent in any normal language, where a more flexible set of grammatical rules determine the order in which words can be reasonably and logically used.

In Mexico work on housing projects using APL recommended that although structures can be built, this strict sequencing does not always work, and the project was missing things that makes a building a 'living structure'. The used sequence for creating a building as given in A Timeless Way does not follow the order offered in A Pattern Language. There is therefore a noticeable tension between the use of patterns in a sequence for building on the one hand, and the sequence in which the patterns illustrate a pattern language. It appears that sequences are fundamental to the building of systems with patterns, but if used for presenting and documenting the patterns in a language it may impose inflexibility.

Alexander presented that buildings could be created using patterns in a specific sequence. These buildings would demonstrate what he termed in the seventies 'the quality without a name (QWAN)' [2] and in his recent work called 'wholeness' [4, 5, 6, 7].

Pattern languages as they are currently depicted seem to present only an ambiguous notion of the order in which patterns should be applied during the construction process. Typically, in APL for example, the patterns are presented in the language in order, with the larger patterns are applied first before the smaller patterns, and more detailed constructional patterns will follow later to embellish those bigger patterns. This order forms a more or less direct sequence, based on the relations between the 'larger' patterns, which come before the 'smaller' patterns. Where a pattern map is used, larger patterns are mostly shown higher in the language map than smaller patterns, and arrows run from larger to smaller patterns to indicate the flow of the use of patterns.

Alexander explains that adjacent patterns need to be applied as close in sequence as possible, but neither Alexander's theory nor language maps specify what order adjacent patterns ought to be used. Furthermore, most system designers using languages work only with the individual patterns and language map, and may not even be familiar with Alexander's underlying theory.

In which order to apply patterns, plus adjacent patterns, is important to the right use of a pattern language: but, as have been established, this is mostly determined by the specific context supplied by the current state of the system in the building process. This is mainly why the key problem of composing pattern sequences is more temporal and dynamic than it is static and structural. In so far as pattern languages a particular sequence is suggested, for example through a patterns map, they can only refer to these structural relations, ones that can be inferred in advance independently of any specific system or context. For example, a large pattern and a smaller pattern can be shown to be reliant on each other in the sense that the smaller pattern always, or at nearly always, refines the larger pattern. This sort of dependency implies that the use of a smaller pattern should not come before the larger pattern. However, current presentations of patterns have no way of capturing or presenting the detailed contextualisation required for the actual construction of a specific system. Very often, even in current maps a pattern at one 'level' may be connected to two or more patterns at the next lower level. The decision as to which one to use is temporally constrained in the sense that the choice is made only at a particular point in the construction process of some specific system, and may well be determined, or at least further constrained, by the current state of that system. Add to this the further complication of multiple variants for the implementation of any given pattern, and that can be considered as a set of instructions to build something *specific,* then the current forms of Pattern Languages are inadequate. They leave out entirely these dynamic aspects. This will need more investigation because, as mentioned earlier, the key problem of composing pattern languages is more temporal than structural.

Some of the issues of the choice of which pattern to apply next can be illustrated with an example offered by Alexander himself. Assume creating a half-hidden garden using patterns from the Figure 2.3. as can be seen from the map that *Half-Hidden Garden* is the first pattern. The application of any of the other patterns which follow in the map may be the next choice. Also the designer may choose *not* to start with *Half-Hidden Garden* as the first pattern but start with *Entrance Transition* followed by *Private Terrace on the Street*. The pattern language map does not specify the order in which these patterns should be applied and that is because of the reasons just discussed. But the actual sequence adopted is crucial to successful design. The presence of *Entrance Transition* may affect the location or application of the *Private Terrace on the Street*. Similarly, if the *Private Terrace on the Street* is applied before *Entrance Transition*, a different design emerges. Alternatively, the *Private Terrace on the Street* may not exist at all. It is impossible to be specific about the sequence in which to use the patterns without considering the emerging properties of the specific system being built.

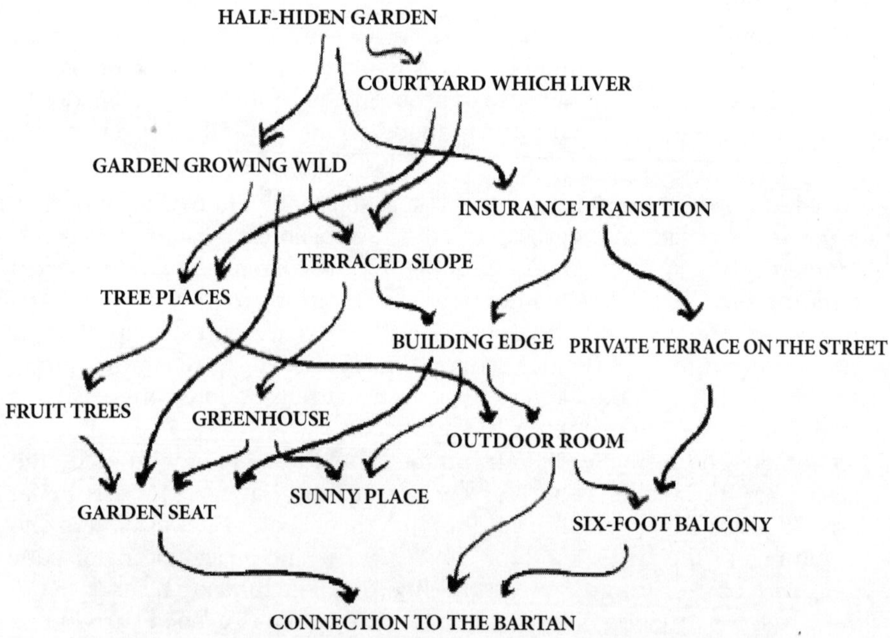

Figure 2.3: A Language for Half-Hidden Garden from Alexander [2]

If these difficulties in presenting sequences within a particular pattern language were not enough, the picture is further complicated in the world of software patterns in that any meaningful sequence of patterns for construction of a specific system, or even subsystem, are likely to draw upon different patterns, from different catalogues, systems and already published pattern languages. The collected patterns are also likely to be published in an arbitrary number of forms, as a result. Recently James O. Coplien and his colleagues have been looking at the issue of composing pattern sequences from different sources [75]. They discussed the possibility of using sequences to combine general patterns with pattern languages, as some pattern languages may possibly have similar patterns or patterns that overlap. Their work also looks at the use of different pattern from different sources to be used in sequences to compose languages, but their study did not look at sequences in the use of a pattern language [75].

Pattern sequences present one way of making logic of the popular notion of compound patterns [77, 90]. From the perspective of pattern sequences compound patterns can be considered as an identifiable and general sequence of patterns that can be considered as a whole with reference to the problem it concentrate on and the design it accomplish [54].

Henney stated that:

> "The definition of a language as a graph offers a simple and powerful pictorial view of a pattern language's connections, but it lacks some of the rules of combination necessary for understanding the composition of pattern sequences. The process definition can be considered to be like the grammar of a language" [54].

Henney [54] used some operators to compose patterns in a better way in addition to the widely used now pattern languages graphs or maps. He used the following symbols to represent his operators:

1. → to indicates the sequential composition,
2. | for alternation, and
3. □ for the completion in this improvised notation
4. Ø for the starting state, and
5. →○ For optional sequential composition.

Also Zdun used pattern language grammar in his paper *'Systematic Pattern Selection Using Pattern Language Grammars and Design Space Analysis'* for providing an approach to better support the selection of patterns and systematic design decisions based on patterns. He proposed a two step approach where he formally document the grammar of a pattern language and annotate it with the effects on quality goals. The idea was that the pattern sequences of a pattern language can be driven from the pattern language grammar [92].

Another example, for the same issue as Alexander above, is from the software pattern area. Taking any of Ian Graham's Web Usability (WU) pattern language maps it is not clear which pattern to apply next and it is in some cases very confusing to the designer or the user to figure out what some of the arrows point to. In order to start building a website by using Figure 2.4 (***Getting started on your site***) the sequence used in the diagram demonstrates the following:

- P1(*Establish the business objectives)* will be used initially
- Then P2 (*Business process model*) follows
- Then P3 *(Establish the use cases)* follows

- Then there are several choices: P17 (*Context-sensitive help*) or P11 (*Classify your site*) or P4 (*Timeboxes*) or P6 *(Automated testing)*.
- Questions that arise: From Pattern 3, should Pattern 4 (*Timeboxes*) be used once or twice? It can be understood from the diagram in (Box 2.4-1) that P4 (arrow A) will be used, but (line B) is a line with no arrowhead, so it cannot be determined whether P4 is to be used again or whether the next pattern to be used is P6 (*Automate testing)*, thus skipping P5 (*Gradual stiffening)*.
- Do lines B and C are point to P4 and P5 from P3, or do they come from P4 and P5 to P6?
- From (Box 2.4-2) in the diagram it can also be seen that there is a (line D) connecting P12 and the arrow from P3 to P17. But does this line go from P3 to P12 or from P12 to P17? This makes it unclear as to whether P12 will be used as one of the choices after P3.
- P6 is refined by P7, P8, P3 and P10 but the same type of arrow is used (solid) as the sequential order.

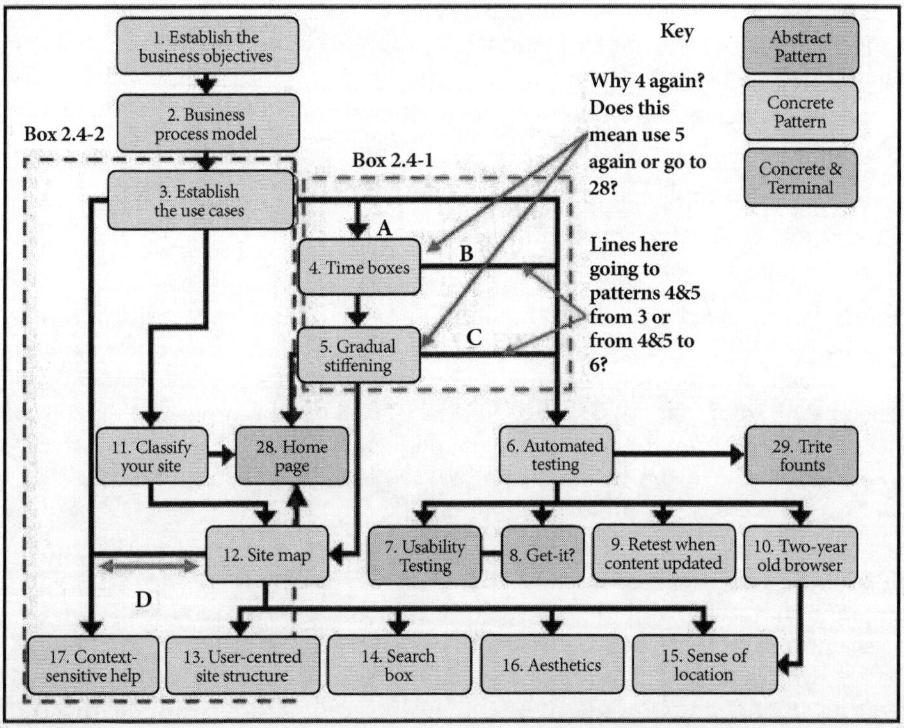

Figure 2.4: Illustration of the ambiguities in Diagram 1 (Getting started on your site) from WU [45] in Boxes 2.4-1 and 2.4-2

Welie and Veer also discussed the issue of structuring a collection of patterns into pattern languages in Interaction Design and they proposed that this language can be organized hierarchically, from high-level design problems to low-level design problems [87]. They also stated in their paper (*Pattern Languages in Interaction Design: Structure and Organization*) that "the hierarchical nature of architectural patterns can also be interpreted as a hierarchy of problems. The highest level problems are broken up in smaller problems for which solutions appear to exist. They just happen to map directly to a geometrical metaphor in architecture, working from large areas to small areas. The important thing to understand is that such a problem-hierarchy approach can be applied to other domains as well" [87].

Figure 2.5 illustrate their partial pattern language for web design centred on "shopping" [87].

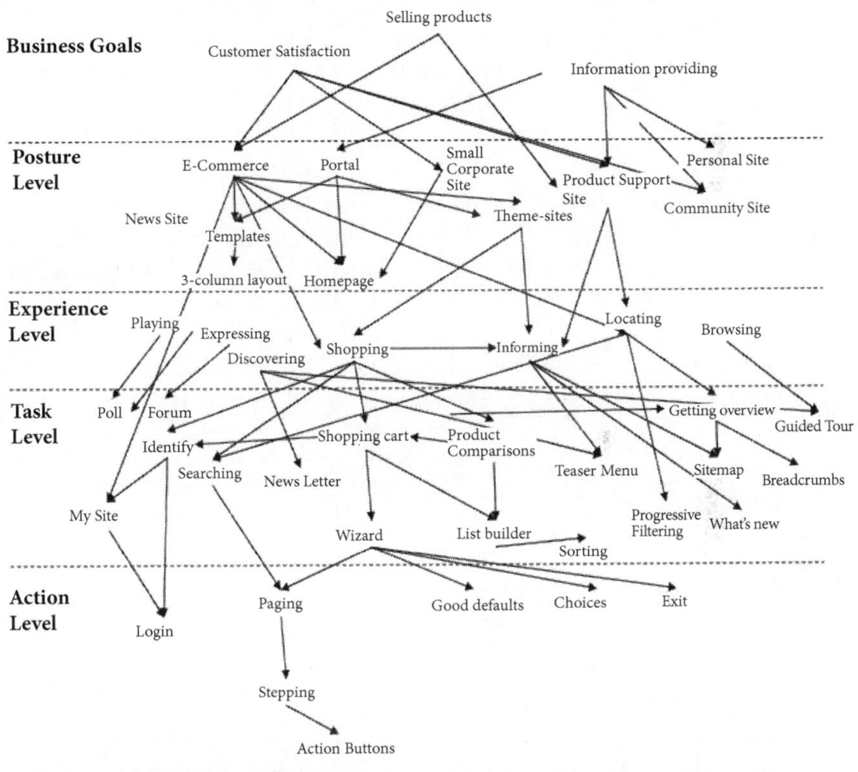

Figure 2.5: Welie partial pattern language for web design "shopping" [87]

2.7 Summary

The main points that can be drawn from the discussion above are as follows:

- A pattern can be defined by a three-part rule: a general solution to a recurring problem in a particular context.
- The perception of patterns within the software development community has grown closer to Alexander's original conception over time even though his own thought has developed further in the 35 years or so since he first

wrote about patterns. The most critical aspect of this evolving consensus has been a growing awareness of the significance of 'context'.

- It is clear that when considering the use of sequences of patterns to be used in construction, 'context' presents a number of difficulties. In particular pattern templates can at best capture only in very general terms the type of context in which a given pattern might be considered. This is a valuable and necessary component of a pattern's description, but one which is insufficient as guidance as to what order patterns might be used in a specific project, and what implementation variant should be adopted.
- For such guidance the more dynamic and temporal aspects of context, those that only emerge in the process of construction itself, must also be captured and presented in some way. Currently the various ways in which pattern languages are presented (for example, with arrowed vectors on pattern maps, or alternatively in hierarchically composed lists) only reflect the more structural ('static') relationships between patterns and not at all in an unambiguous way.

These understandings will be taken forward into the subsequent chapters of this book. Chapter 3 will focus on new ways of representing the dynamic relationships implied by pattern sequences, and in chapter 4 will present operators which more accurately reflect the static relationships that are found commonly in currently published pattern languages. The remainder of the book will seek to validate these innovations and demonstrate their usefulness, before these conquests can be finally summarize and suggest further research paths which they indicate.

CHAPTER 3

Compositional Framework for Pattern Applicability

3.1 Introduction

This chapter gives an overview of the framework for the analysis of pattern applicability. It introduces the concept of Assumption and Commitment constraint pairs (*A-C*) as a mechanism for characterising pattern context [33]. It also discusses how these constraints determine the applicability of patterns, as they guide the decisions on the application of subsequent patterns. The successful application of one pattern to solve a problem within a given context, results in the generation of a new context which needs to be understood before the application of another pattern.

Further, how to integrate a pattern into a partially existing design? What kinds of patterns should be applied in which order? How to solve problems that cannot be solved by a single pattern in isolation? Answering such questions is important for being able to use patterns effectively. The framework introduced in this chapter will help to answer these questions thereby facilitating the applicability of patterns in system design.

3.2 Characterising Context

This section will discuss first the need for context in patterns by giving an example of pattern context. Then various definitions of context in general will be discussed and then of context as used within the pattern community followed by the book definition. Some examples will be given to illustrate the need for context.

3.2.1 What is the Context

This subsection will specifically discuss what context is and give general definitions of context and why it is needed in the book and the definition as used in this book plus a comparison with the other definitions.

Context is defined as the interrelated conditions in which something exists or occurs [91]. This means that context is the mutual relationship between the many conditions that obtain in a given actor's situation or the occurrence of an event. In Software Engineering many definitions for context have been conceived. Appleton sees it as *tells how the problem occurs / when the solution works* [12]. In Artificial Intelligence Guha and McCarthy, context appears as *means of partitioning a knowledge base into manageable sets or as logical construct that facilitates reasoning activities* [47, 67]. In Information Bases, Theodorakis et al for example, context appears as a *conceptual entity that describes a group of other conceptual entities from a particular standpoint* [84]. In Ubiquitous Computing domain many definitions for context have been conceived. For instance Dey, defines context as "*the user's emotional state, focus of attention, location and orientation, date and time, objects, and people in the user's environment* " [34]. Context means situational information, or as Dey and Abowd [35] state:

> *Context is any information that can be used to characterise the situation of an entity. An entity is a person, place, or object that is considered relevant to the interaction between a user and an application, including the user and application themselves.*

Schilit and Theimer [81] refer to context as location, identities of nearby people and objects, and changes to those objects. In a similar definition, Brown defines context as location, identities of people in the user's environment, the time of day, season, temperature etc. Brown defines context as the elements of the user's environment that the user's computer knows about [15]. For Ryan, context is the user's location, environment, identity and time [79]. In computer science, context is the circumstances under which a device is being used [39]. In Architectures Alexander, context appears as *a situation giving rise to a problem* [1].

As seen in the previous paragraph the term "context" is burdened with a vast selection of meanings depending on the purposes of the particular application and/or on the research community perspective. However, several definitions for context have been put here, serving different purposes.

A definition for context with respect to patterns needs to make explicit the relationships between context (environment) and the solution provided by the pattern. This will make the application of a pattern within a certain context easier for the system designer. Therefore the definition introduces a pair of constraints: one is placed on the environment within which the system that is being developed by using the patterns and the other is what the designed system will commit to (called *Commitment*). Context in this book is thus defined as:

> *Context refers to all constraints under which the problem and its solution seem to recur, and for which a solution is desirable. Specifically, context is characterised by two elements. One describes the Assumption on the context which describes the forces from the context towards the solution whilst the other describes the Commitment of the solution towards the context.*

As can be seen from the above definition, there are two directional types of forces:

$$\text{Context} \rightarrow \text{Solution}$$
$$\text{Solution} \rightarrow \text{Context}$$

In the current pattern description formats this direction is not made explicit. The book will introduce the Assumption and Commitment elements to characterise the context and to make this direction of forces explicit.

In general, the Assumption is a constraint placed on the context and the Commitment is a constraint placed on the solution. Consequently, if the Assumption and Commitment are not both taken into consideration, the system being developed by using that pattern might fail. Two questions concern exactly what Assumptions are being made about the Context, and what solution the pattern guarantees. It will be noted that Assumption and Commitments are elements that constrain the use of the pattern. In order for the pattern to work, the Assumption and Commitment constraints should be satisfied. This means that not only the context in which this pattern exists is important, but also both Assumption and Commitment must be taken into consideration while developing the system. Assumption and Commitment will be used to select the "right" pattern in a given context.

Assumption and Commitment are the key elements of any sequence of pattern applications. Patterns as such do not communicate which each other but there is a possibility that patterns interact (interfere, cooperate) with each other when they are applied in a sequence. Now the use of Assumption and Commitment will lead to good interactions between patterns.

Assumption and Commitment will also help in the way patterns are applied in sequence and in analysing pattern applicability. The diagram below is illustrating the role of the Assumption and Commitment in characterising context.

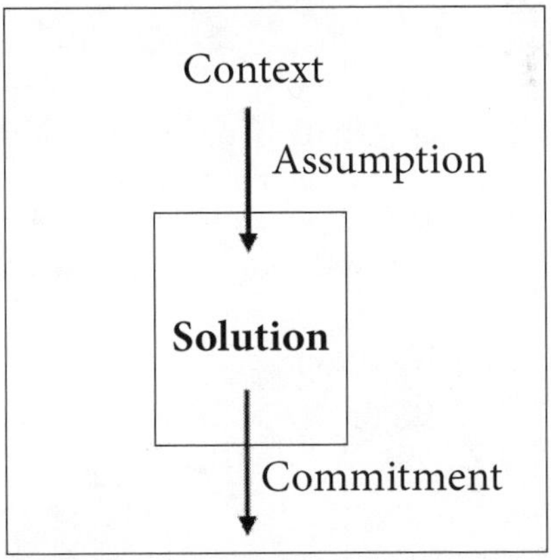

Figure 3.1: Illustrates the role of the Assumption and Commitment

Several different formats for describing patterns are used in the pattern community, none of which has achieved widespread acceptance (see Chapter 2 section 2.5). However, there is broad agreement on the types of elements that a pattern should contain. The different patterns formats all have particular qualities to them, and any pattern's author will tend to pick a format that works well with their preferences.

The book is not making any changes to those formats or suggesting a new one, all what the book is proposing that what ever the type of pattern format being used the context will be characterised with those two elements Assumption and Commitment as explicit elements.

3.2.2 The Need for Context

Context plays a very important role in the course of interaction between things (patterns, objects, people....etc) and its surrounding environment. It decides whether the interaction can continue successfully.

Context is the environment or situation in which something exists or occurs. People can recognize the contexts they are in and know what information is applicable to each context, and derive information from each context. The human brain uses context to manage a huge amount of information from many different situations, such as family, friends, work, and society. Using context, people quickly translate what information is appropriate in any given situation. While context is essential to human mental function and for his decisions, it is not widely present for the modern information technology infrastructure.

Patterns also need context, and who is adding context to the pattern is the system designer when using them to design a system using patterns. Context is part of some pattern description formats, but some pattern writer like for example Welie [88] and Tidwell [86] do not describe the context as part of their pattern description formats. Not knowing what is context will make the application of the pattern not clear, i.e., in what context should this pattern be used? For example, a pattern from Alexander to build a garden can not be used as user interface to build a website for E-commerce.

This example is from the WU patterns [45], the full pattern descriptions are in Appendix A, shows that the context of a given pattern can result in different solutions depending on the context. This pattern *Establish the business objectives* is a pattern that can be used in different context. As stated by Ian Graham "This pattern is one of several in this language whose applicability is far wider than web design and could – no should – be adopted usefully on non-web projects. It is a process pattern".

The pattern description is as follow:

Pattern's name:

Establish the business objectives

Pattern's description:

The problem this pattern wants to solve is to create a new website or modify an existing one. This pattern is as fundamental to the success of web projects as to others and because it is one of the patterns most often ignored by web developers– to the ultimate detriment of their projects. It is a process pattern. Business objectives allow teams to validate their use case and business process models. How should they be discovered?

Assumption:

The Assumption for this pattern for any general usage in any domain is that there are business objectives.

Commitment

For the application of this pattern in this web design context the specific Commitment is a website that satisfies the business objectives. The Commitment for this pattern for any general usage in any domain is that the pattern will create a process that satisfied the business objectives.

So from the above pattern description it can be seen that when the system designer uses this pattern in designing a website for E-commerce the context of it is totally different from designing an E-government website, in terms of the type of solutions they provide, i.e., service. Even though both services are provided online through a website but the services they are providing are different in their context.

3.2.3 Capturing Context

This subsection will discuss the characterisation of the context with the two elements Assumption/Commitment.

3.2.3.1 Assumption/Commitment (Constraints)

In this subsection two main questions arise when trying to capture the context via the Assumption/Commitment constraints:

1. What do I need in order to apply the pattern? (The answer to this question is described in the Assumption)
2. What is the result of applying the pattern? (The answer to this question is described in the Commitment)

So in order to capture them the designer needs to start by answering these two questions. The answer is embedded inside the pattern description and the system under development, this will be shown in the next subsection.

3.2.3.2 How can the Assumption/Commitment Constraints be Captured from the Available Information Sources

The Assumption and Commitment are constraints placed on the context. These constraints can come from many different sources and the system designer, must consider the context in order to find the right pattern to apply.

The *Assumption* can be identified from many sources and the main ones are:

a. The pattern name
b. The problem descriptions
c. The solution descriptions
d. The information of the system under development

The *Commitment* can be identified from the solution provided by the pattern and can be also identified from the problem it is solving.

a. The solution descriptions
b. The problem description
c. The information of the system under development

3.2.3.3 Example of Assumption/Commitment Capture

This example is from Welie pattern collection website [88], and the full pattern descriptions are in Appendix B, to show how to extract the Assumption/Commitment from the information available in the pattern description format. Welie used a format which did not include the context in the description of his patterns. The pattern information is as follow:

Pattern's name:

View

Pattern's description:

The problem this pattern wants to solve is that the users need to manage a collection of objects. A view usually is an overview of a set of objects, e.g. email messages, orders, appointments, products, and images. Users need to manage objects such as shopping orders, emails, bank accounts, stocks, and so on.

Assumption:

There is a set of objects.

Commitment

Is the creation of an overview of objects that together is meaningful to users and can be seen and navigated through very easily.

3.3 The Framework

How to solve problems that cannot be solved by a single pattern? What kind of patterns should be applied in which order? Answering such questions is important for being able to use patterns successfully. Otherwise patterns are applied, but the resulting design will likely expose unnecessary complexity. Even with the fact that every well-described pattern provides information about its implementation, refinement and combination with other patterns [42, 18]. But all this information is pattern-specific. The application of patterns in general is not supported by that information when building a real-world software system.

This framework is an approach for supporting the effective use of patterns in software engineering to solve problems that have no specific patterns that provide a solution. First a categorisation of patterns is introduced that characterise the role that a pattern can play in the framework. This characterisation is orthogonal to the other used types (architectural patterns, design patterns and idioms or coding patterns) which are introduced in chapter 2. Although the terminology is the same as used in WU [44, 45] the definition is however different. These patterns are:

- *Abstract pattern*. This pattern is defined as the specification of a problem which the system designer is trying to solve.
- *Concrete pattern*. This pattern is defined as any pattern available in any pattern bank, i.e., any pattern which will solve a particular problem.

Pattern refinement denotes the 'implementation' of an abstract pattern by a concrete pattern. Again since application of a pattern is context dependent, refinement will be context dependent as well. Refinement is represented as a dashed line. So a concrete pattern 'implements' an abstract pattern in a certain context if the following two conditions hold:

1. The Assumption of the Abstract pattern (**A**) implies the Assumption of the Concrete pattern (**Ax**).

   A implies **Ax**

2. The Commitment of the Concrete pattern (**Cx**) implies the Commitment of the Abstract pattern (**C**).

   Cx implies **C**

So intuitively refinement of patterns in certain context means that an abstract pattern can be replaced by a concrete pattern if and only if those conditions hold.

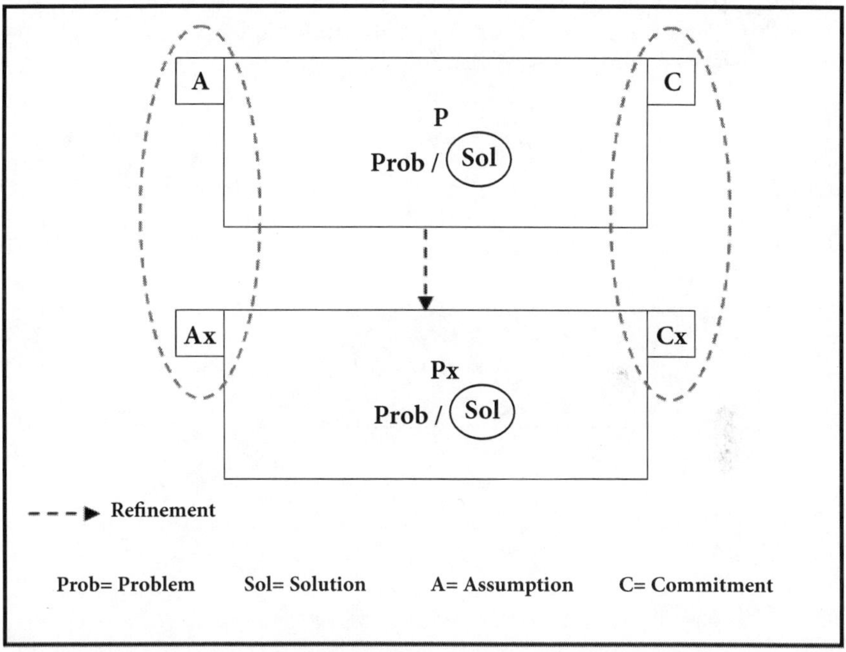

Figure 3.2: Illustrates the refinement condition need to be hold between two patterns

This framework would not only provide solutions to specific design problems, but it will also provide a process of how to apply patterns, which will help in the process of applying them: when, how, and in which order. The framework consists of two stages described in the following subsections.

In this framework a pattern is presented as a problem/solution pair together with an Assumption/Commitment pair (**Prob, Sol, A, C**). The system designer starts with an abstract pattern (**Prob, Sol, A, C**) that is a specification of the system to be built, i.e., **Prob** is the specification and **Sol** is the solution the designer is constructing to solve **Prob** within a context described by the Assumption / Commitment pair (**A, C**).

3.3.1 Stage 1: Use/Adapt Existing Patterns

Firstly the designer will look for a concrete pattern to solve the problem **Prob**. If there is a pattern in a particular pattern bank that solves this problem then the designer will use it. This pattern must solve the whole problem.

Secondly, if there is no pattern in a particular pattern bank that solves the problem **Prob** the designer has to search for a solution and the designer will have the following 2 options:

A. To search for a concrete pattern that solves a bigger problem. In this case there is a concrete pattern **P (Prob_p, Sol_p, Ap, Cp)** such that **Prob** is contained in **Prob_p** because then pattern **P** will provide a solution **Sol_p** for it. So if **Prob** is contained in **Prob_p**, i.e., **Prob** is smaller than **Prob_p**, and **Sol_p** is a solution for **Prob_p** then obviously **Sol_p** is also a solution for the smaller **Prob**. Since also the context need to match then the following conditions need to hold:

 A implies **Ap** (because of refinement)

 Cp implies **C** (because of refinement)

In that case **Sol_P** provides a solution for problem **Prob** in the context described by **A** and **C**. Figure 3.3 illustrates this relation.

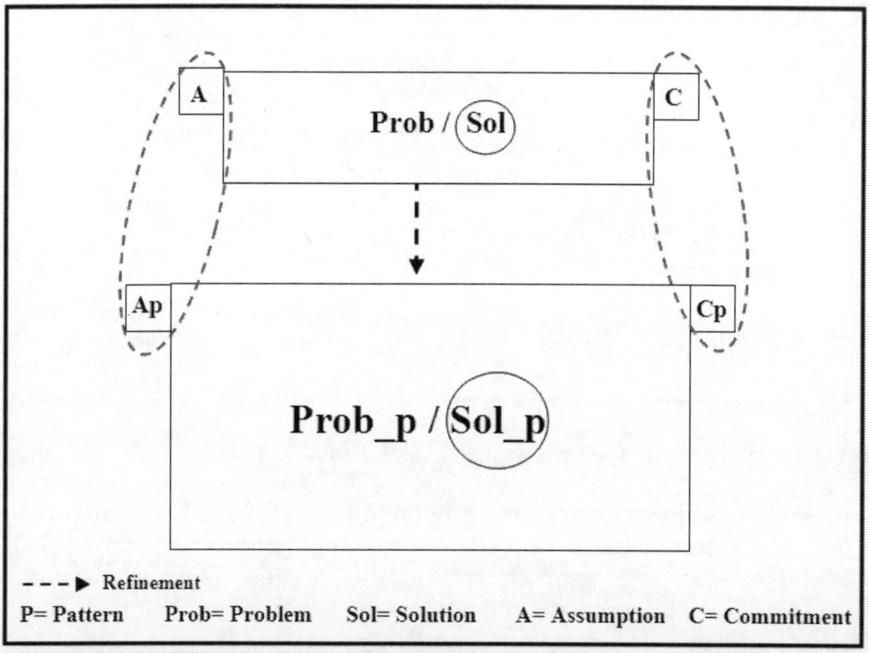

Figure 3.3: Illustrates the use of part of a bigger pattern solution to solve smaller problem

B. To invent a new concrete pattern. This new pattern needs to be examined and used over and over again to become an accepted pattern.

If none of the above is appropriate or no solution is found using ***Stage 1*** then the system designer proceeds to ***Stage 2***.

3.3.2 Stage 2: Divide and Conquer

If the designer faces a problem where there exists no concrete pattern in any bank to solve that particular problem then the designer has to decompose this problem into sub-problems and find concrete patterns that will provide a solution for these sub-problems. The rationale is that for a complex system, there may not be an existing concrete pattern that can be used directly to solve this big problem.

The stages of Divide and Conquer are as follows:

Stage I: Decompose the Problem into Sub-problems (Divide)

If there are no concrete patterns available for solving a specific problem directly then the designer decomposes the big/complex problem using operator **OPd** into smaller sub-problems.

The context described by **A** and **C** remain the same for these sub- problems. Figure 3.4 shows a problem decomposition into two sub- problems using operator **OPd**.

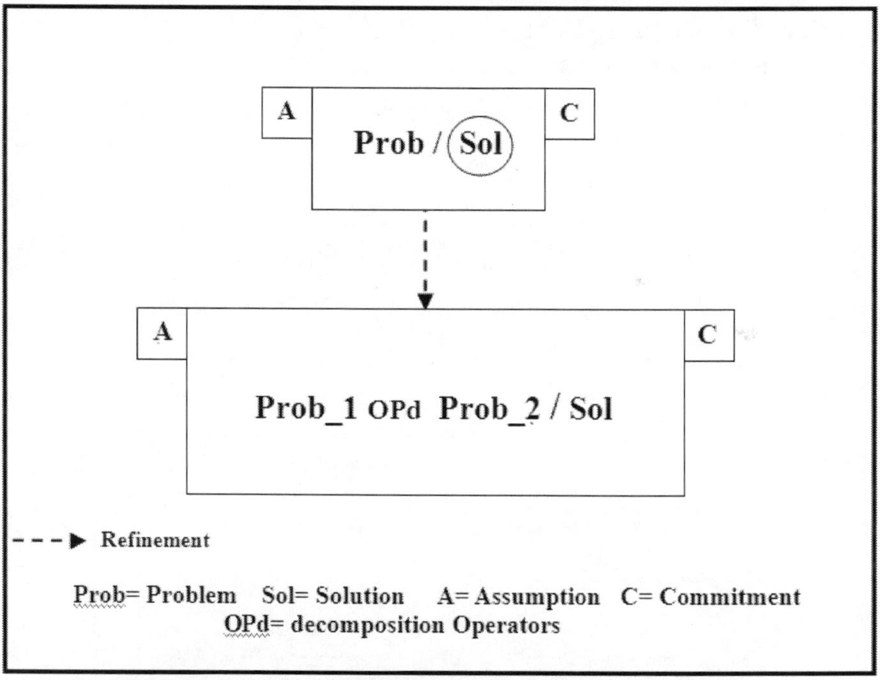

Figure 3.4: Illustrates the decomposition of the problem

Stage II: Compose the Solutions for the Sub-problems (Conquer)

After decomposing the problem the focus is now on how to compose the solutions of the sub-problems to form the solution to the problem **Prob**. Instead of looking for patterns that will solve **Prob** the designer needs to find patterns that will solve the sub-problems.

If the designer finds concrete patterns **P1** and **P2** that will provide solutions **Sol_1** and **Sol_2** for respectively **Prob_1** and **Prob_2** then **Sol_1 OPc Sol_2** will provide a solution for the original problem Prob.

Sol_1 OPc Sol_2 will only provide a solution for problem **Prob** if the context of patterns **P1** and **P2** matches that of the abstract pattern. If the operator **OPd** and **OPc** are the sequential operator then the matching of context is expressed as follows:

A implies **A1** (because of refinement)

C2 implies **C** (because of refinement)

C1 implies **A2** (because of sequential application/composition)

In Chapter 4 the matching of context with respect to various operators, i.e., Sequential, Choice and Parallel will be discussed.

From Figure 3.5 it can be seen that the problem is decomposed into sub-problems and then the concrete patterns solving those sub-problems can be composed to solve the original problem, i.e., the designer performs the following steps:

(Prob, Sol, A, C)

(Prob_1 OPd Prob_2, Sol, A, C)

(Prob_1 OPd Prob_2, Sol_1 OPc Sol_2, A, C)

(Prob_1, Sol_1, A1, C1) OP (Prob_2, Sol_2, A2, C2)

So composing two concrete patterns applications denotes first the decomposition of the problem **Prob** and then the composition of the solutions for the sub-problems.

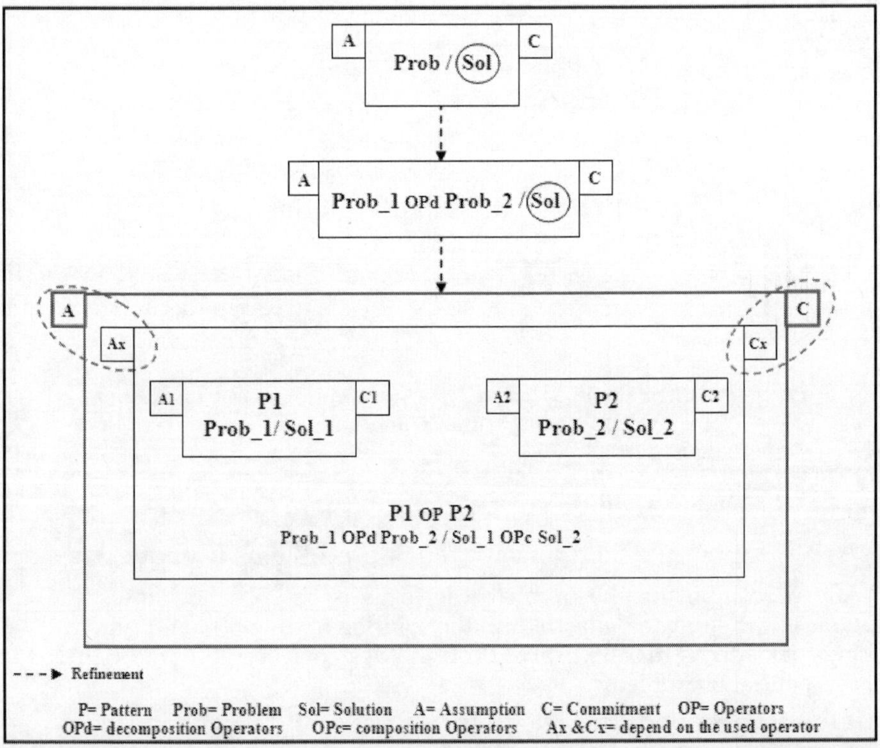

Figure 3.5: Illustrates the decomposition of the problem and composition of the solution

The **Ax** and **Cx** stand for the Assumption and commitment of the composed patterns.

3.3.3 The Role of the Operators in the Framework

When using the framework to solve a problem the operators play two roles:

To decompose the problem into sub-problems:

Figure 3.5 above shows that the problem **Prob** is decomposed into two sub-problems (**Prob_1** and **Prob_2**) using operator **OPd**. The operator **OPd** could be for example sequence.

To compose the sub-solutions to form a solution:

The sub-problems created in **Stage 2 I** might have concrete patterns that provide a solution to those sub-problems. These sub-solutions need to be composed together using operator **OPc** to form a solution for the overall problem **Prob**. Again this operator could be for example sequence.

In general the operator **OPd** for decomposition matches the one for composition **OPc**. An example where this is not the case is when the **OPd** is the Parallel operator and the **OPc** could be in sequence. In this case the designer opted to provide a sequential solution for a parallel problem.

3.3.4 Example of the Use of the Framework

This example uses design patterns from the Welie pattern collection website [88] and the full patterns descriptions are in Appendix B. although the framework can be applied using architectural patterns and idioms (or coding patterns) the examples and the case studies in the book will only consider design patterns. The example will show the design of a specific part of a shopping website. What is the problem to be solved? The problem is specified as follows:

The user wishes to buy items and wants to see those items listed before check out. One of the most common patterns is the Shopping Cart pattern. This Shopping Cart pattern can not be used as is because it is an abstract pattern that requires the concrete pattern List Builder and Collector to solve specific sub-problems. First the description of these 3 patterns will be given and then the use of the framework to show the relationships between the 3 patterns.

The next two tables summaries all the needed information about the used design patterns in the example.

Table 3.1: Problem/Solution of the used patterns from Welie [88]

Pattern name	Problem	Solution
Pattern 7: Shopping Cart	Users want to buy a product	Introduce a shopping cart where users can put their products in before they actually purchase them.

Pattern name	Problem	Solution
Pattern 8: Collector	Users need to temporarily gather a set of items for later use	Allow users to build their list of items by selecting the items as they are viewing them. Place a link to the collected items list on every page in the site.
Pattern 9: List Builder	The users need to build up and manage a list of items	Present the total list and provide editing functionality next to it.

Table 3.2: Assumption/Commitments pairs of the used patterns

Pattern name	Assumption	Commitment
Pattern 7: Shopping Cart	A collection of objects the user can buy	List the objects the user wants to buy.
Pattern 8: Collector	There are objects that the user can select.	Set of objects selected by the user.
Pattern 9: List Builder	There is a set of objects selected by the user	To list the objects in the set selected by the user in a particular order.

The framework is used to solve the Shopping Cart problem:

Stage 1: there is no concrete pattern in the system designer's pattern bank that can solve this problem and there is also no bigger concrete pattern that will provide a solution. Then the next stage in the framework is applied.

Stage 2: will have the following steps:

I. to decompose this problem into sub-problems (Divide). The Shopping Cart pattern problem can not be solved by applying only one pattern. The Shopping Cart problem is decomposed into two sub-problems: the Collector and List Builder. The decomposition is done using the sequential operator.

II. to compose the solutions of the sub-problems Collector and List Builder (Conquer). Since the sub-problems of both patterns are representing part of the solution for the problem of the Shopping Cart pattern the sequential composition of the solutions of Collector and List Builder patterns will solve the Shopping Cart problem.

The Collector and List Builder patterns need to be applied in the right context. The Assumption and Commitment of each patterns is listed in Table 3.2. Since the operator **OPd** and **OPc** are both the sequential operator the matching of context is expressed as follows:

In circle 1: **A7** implies **A8** (because of refinement)

In circle 2: **C8** implies **A9**

In circle 3: **C9** implies **C7** (because of refinement)

Where

A7 is the Assumption of the Shopping Cart pattern

A8 is the Assumption of the Collector pattern

A9 is the Assumption of the List Builder pattern

C7 is the Commitment of the Shopping Cart pattern

C8 is the Commitment of the Collector pattern

C9 is the Commitment of the List Builder pattern

So the system designer needs to check those three conditions. In this case the three conditions trivially hold.

Figure 3.6 illustrates the relation between the three patterns.

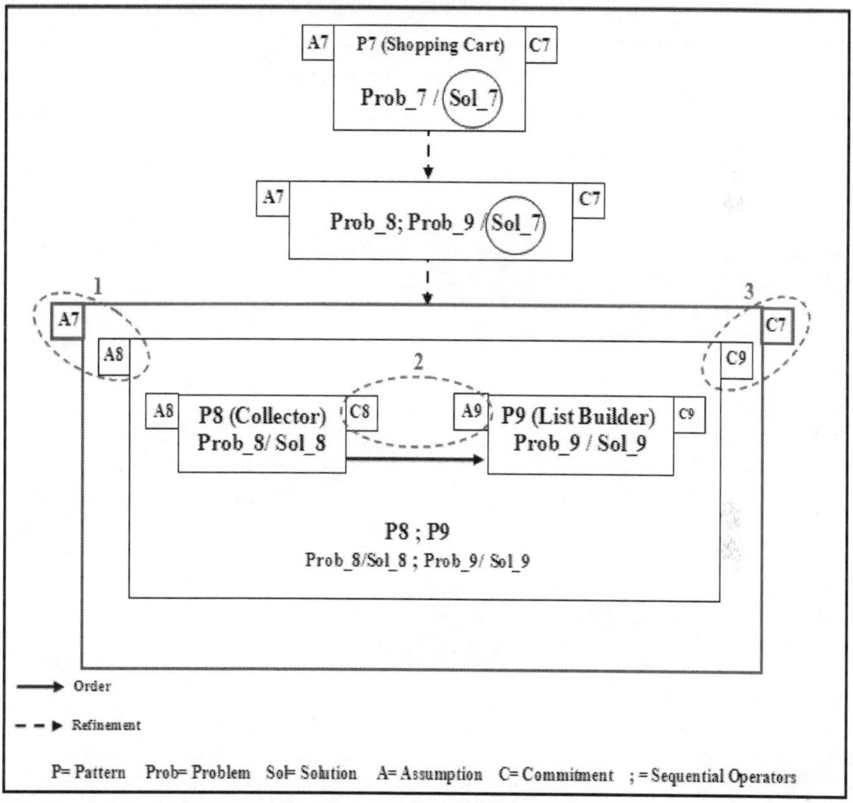

Figure 3.6: Illustrates the decomposition of the problem and composition of the solutions for the Shopping Cart pattern

3.4 Summary

This chapter started with discussing the various definitions of context and then introduced the book definition of context. The context in the book is characterised via Assumption and Commitment constraints which will facilitate the way of applying patterns. The ways of capturing context from the available information sources were also introduced. Then the chapter outlined the framework within which pattern application can be studied and analysed. A categorisation orthogonal to the existing one was introduced reflecting the role that pattern plays during the design of the system. They are the Abstract and Concrete patterns. Some of the patterns can be Abstract in one context and they can be Concrete in another context and chapter 5 will illustrate this.

The framework also provided a process of applying patterns and the stages the designer will be able to use in solving a problem. They are two stages. Stage 1: Use/Adapt Existing Patterns. Stage 2: Divide and Conquer. Stage 2 will allow the designer to divide the problem into sub- problems and compose their solutions to solve the main problem. This framework uses three operators to help in decompose the problem into sub-problems and compose solutions of sub-problems. These operators also used to indicate the composition of patterns. These operators are the Sequential, Choice and Parallel and their role is fully discussed in chapter 4.

CHAPTER

4

Operators

The previous chapter introduced the key elements of the framework for patterns analysis and applicability. The focus now turns to the operations which will help in applying the framework. In order to do so it is necessary to provide operators that will be used for:

1. Decomposition of problem into sub-problems.
2. Composition of solutions.
3. The indication of the order in which patterns are applied.
4. Making the use of the pattern maps more precise and clearer.

The operators are listed in the table 4.1 below.

Table 4.1: Operators table

Symbol	Name	Example	Descriptions	Purpose
;	Sequential	P1 ; P2	Indicates the sequence of the act	Apply P1 and then apply P2
□	Choice	P1 □ P2	Indicates the choice of the act	Apply at least one P1 or P2
|	Parallel	P1 | P2	This is a combination of the sequential and the choice operators. It is used for ease of writing.	Apply both P1 and P2 in any sequence

The operators are similar to the ones used in The Guarded Command Language (GCL) by Edsger Dijkstra [36]. The following sections will introduce each operator in more detail and provide rules for applying patterns in certain order and context.

4.1 The Role of the Operator at Problem/Solution Level

As mentioned in Chapter 3, the operators are used to:

1. Decompose the problem into sub-problems.
2. Compose the solutions of the sub-problems.

The Sequential, Choice and Parallel operators satisfy the following Axioms, i.e., these axioms hold for the language used to describe problem and solution.

Axioms for decomposition and composition

Let Xi be a problem or solution $(1 \leq i \leq 3)$

X1; (X2; X3) = (X1; X2) ; X3	(; is associative)
X 1 □ X 1= X 1	(□is idempotent)
X 1 □ X 2 = X 2 □ X 1	(□is commutative)
X 1; (X 2 □ X 3) = (X 1; X 2) □ (X 1; X 3)	(; is distributes over □)
X 1 □ (X 2 □ X 3) = (X 1 □ X 2) □ X 3	(□is associative)
X 1 | X 2 = X 2 | X 1	(|is commutative)

In the following sections the operators are defined at pattern level, i.e., patterns are applied in certain context using those operators. Above axioms are then lifted to pattern level in form of rules.

4.2 Sequential Operator

This is an operator that indicates the sequence of the act, and it is used to show the flow or direction of usage of the patterns. P1 ; P2 means that pattern P1 must be applied first and then pattern P2 is applied.

4.2.1 Applying Patterns Sequentially in Certain Context

Assumption and Commitment constraints are used to allow the Sequential application of patterns in a certain context.

The assumption and commitment and the use of the sequential operator is depicted in Table 4.1.

As seen in chapter 3 patterns applied sequentially in certain context needs to satisfy conditions. If **P1 ; P2** then the Assumption of the **P2** must be implied by the Commitment of **P1**. The matching of context is expressed in Figure 4.1 by the red circles which means the following:

Let $1 \leq i \leq 2$

A is the Assumption of abstract pattern

Ai is the Assumption of concrete pattern **Pi**

C is the Commitment of abstract pattern

Ci is the Commitment of concrete pattern **Pi**

In circle 1, **A** implies **A1** (usually **A** is equal to **A1**)

In circle 2, **C2** implies **C** (usually **C2** is equal to **C**)

In circle 3, **C1** implies **A2**

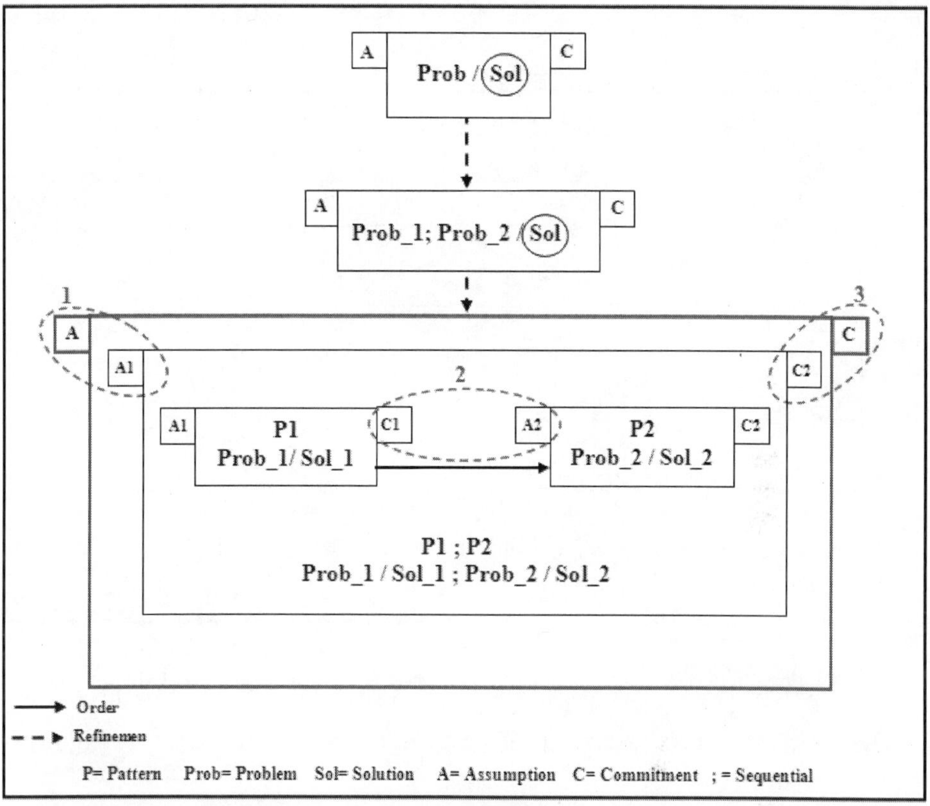

Figure 4.1: The Assumption and Commitment and the use of the sequential operator

4.2.2 Algebraic Rules

These algebraic rules are used to show how certain rules will determine the application order of the patterns.

The following are rules for the Sequential operator:

Sequential

Rule 1

- **P1; (P2; P3) = (P1; P2) ; P3**

Applying P1 then P2 followed by P3 is the same as applying P1 followed by P2 and then P3.

Figure 4.2 will demonstrate the first half of the algebraic **Rule 1** which is **P1; (P2; P3)** and the role the Assumption and Commitment.

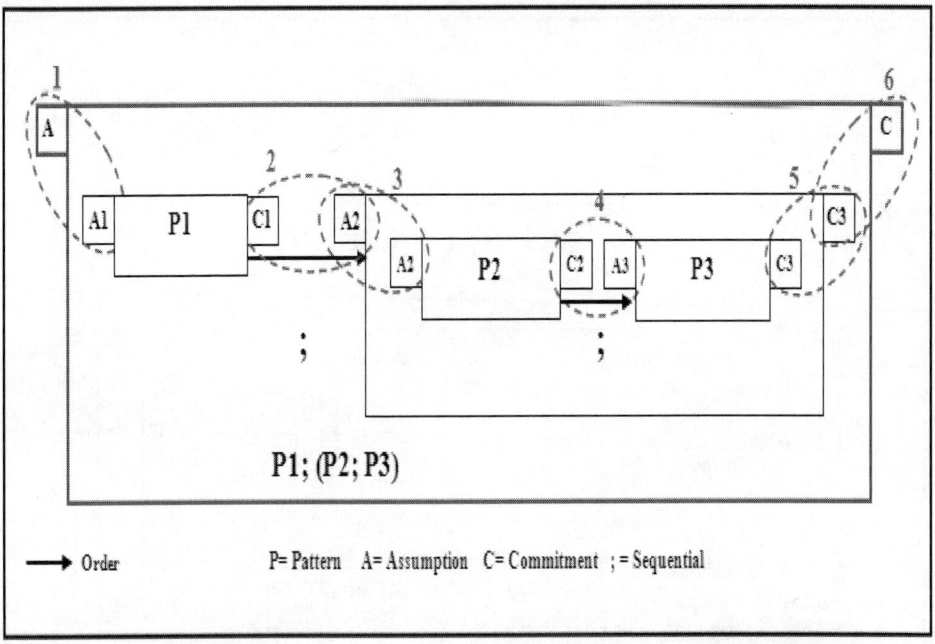

Figure 4.2: Illustrate the first half of the sequential algebraic Rule 1

The matching of context is expressed in Figure 4.2 by the circles which means the following

Let 1 ≤ i ≤ 3

A is the Assumption of abstract pattern

Ai is the Assumption of concrete pattern **Pi**

C is the Commitment of abstract pattern

Ci is the Commitment of concrete pattern **Pi**

In circle 1, **A** implies **A1** (usually **A** is equal to **A1**)

In circle 2, **C1** implies **A2**

In circle 3, **A2** implies **A2** In circle 4, **C2** implies **A3**

In circle 5, **C3** implies **C3**

In circle 6, **C3** implies **C** (usually **C3** is equal to **C**)

Figure 4.3 will demonstrate the second half of the algebraic **Rule 1** which is **(P1; P2) ; P3** and the role the Assumption and Commitment.

In order for this application to happen the Assumption and Commitment condition of the sequential operator rule must be met (the Commitment of the first applied pattern is the same as the Assumption of the next pattern).

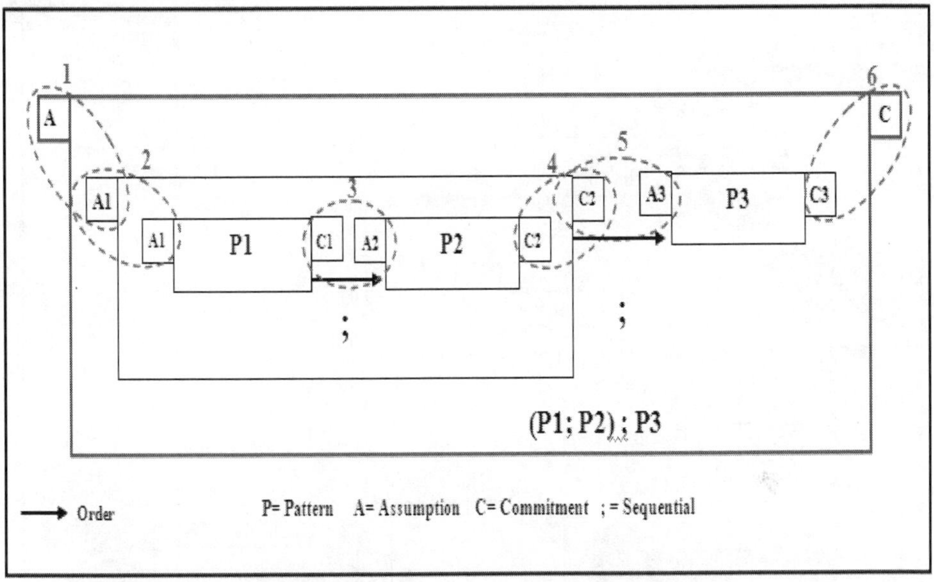

Figure 4.3: Illustrate the second half of the sequential algebraic Rule 1

The matching of context is expressed in Figure 4.3 by the circles which means the following:

Let $1 \leq i \leq 3$

A is the Assumption of abstract pattern

Ai is the Assumption of concrete pattern **Pi**

C is the Commitment of abstract pattern

Ci is the Commitment of concrete pattern **Pi**

In circle 1, **A** implies **A1** (usually **A** is equal to **A1**)

In circle 2, **A1** implies **A1**

In circle 3, **C1** implies **A2** In circle 4, **C2** implies **C2**

In circle 5, **C2** implies **A3**

In circle 6, **C3** implies **C** (usually **C3** is equal to **C**)

This will proves that both side of **Rule 1** are equal.

4.2.3 Example

The example used in this section is from Ian Graham's (WU), which appears in *A Pattern Language for Web Usability* [44], which is a pattern language for designing and building websites. WU will be discussed in detail in Chapter 5. The full patterns descriptions are in Appendix A.

WU patterns, the diagram (**Getting started on your site)** will be used to illustrate the use of the Sequential operator in applying patterns by using some of the patterns in Figure 4.4:

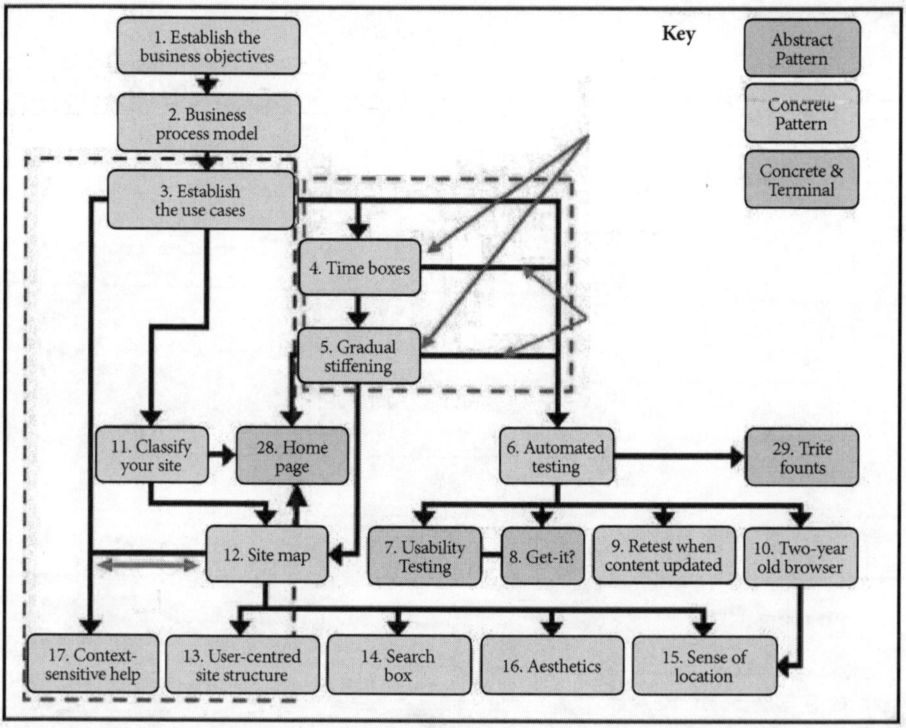

Figure 4.4: Illustration of the use of the sequential operator in the application of the patterns in Box 4.4-1 from WU [45]

The chosen patterns from Figure 4.4 are:

P1 (*Establish the business objectives*), P2 (*Business process model*) and P3 (*Establish the use cases*), which need to be applied in the sequence (**P1; P2; P3**) shown in the diagram above. This will consequently illustrate the sequential operator. The conditions of the sequential operator rule are satisfied:

The Assumption **A2** of **P2** is the same as the Commitment **C1** of **P1**. The Assumption **A3** of **P3** is the same as the Commitment **C2** of **P2**.

Where the Assumption and Commitment are as follows:

P1 (*Establish the business objectives*)

A1: there are business objectives.

C1: List of chosen business objectives.

P2 (*Business process model*)

A2: list of chosen business objectives.

C2: list of business process corresponding to the business objectives.

P3 (Establish the use cases**)**

A3: list of chosen business process.

C3: list of use cases corresponding to the business process.

4.3 Choice Operator (□)

This is an operator that indicates a choice between more than one possibility. This operator is used to show that any pattern or patterns that meet a need for the usage of the patterns can be used. It also means that the designer have the choice to pick at least one pattern, but more than one can be picked.

4.3.1 Choice of Applying Patterns in Certain Context

Assumption and Commitment constraints are used to allow the choice of patterns in certain context (see Figure 4.5).

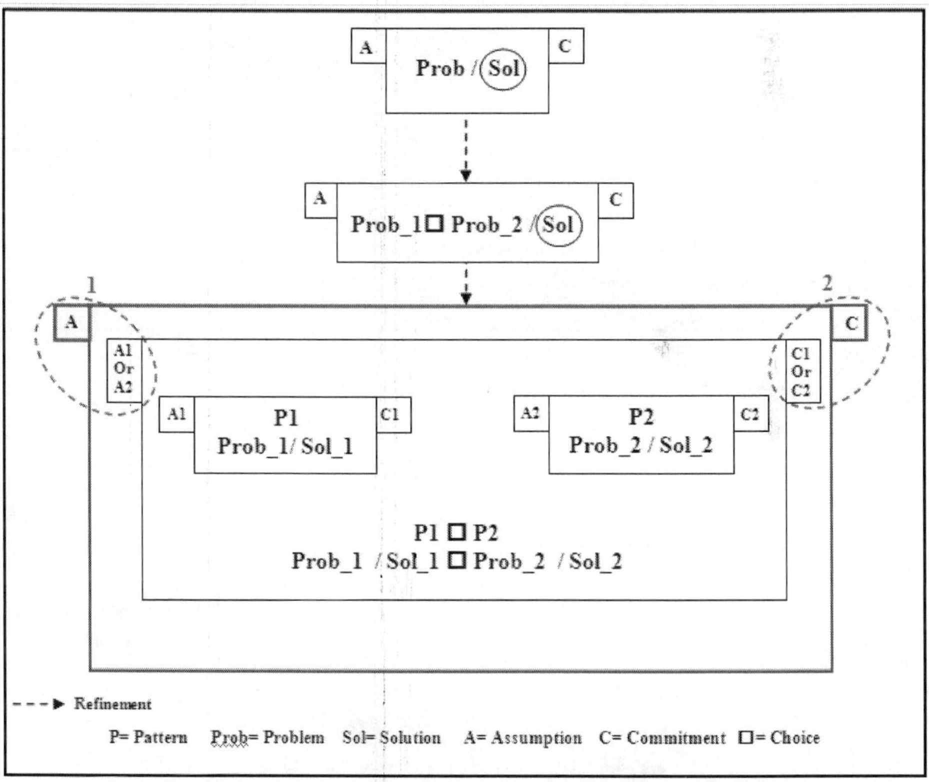

Figure 4.5: The Assumption and Commitment and the use of the Choice operator

If **P1** □ **P2** is applied in a certain context then the following conditions need to be satisfied:

The Assumption '**A1** or **A2**' must be implied by the Assumption **A** and '**C1** or **C2**' must imply the Commitment **C**. The matching of context is expressed in Figure 4.5 by the red circles which means the following:

Let $1 \leq i \leq 2$

A is the Assumption of abstract pattern

Ai is the Assumption of concrete pattern **Pi**

C is the Commitment of abstract pattern

Ci is the Commitment of concrete pattern **Pi**

In circle 1, **A** implies (**A1** or **A2**)

In circle 2, (**C1** or **C2**) implies **C**

4.3.2 Algebraic Rules

These algebraic rules are used to show how certain rules will be used in the application order of the patterns.

The following are rules for the choice operator:

Choice

Rule 2

- **P1 □ P1= P1**

A choice between the same pattern will result in applying the pattern once.

Figure 4.6 will illustrate the algebraic **Rule 2** and the role of the Assumption and Commitment.

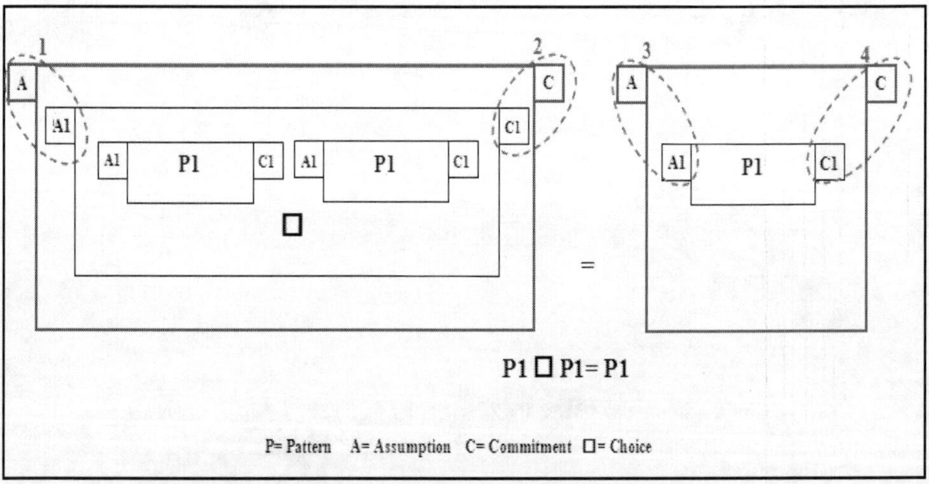

Figure 4.6: Illustrate the Choice algebraic Rule 2

The matching of context is expressed in Figure 4.6 by the red circles which means the following:

A1 is the Assumption of concrete pattern **P1**

C1 is the Commitment of concrete pattern **P1**

In circle 1, **A** implies **A1**

In circle 2, **C** implies **C1**

In circle 3, **A** implies **A1**

In circle 4, **C** implies **C1**

Rule 3

❖ **P1 □ P2 = P2 □ P1**

Order of choice is not relevant.

Figure 4.7 will illustrate the algebraic **Rule 3** and the role of the Assumption and Commitment.

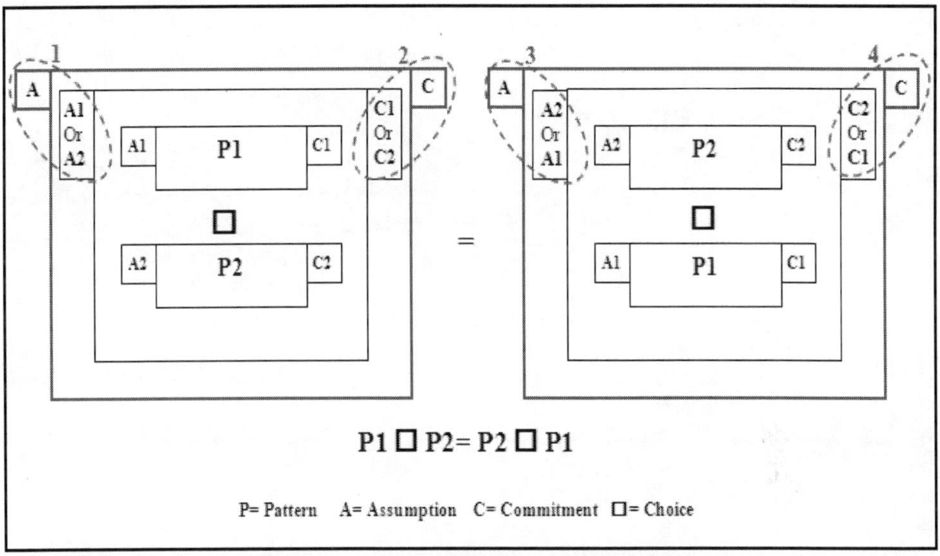

Figure 4.7: Illustrate the Choice algebraic Rule 3

Figures 4.7 shows that for both side of the algebraic rule equation the end result is the same. The matching of context is expressed in that figure by the red circles which means the following:

Let $1 \leq i \leq 2$

A is the Assumption of abstract pattern

Ai is the Assumption of concrete pattern **Pi**

C is the Commitment of abstract pattern

Ci is the Commitment of concrete pattern **Pi**

In circle 1, **A** implies (**A1** or **A2**)

In circle 2, (**C1** or **C2**) implies **C**

In circle 3, **A** implies (**A2** or **A1**)

In circle 4, (**C2** or **C1**) implies **C**

This proves that both side of **Rule 3** are equal.

Rule 4

- **P1; (P2 □ P3) = (P1; P2) □ (P1; P3)**

Applying P1 in sequence (or followed by) with P2 or P3 is the same as applying P1 followed by P2 or P1 followed by P3.

Figure 4.8 will demonstrate the first half of the algebraic **Rule 4** which is **P1; (P2 □ P3)** and the role the Assumption and Commitment.

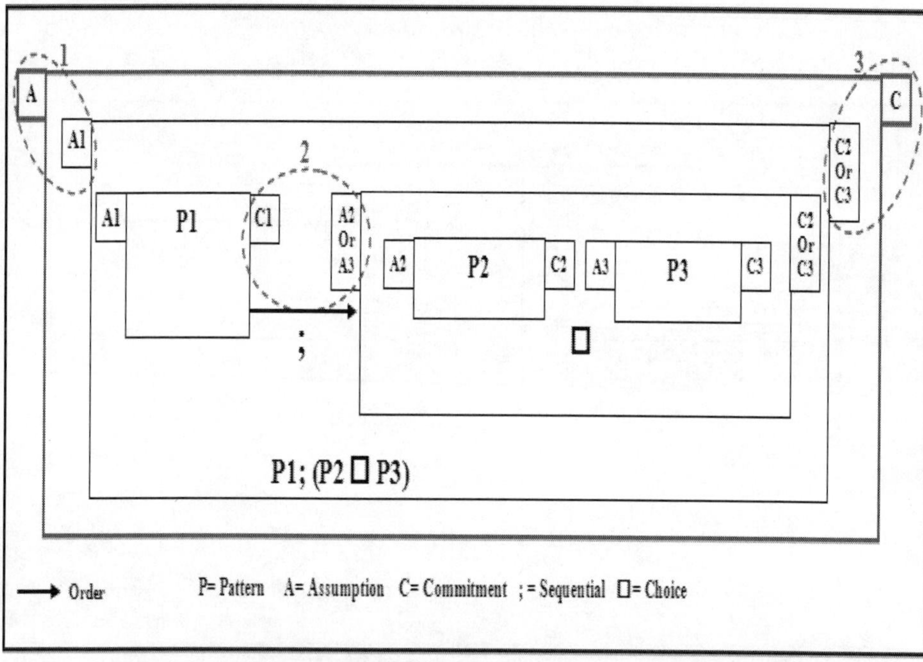

Figure 4.8: Illustrate the first half of the choice algebraic Rule 4

The matching of context is expressed in Figure 4.8 by the red circles which means the following:

Let $1 \leq i \leq 3$

A is the Assumption of abstract pattern

Ai is the Assumption of concrete pattern **Pi**

C is the Commitment of abstract pattern

Ci is the Commitment of concrete pattern **Pi**

In circle 1, **A** implies **A1**

In circle 2, **C1** implies (**A2** or **A3**)

In circle 3, (**C2** or **C3**) implies **C**

Figure 4.9 will illustrate the second half of the algebraic **Rule 4** which is **(P1; P2) □ (P1; P3)** and the role the Assumption and Commitment.

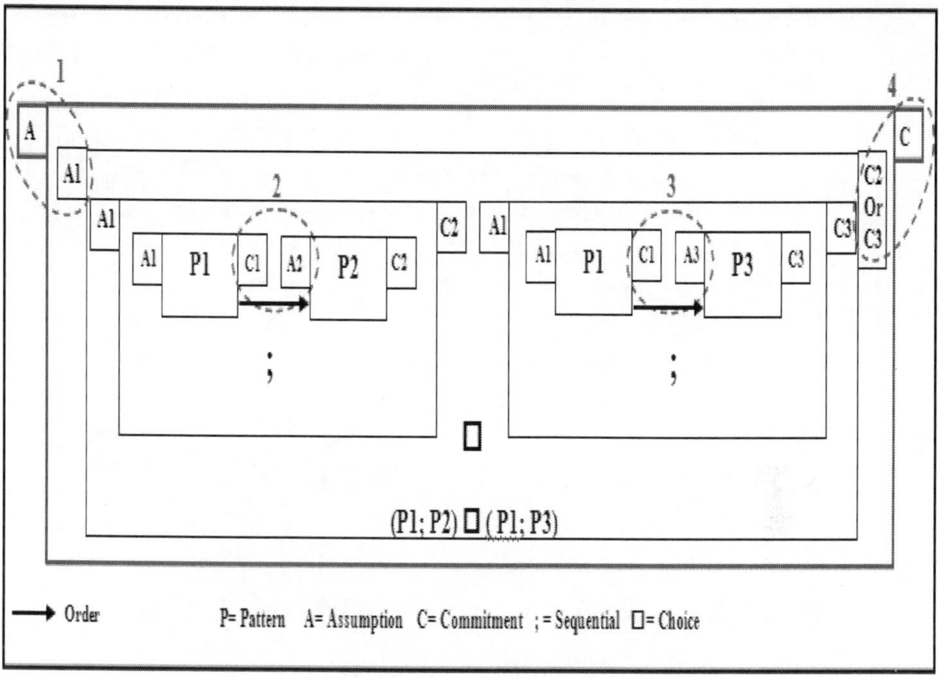

Figure 4.9: Illustrate the second half of the choice algebraic Rule 4

Both figure 4.8 and 4.8 shows that for both side of the algebraic rule the end result is the same. **Rule 4** is expressed as follows:

Let $1 \leq i \leq 3$

A is the Assumption of abstract pattern

Ai is the Assumption of concrete pattern **Pi**

C is the Commitment of abstract pattern

Ci is the Commitment of concrete pattern **Pi**

In circle 1, **A** implies **A1**

In circle 2, **C1** implies **A2**

In circle 3, **C1** implies **A3**

In circle 4, (**C2** or **C3**) implies **C**

This proves that both side of **Rule 4** are equal.

Rule 5

P1 □ (P2 □ P3) = (P1 □ P2) □ P3

The choice is associative.

Figure 4.10 will demonstrate the first half of the algebraic **Rule 5** which is **P1 □ (P2 □ P3)** and the role of the Assumption and Commitment.

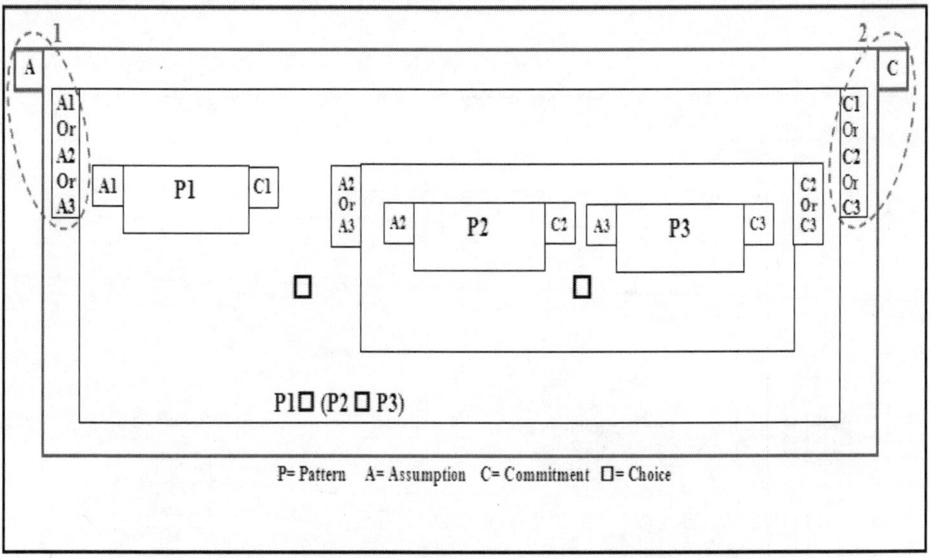

Figure 4.10: Illustrate the first half of the choice algebraic Rule 5

The matching of context is expressed in Figure 4.10 by the red circles which means the following:

Let $1 \leq i \leq 3$

A is the Assumption of abstract pattern

Ai is the Assumption of concrete pattern **Pi**

C is the Commitment of abstract pattern

Ci is the Commitment of concrete pattern **Pi**

In circle 1, **A** implies (**A1** or **A2** or **A3)**

In circle 2, (**C1** or **C2** or **C3)** implies **C**

Figure 4.11 will illustrate the second half of the algebraic **Rule 5** which is **(P1 □ P2) □ P3** and the role the Assumption and Commitment.

4.3.3 Example

The example will illustrate the use of the choice operator with the Assumption and Commitment to guide the selection of the application of the next pattern in the pattern map. WU patterns [45], The full patterns descriptions are in Appendix A, the diagram **(Dealing with workflow and security)** will be used to illustrate the application of the choice operator in applying patterns by using some of the patterns in Figure 4.12:

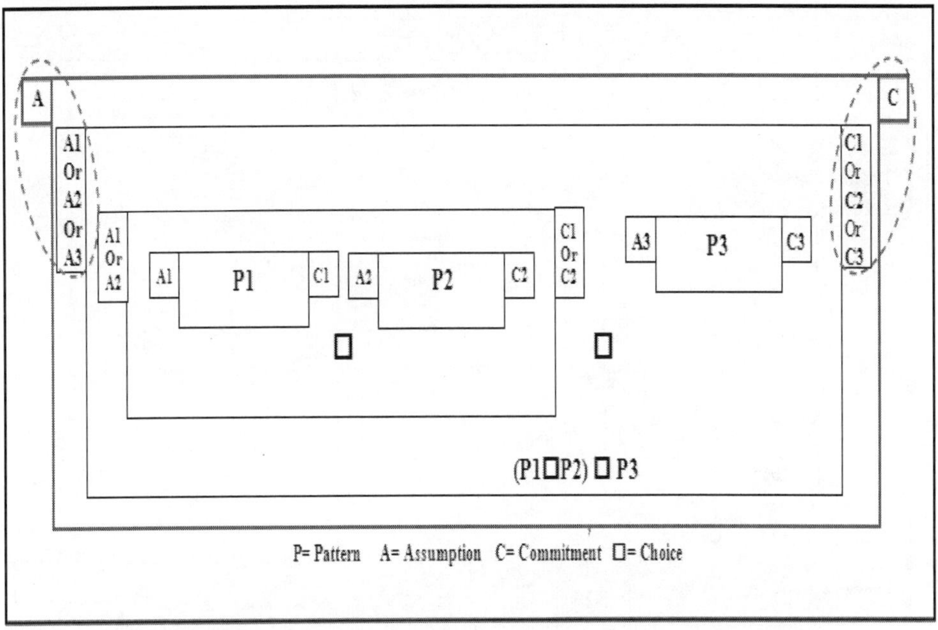

Figure 4.11: Illustrate the second half of the choice algebraic Rule 5

The matching of context is expressed in Figure 4.11 by the red circles which means the following:

Let $1 \le i \le 3$

A is the Assumption of abstract pattern

Ai is the Assumption of concrete pattern **Pi**

C is the Commitment of abstract pattern

Ci is the Commitment of concrete pattern **Pi**

In circle 1, **A** implies (**A1** or **A2** or **A3)**

In circle 2, (**C1** or **C2** or **C3)** implies **C**

This proves that both side of **Rule 5** are equal.

4.4 PARALLEL OPERATOR (|)

This is an operator that indicates that two patterns can be applied simultaneously. The choice here is in the order of applying which first and which second. This operator is used to simplify the writing of applying patterns in any order. P1|P2 means that P1 and P2 can be applied in any order, i.e., apply P1 first and then P2 or apply P2 first and then P1. The parallel operators is defined as follows

P1|P2 = P1 ;P2 □ P2 ;P1

Which mean there is a choice in the application order of these patterns.

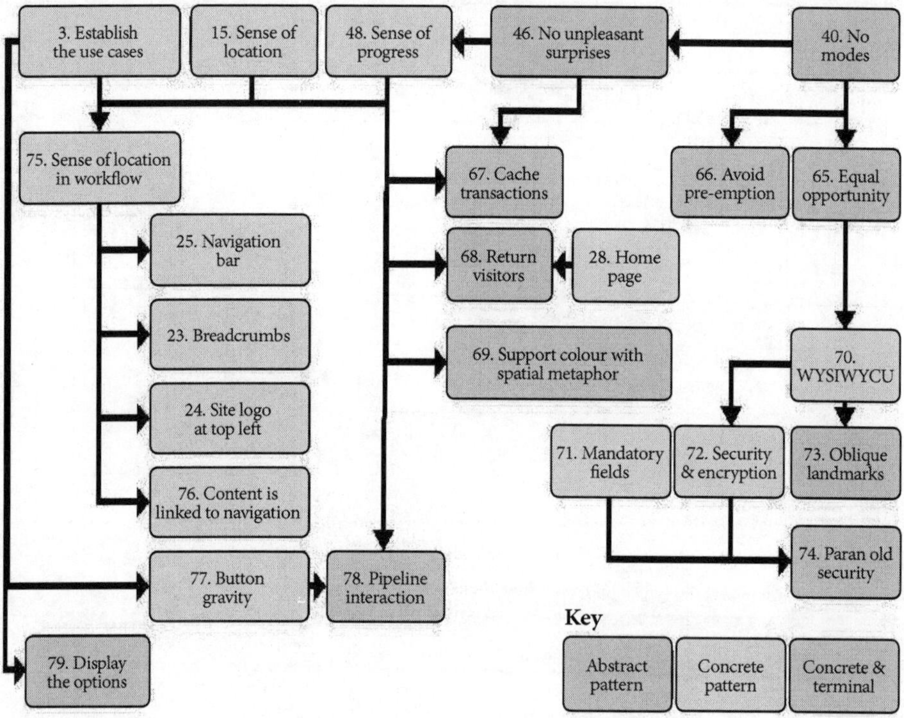

Figure 4.12: Illustration of the use of the choice operator in the application of the patterns in Box 4.12-1 from WU [45]

The use of choice operator will give the designer limited freedom in choosing the next pattern(s) to be applied.

The chosen patterns from Figure 4.12 are:

Pattern 25 (Navigation bar), Pattern 23 (Breadcrumbs), P24 (Site logo at top left) and P76 (Content is linked to navigation). At least one of them needs to be applied. This will therefore illustrate the choice operator.

Where the Assumption and Commitment are as follows:

Pattern 25 (Navigation bar)

A25: there is a current webpage to be displayed.

C25: is navigation bar dependent on the location

Pattern 23 (Breadcrumbs)

A23: there is a current webpage to be displayed.

C23: to put breadcrumbs at this webpage.

P24 (Site logo at top left)

A24: there is a current webpage to be displayed.

C24: to put a logo at his webpage.

P76 (Content is linked to navigation)

A76: there is a current webpage to be displayed.

C76: link contents of current webpage to navigation.

As can be seen from the Assumption of the above patterns that they are the same.

So the Assumption of **P25 □ P23 □ P24 □ P76** is: there is a current webpage to be displayed.

The Commitment of **P25 □ P23 □ P24 □ P76** is at least one of the Commitments of **P25, P23, P24** and **P76.**

4.4.1 Applying Patterns in Parallel in Certain Context

Assumption and commitment constraints are used to allow the parallel operator of patterns in certain context (see Figure 4.13).

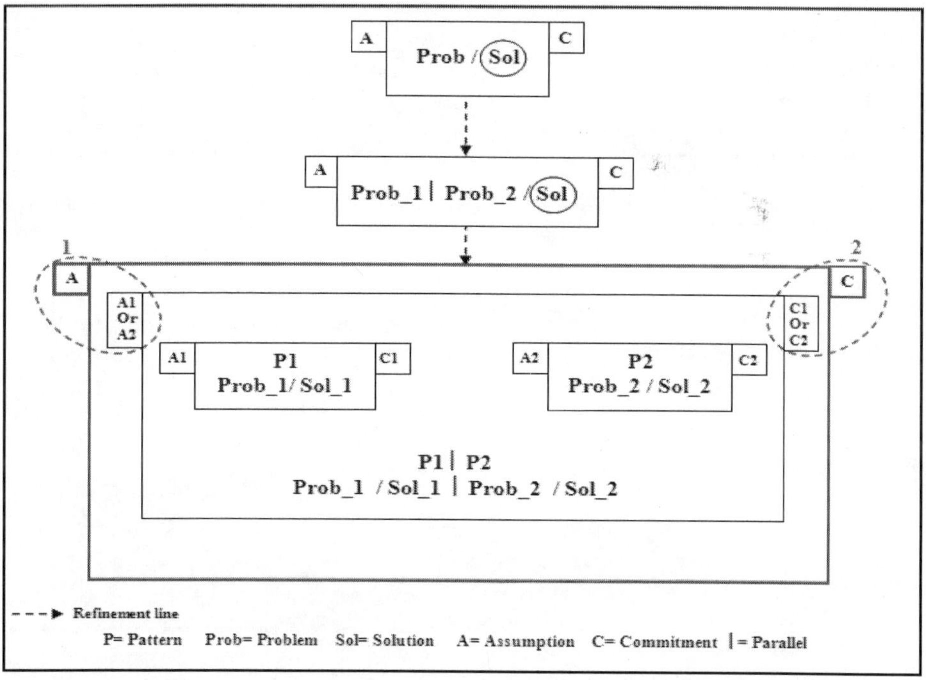

Figure 4.13: The Assumption and Commitment and the use of the parallel operator

The matching of context is expressed in Figure 4.13 by the red circles which means the following:

Let 1 ≤ i ≤ 2

A is the Assumption of abstract pattern

Ai is the Assumption of concrete pattern **Pi**

C is the Commitment of abstract pattern

Ci is the Commitment of concrete pattern **Pi**

In circle 1, **A** implies (**A1** and **A**2)

In circle 2, (**C1** and **C2**) implies **C**

4.4.2 Algebraic Rules

The following is a rule for the parallel operator:

Parallel

Rule 6

- **P1 | P2 = P2 | P1**

Applying P1 and P2 in parallel is the same as applying P2 and P1 in parallel.

Where **P1 | P2 = P1 ;P2 □ P2 ;P1**

And **P2 | P1 = P2 ;P1 □ P1 ;P2**

Figure 4.14 will illustrate the first half of the algebraic **Rule 6** which is **P1 | P2** and the role the Assumption and Commitment.

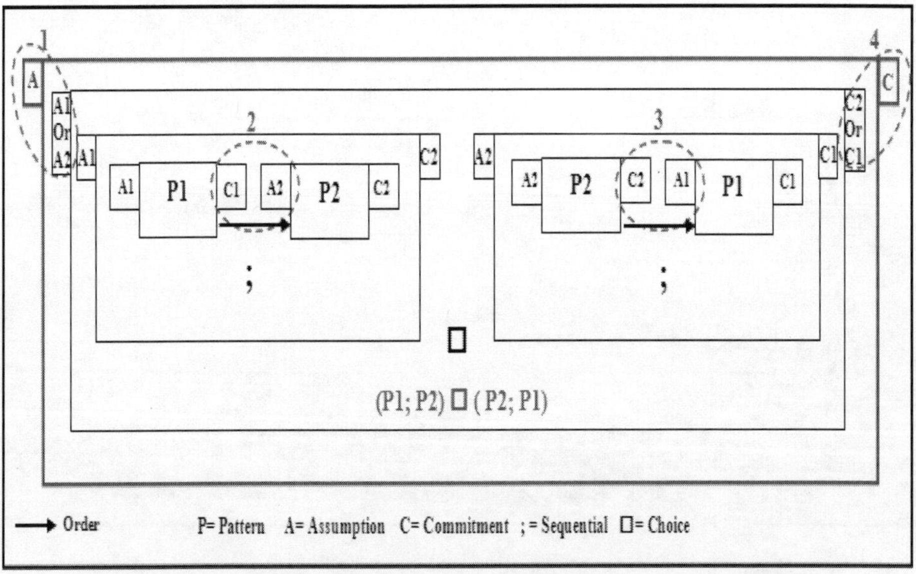

Figure 4.14: Illustrate the first half of the parallel algebraic Rule 6

The matching of context is expressed in Figure 4.14 by the red circles which means the following:

Let 1 ≤ i ≤ 2

A is the Assumption of abstract pattern

Ai is the Assumption of concrete pattern **Pi**

C is the Commitment of abstract pattern

Ci is the Commitment of concrete pattern **Pi**

In circle 1, **A** implies (**A1** or **A2**)

In circle 2, **C1** implies **A2**

In circle 3, **C2** implies **A1**

In circle 4, (**C2** or **C1**) implies **C**

Figure 4.15 will illustrate the second half of the algebraic **Rule 6** which is **P2|P1** and the role the Assumption and Commitment.

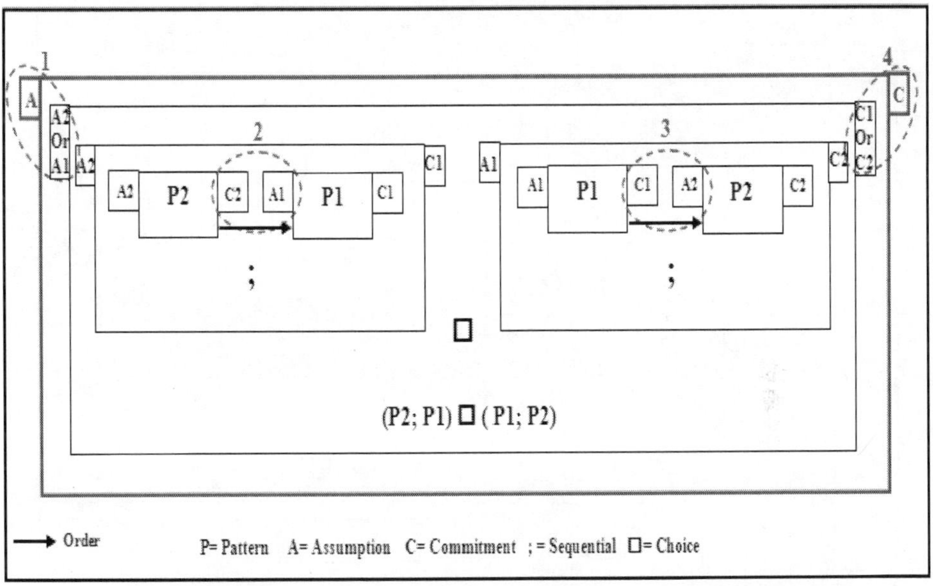

Figure 4.15: Illustrate the second half of the parallel algebraic Rule 6

The matching of context is expressed in Figure 4.15 by the red circles which means the following:

Let 1 ≤ i ≤ 2

A is the Assumption of abstract pattern

Ai is the Assumption of concrete pattern **Pi**

C is the Commitment of abstract pattern

Ci is the Commitment of concrete pattern **Pi**

In circle 1, **A** implies (**A1** or **A2**)

In circle 2, **C2** implies **A1**

In circle 3, **C1** implies **A2**

In circle 4, (**C1** or **C2)** implies **C**

This proves that both side of **Rule 6** are equal.

4.4.3 Example

The same example as before, WU patterns [45], the full patterns descriptions are in Appendix A, the diagram **Adding detail** will be used to illustrate the application of the parallel operator.

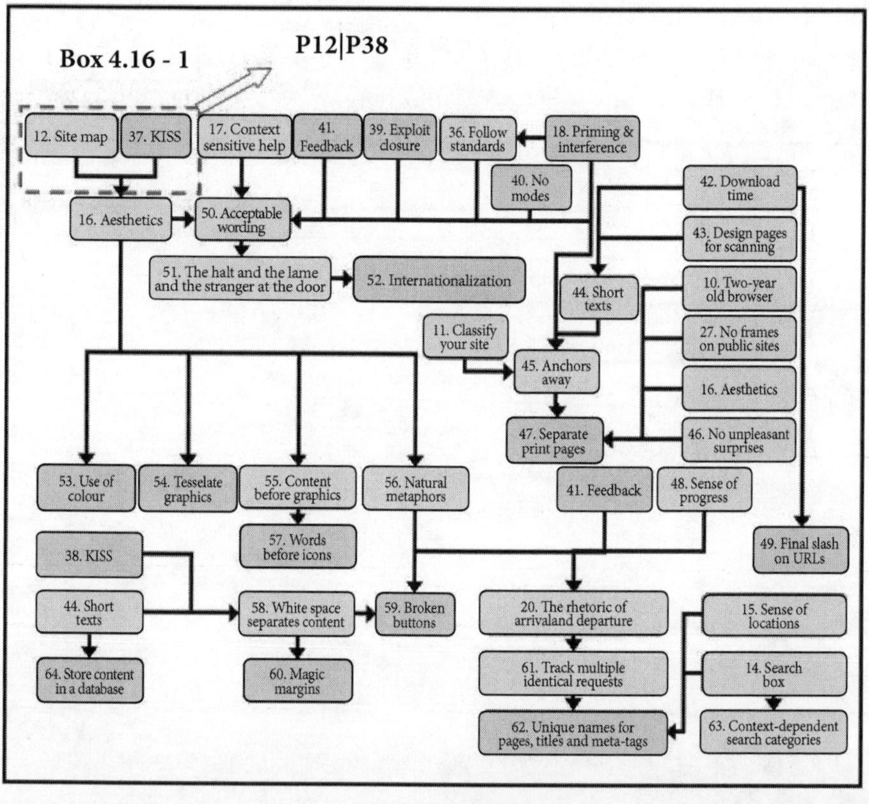

Figure 4.16: Illustration of the use of the parallel operator in the application of the patterns in Box 4.16-1 from WU [45]

The chosen patterns from Figure 4.16 are:

P12 (*site map*), P38 (*KISS*) can be applied in any order, i.e., in parallel. The Assumption/Commitment of them are:

P12 (site map)

A12: there is a website structure

C12: is provide the user with a contextual overview of the site

P38 (Kiss)

A38: there is a website structure

C38: simple site structure

The Assumption of **P12 | P38** is **'A12** or **A38'**

The Commitment of **P12 | P38** is **'C12** or **C38'**

4.5 SUMMARY

This chapter introduced the decomposition and composition operators. In order to decompose a problem into sub-problems and to compose their solutions, a set of operators was defined: Sequential, Choice, and Parallel. Their definition and meaning were illustrated and some algebraic rules for using them with respect to the Assumption and Commitment constraints. The method of writing them is described as an algebraic expression. Examples were also given to demonstrate Sequential, Choice, and Parallel operators.

CHAPTER

5

Case Studies

5.1 Introduction to WU and Welie Patterns Collection

This chapter will analyse parts of the design of two existing websites using the Assumption/Commitment framework.

The patterns used in the design are from WU and Welie [44, 45, 88], the full patterns descriptions are in Appendix A and B, as a building guide in the examination of the design of the two websites. The first case study examines the design of an existing shopping website- etidy. The second case study examines the design of an existing E-government website for Child Benefits.

WU is a pattern language for designing and building usable websites. The way this language is built will be noted in section 5.1.1.

Welie pattern library for interaction design is a collection of patterns that can be help designer as reference or bank when designing websites. The way this library is constructed will be noted in section 5.1.2.

5.1.1 The Web Usability (WU)

The Web Usability (WU) [44, 45] pattern language is used in the design of the websites analysed in both case studies.

The language sprang from a workshop organised by Ian Graham at the OT2001 conference in Oxford. In this workshop he suggested the names and outlines of about 70 patterns with performances that were completed and discussed by participants working in pairs. The language grew organically in this manner, and in its final published form consists of a network of 79 highly interconnected patterns, each of them divided into four sections that take the form of pattern maps. The four sections have been labelled for the following functions:

- ❖ Getting started on your site (see Fig. 5.1)
- ❖ Enhancing usability (see Fig. 5.2)

- Adding detail (see Fig. 5.3)
- Dealing with workflow and security (see Fig. 5.4)

Some patterns in these maps appear in more than one section. In these maps, the patterns are classified into abstract, concrete and terminal patterns and are shown by their colour coding.

These sections broadly follow the order in which they might be dealt with in an actual scenario, in a similar fashion to Alexander's APL. Graham suggests that one should use an actual problem in order to fully appreciate the workings of these patterns, and to begin with Pattern 1: ***Establish the business objectives***. One should then continue until one reaches a terminal pattern. Particular design problems or kinds of site can be handled using sublanguages. A sequence can be built using the following questions:

- Is the pattern relevant?
- Can it be ignored?
- How does it apply in this case?
- What solution will it generate?

The completed sequence results in a preliminary list of patterns useful for a particular problem. The next stage is to go through the list in order, asking the same questions of each pattern and remembering to consider each pattern in its opening context in order to eliminate repetitions. Finally, Graham says, there emerges a working subset of the pattern language applicable to a particular problem.

The patterns in the WU pattern language are described as being of three types: Abstract, Concrete and Terminal. Figures 5.1- 5.4. Shows the WU pattern maps, which are divided into four diagrams.

5.1.2 Welie Patterns Library for Interaction Design

Welie pattern library [88] for interaction design is a collection of patterns or a pattern bank or as he stated "they are references or basic 'toolkit' ". The website contains a lot of patterns as Welie called them "best practices in Interaction Design patterns". The patterns are listed in meaningful groups which are divided into three main groups. These three groups are divided into sub-groups containing a collection of patterns. They are as follow:

1. **User needs:** list the Patterns that meet the user direct need. They are divided into the following sub-groups:
   b. Navigating around (for example contains 25 patterns)
   c. Basic interactions
   d. Searching
   e. Shopping
   f. Dealing with data
   g. Personalizing
   h. Making choices
   i. Giving input
   j. Miscellaneous

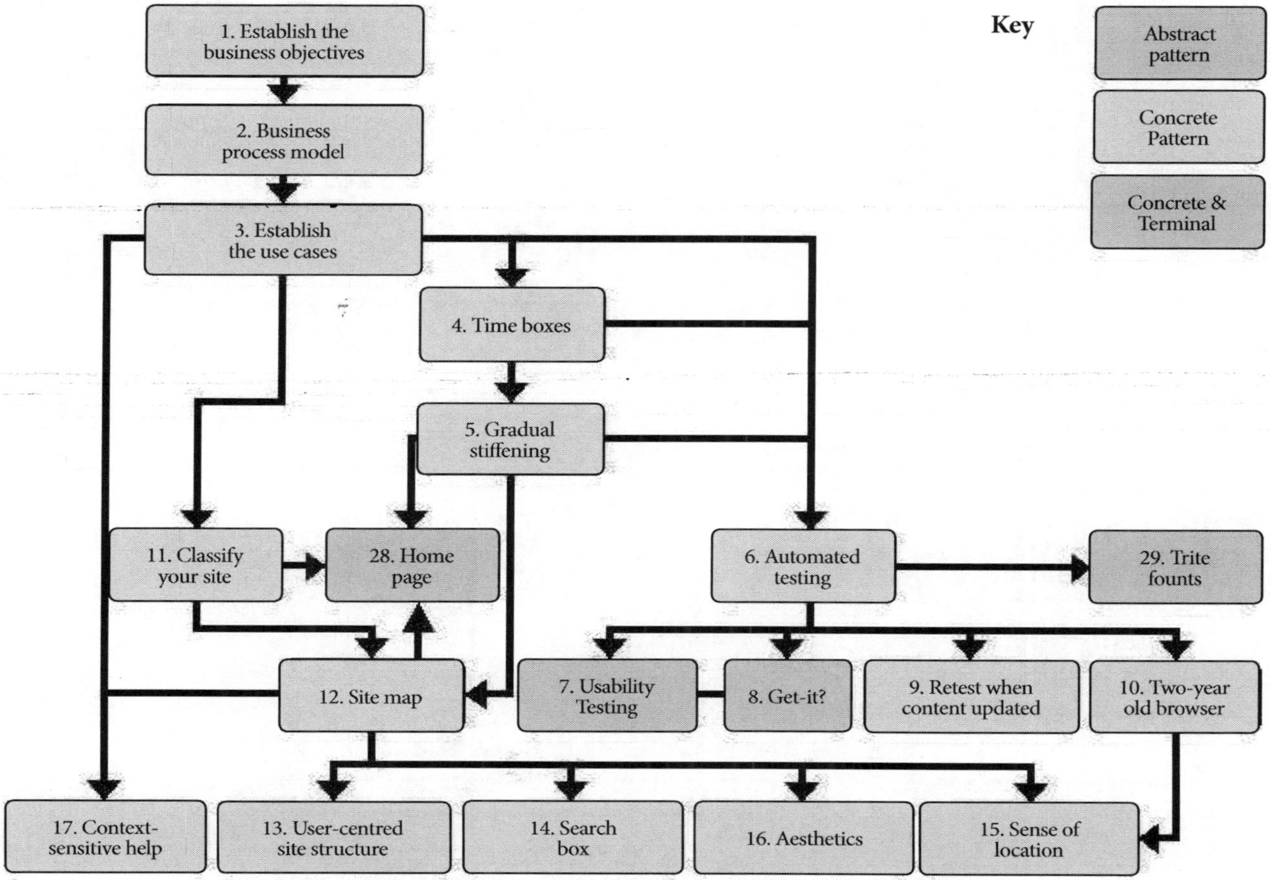

Figure 5.1: Diagram 1 (Getting started on your site) from WU [45]

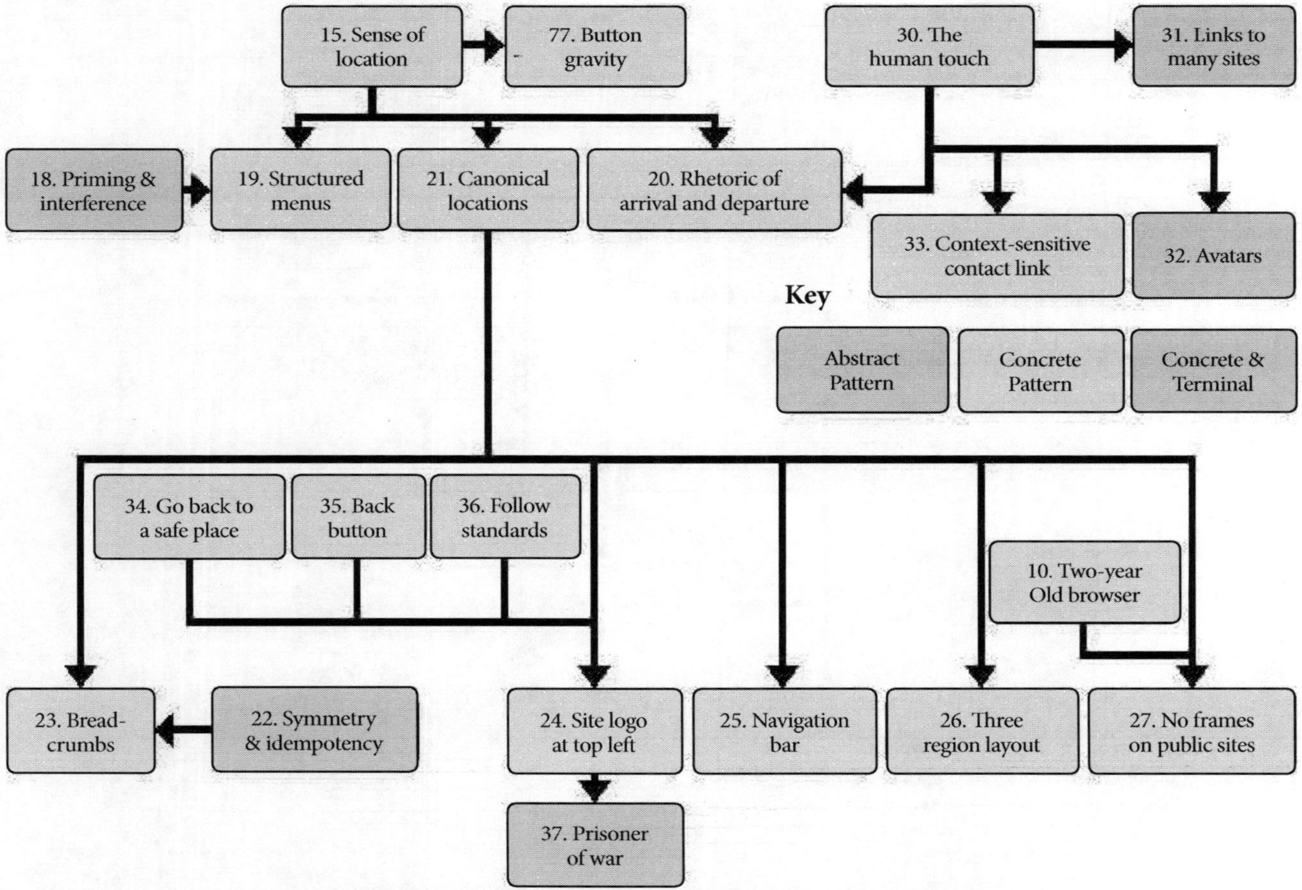

Figure 5.2: Diagram 2 (Enhancing usability) from WU [45]

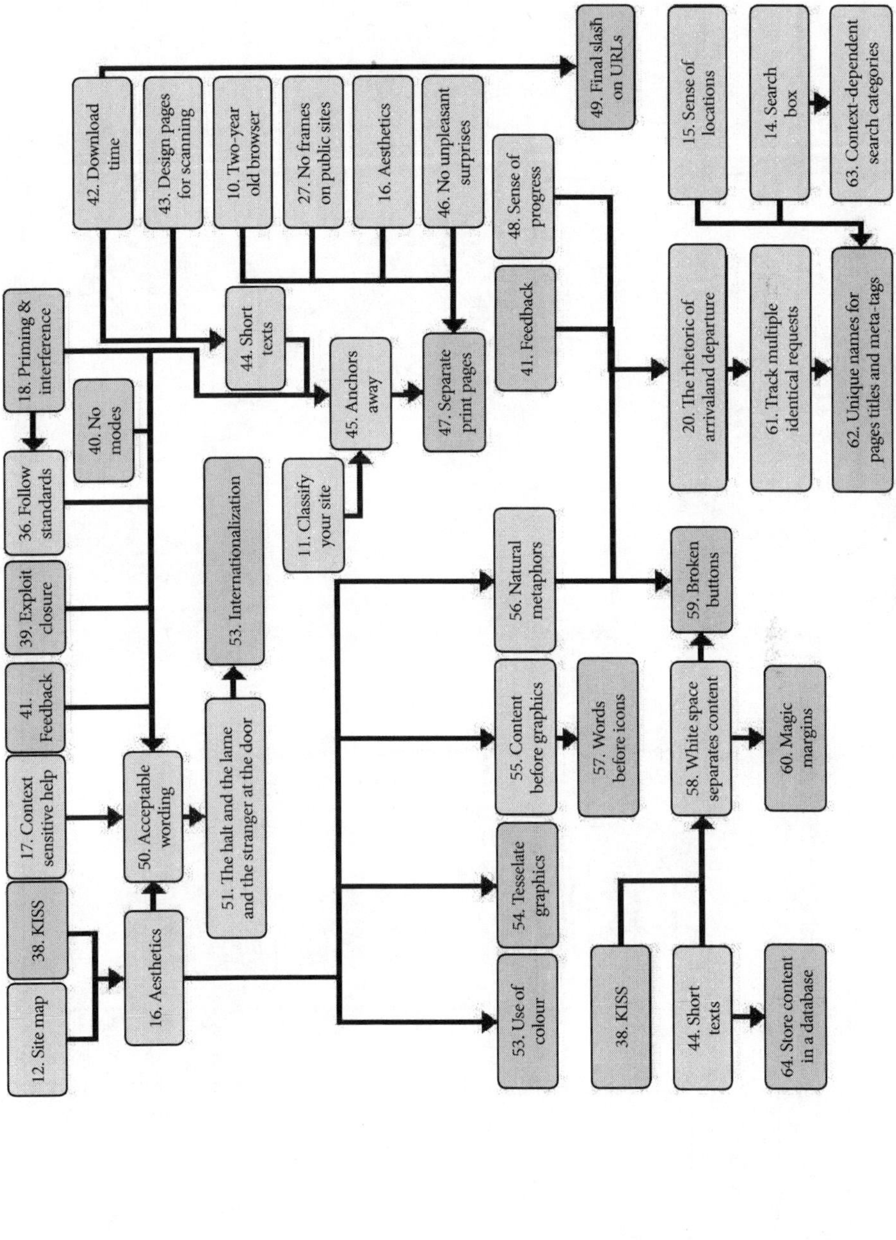

Figure 5.3: Diagram 3 (Adding detail) from WU [45]

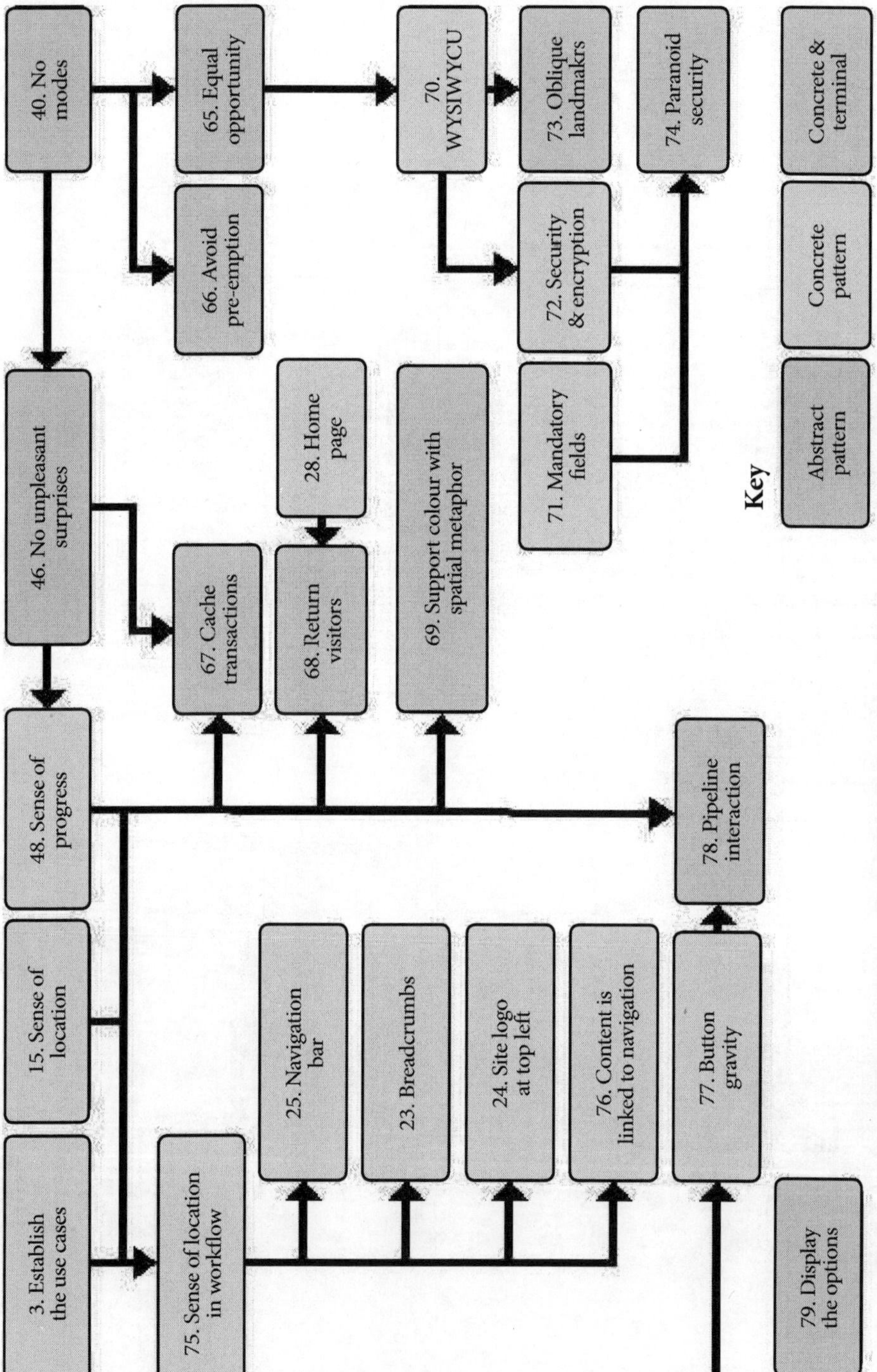

Figure 5.4: Diagram 4 (Dealing with workflow and security) from WU[45]

2. **Application needs**: list the Patterns that help the designer and the application to communicate better with the user direct need. They are divided into the following sub-groups:
   c. Drawing attention
   d. Feedback
   e. Simplifying interaction
3. **Context of design**: list the Patterns that deal with the context of the design. They are divided into the following sub-groups:
   d. Site types
   e. Experiences
   f. Page types

5.2 A Shopping Website Case Study

5.2.1 Introduction

The case study is examining the design of an existing shopping website called etidy [38] (see Figure 5.5). This website sells only one product and it is a necklace hanger. A closer examination of the website reveals that the designer used a selection of User Interface patterns (UI) patterns (see Figure 5.5) for the design of the website. User Interface patterns, taken from WU and Welie [44, 45, 88] are used in the design of many shopping sites like Amazon, Ebay, Tesco ...etc. The selected patterns are the essential patterns needed to build a small shopping website.

The purpose of this case study is to evaluate the book findings, i.e., the evaluation of the Assumption /Commitment framework and the use of the operators in the application of patterns to build a small shopping website.

The case study will be divided into two parts. In the first part the existing website will be examined. In the second part, the design of the website is modified to examine the ability of the framework in supporting any extension or modification in the form of adding or removing patterns.

5.2.2 The First Part of the Case Study

The patterns used in the design of the etidy website [38] (see Figure 5.9) are basic patterns and can be used to build any shopping website. The aim here is to examine the use of the Assumption /Commitment framework in applying those patterns and determined the order in which they can be applied.

In this first part a total of 10 basic patterns are picked from WU and Welie [44, 45, 88], the full patterns descriptions are in Appendix A and B. The first four patterns are picked to determine the type of website to be built. The rest of the patterns are selected to show the design of the basic functionality of shopping website. Figure 5.6 show the two sets of patterns.

Figure 5.5: The etidy website main page [38]

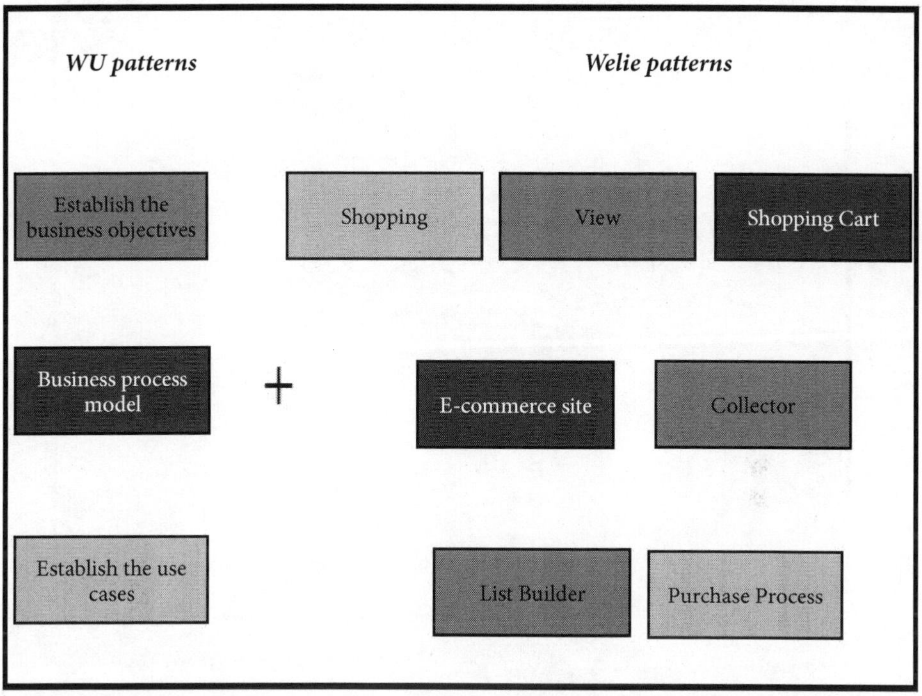

Figure 5.6: Illustrates the main patterns from two different pattern banks used in the etidy website

Because the original design of the website is unknown a design in the form of pattern map is proposed. This design is represented as a pattern map and illustrated in Figure 5.9. The proposed design is analysed using the Assumption/Commitment framework. In the analysis the application order of the patterns is determined, i.e., what is needed (Assumption) in order to apply a certain pattern and what is provided (Commitment) in order to apply the next pattern.

For the simplicity the pattern map will be divided to two sections:

a. Section one: ***The Site Type Design (Abstract Patterns)*** In this section the first 3 patterns can be used as a start to design any type of business [45]. These patterns are applied according to the context. The 4th pattern determines the site type and in this case an E-commerce site. The patterns in this section are *Abstract Patterns*. They are illustrated in Figure 5.7.

b. Section two: ***The Site Concrete Design (Concrete Patterns)*** In section one the type of site is determined. In section two a concrete design of the site is given, i.e., a concrete design for the abstract pattern E-commerce site is given. This is illustrated in Figure 5.8.

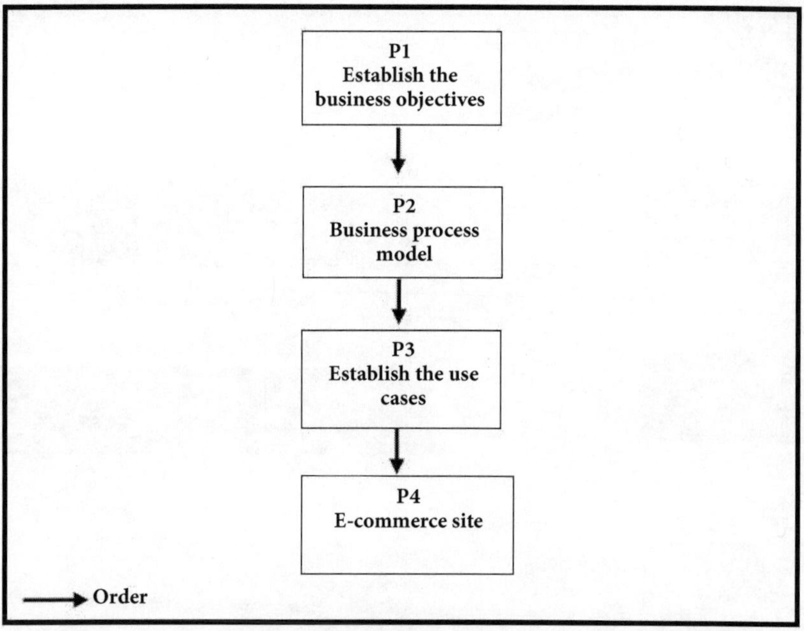

Figure 5.7: The site type design patterns for an E-commerce website

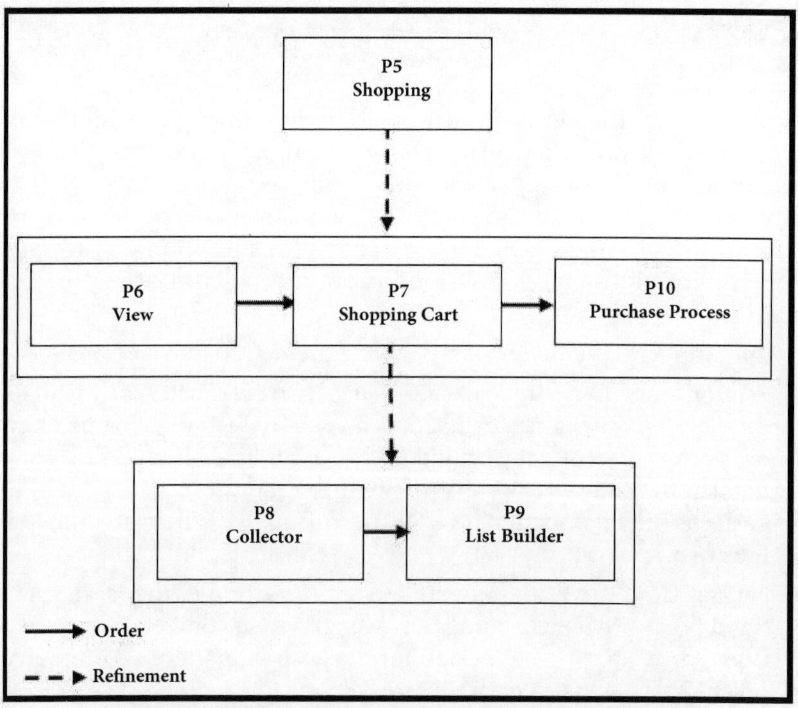

Figure 5.8: The etidy website concrete design patterns

Figure 5.9 illustrates the proposed patterns used in the etidy website.

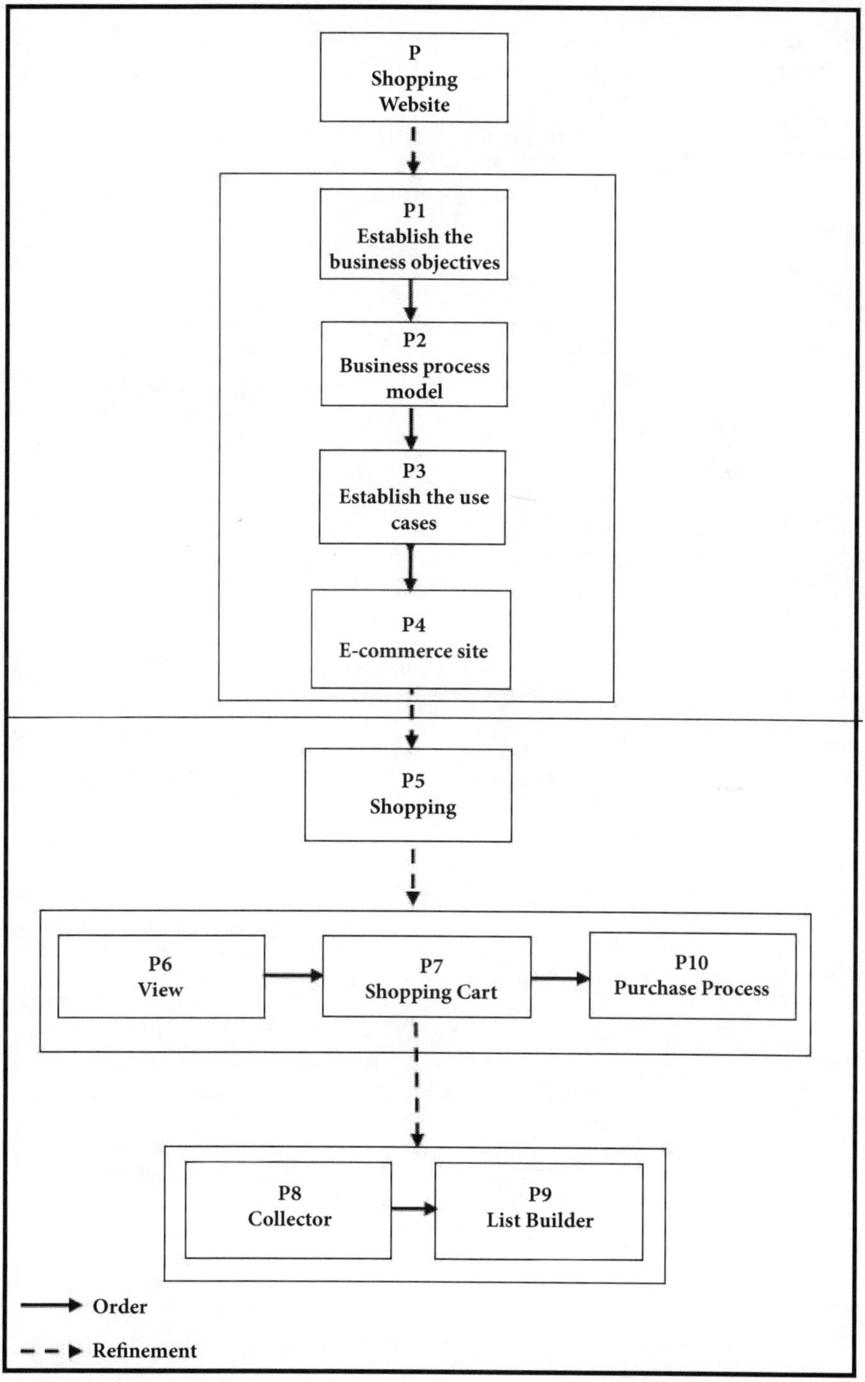

Figure 5.9: Illustrate the proposed patterns map used to build the etidy website

The following tables summarise problem/solution and Assumption/ Commitment for each patter used in the first part of the case study.

Table 5.1: The problem/solution of the used patterns in the etidy website

The problem/Solution of the used patterns			
Pattern name	**Source**	**Problem**	**Solution**
Pattern 1: Establish the business objectives	WU	To create a new website or modify an existing one	Hold a workshop involving as many stakeholders as possible. Make sure that potential users are represented by marketing personnel or the results of focus groups, surveys, etc. Find a good facilitator. Agree a mission statement. Find measures for each objective.
Pattern 2: Business process model	WU	To organise the content in a way that supports several navigation structures simultaneously	An understanding of the network of agents and commitments that make up the business must first be gained. The conversations that take place at an appropriate level of abstraction must be specified, so that they become stereotypes for actual stories. People must tell these stories. Ensure that both 'before' and 'after' business process models are produced. Eliminate conversations that do not correspond to business objectives (or discover the missed objective). Ensure that every objective is supported by a conversation.

The problem/Solution of the used patterns

Pattern name	**Source**	**Problem**	**Solution**
Pattern 3: Establish the use cases	WU	The site must serve at least one significant business purpose. For this reason we must look at all the use cases that we can predict users will want to execute.	Extract the use cases from the conversations in the BUSINESS PROCESS MODEL (2). Record their correspondences to the business objectives. Write post-conditions for each use case. Compare the vocabulary of the post-conditions to the type model. Write use cases in stimulus–response form. Convert the use cases into the user training manual and the test plan. One stimulus/response pair from the use case should correspond to one step in the workflow if the site deals with workflows. If not, do not constrain the user's ability to perform steps in any particular sequence. Ensure that you extract and document a business object type model from the use case goals.
Pattern 4: E-commerce Site	Welie	User wants to shop for a product.	Create a 'virtual' store where visitors can browse, choose and pay for all their selections in one go.
Pattern 5: Shopping	Welie	Users want to look for products of interest and potentially purchase them	Create an online shopping experience that matches off-line shopping experiences
Pattern 6: View	Welie	Users need to manage a collection of objects	Create an overview of objects that together is meaningful to users
Pattern 7: Shopping Cart	Welie	Users want to buy a product	Introduce a shopping cart where users can put their products in before they actually purchase them.

The problem/Solution of the used patterns			
Pattern name	**Source**	**Problem**	**Solution**
Pattern 8: Collector	Welie	Users need to temporarily gather a set of items for later use	Allow users to build their list of items by selecting the items as they are viewing them. Place a link to the collected items list on every page in the site.
Pattern 9: List Builder	Welie	The users need to build up and manage a list of items	Present the total list and provide editing functionality next to it.
Pattern 10: Purchase Process	Welie	Users want to purchase an already selected product	Present users with the purchase steps

Table 5.2: The Assumption/Commitment of the used patterns in the etidy website

The Assumption/Commitment of the used patterns			
Pattern name	**Source**	**Assumption**	**Commitment**
Pattern 1: Establish the business objectives	WU	There are business objectives.	List of chosen business objectives.
Pattern 2: Business process model	WU	List of chosen business objectives.	List of business processes corresponding to the business objectives.
Pattern 3: Establish the use cases	WU	List of chosen business processes.	List of use cases corresponding to the business processes.
Pattern 4: E- commerce Site	Welie	There is a shopping use case for the E-commerce process	Website that provides the E-commerce process shopping.
Pattern 5: Shopping	Welie	There are objects to buy and there is a shopping use case.	A website for buying objects online.
Pattern 6: View	Welie	There is a set of objects.	Display the objects the user can buy
Pattern 7: Shopping Cart	Welie	A collection of objects the user can buy	List the objects the user wants to buy.
Pattern 8: Collector	Welie	There are objects that the user can select.	Set of objects selected by the user.
Pattern 9: List Builder	Welie	There is a set of objects selected by the user	To list the objects in the set selected by the user in a particular order.
Pattern 10: Purchase Process	Welie	There are objects in the shopping cart.	Buy the objects in the shopping cart.

The application of the proposed design in a certain context is checked using the Assumption/Commitment framework. This is proved by applying the framework for each pattern application.

The application steps of these patterns are:

Step Zero:

In this step the designer defines the problem, in this case the creation of a shopping website to provide services to the user through the internet (see Figure 5.10).

Step one:

The first four Abstract patterns, P1: Establish the business objectives, P2: Business process model, P3: Establish the use cases and P4: E-commerce Site, need to be applied in the right context by using the Assumption and Commitment of each patterns listed in Table 5.2. Since they are applied in sequential order the operator is the sequential operator.

The designer will start by applying the following four patterns:

Pattern 1: Establish the business objectives

Pattern 2: Business process model

Pattern 3: Establish the use cases

Pattern 4: E-commerce Site

The framework is used to here aid the designer in solving the problem of building shopping website and the framework stages will be applied as follows:

Stage 1: there are no single concrete patterns in the designer's pattern bank that can be applied to produce this website and solve this problem. Also there is no bigger concrete pattern that will provide a solution to the problem of building this website. Then the next stage in the framework is applied.

Stage 2: will have the following steps:

I. to decompose this problem into sub-problems and find patterns for these sub-problems (Divide). The shopping website problem can not be solved by applying only one pattern. The shopping website problem is decomposed into four sub-problems in this context: the Establish the business objectives, Business process model, Establish the use cases and E-commerce Site. The decomposition is done using the sequential operator.

II. to compose the solutions of the sub-problems Establish the business objectives, Business process model, Establish the use cases and E-commerce Site (Conquer). Since the sub-problems of those patterns are representing part of the solution for the problem of the shopping website problem the sequential composition of the solutions of four patterns will solve the shopping website problem.

These four patterns need to be applied in the right context. Table 5.2 list the Assumption and Commitment of each patterns used. Figure 5.10 illustrates the relation between the Assumption/Commitment of these patterns.

The Assumption of the shopping website (*There are business objectives*) the Commitment of the shopping website (*Website that provide the E-commerce processes shopping*).

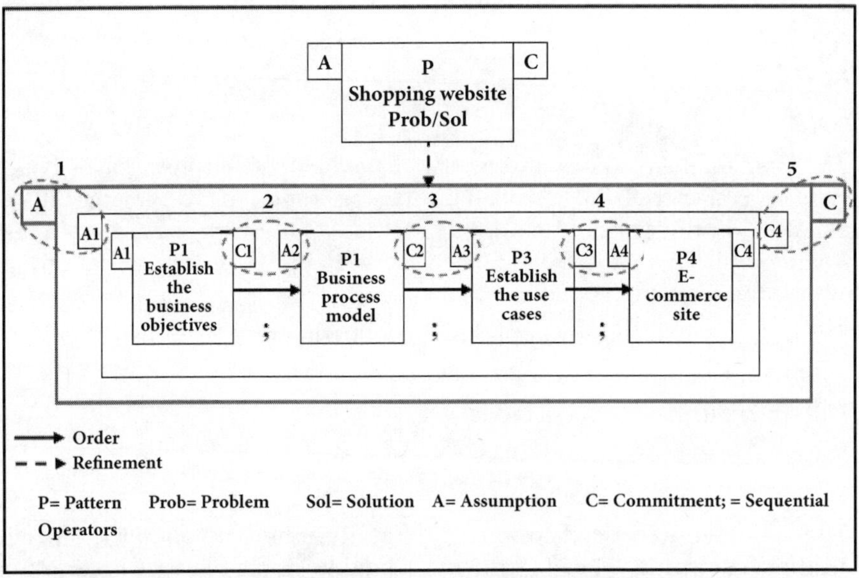

Figure 5.10: The basic patterns to start the design of an E-commerce site

The operator used here is the sequential operator and the relation is expressed as

P is refined by **P1 ; P2 ; P3; P4**

The system designer needs to check the five following conditions to make sure that the sequence of pattern can be applied for the shopping website problem. In this case the five conditions trivially hold and the matching of context is expressed as follows:

In circle 1: **A** implies **A1** which means that

The Assumption of the shopping website (*There are business objectives*) matches the Assumption of the Establish the business objectives pattern (*There are business objectives*).

In circle 2: C1 implies **A2** which means that

The Commitment of Establish the business objectives pattern (*List of chosen business objectives*) matches the Assumption of the Business process model pattern *(List of chosen business objectives).*

In circle 3: C2 implies **A3** which means that

The Commitment of the Business process model pattern (*List of business processes corresponding to the business objectives*) matches the Assumption of the

Establish the use cases pattern *(List of chosen business processes).*

In circle 4: **C3** implies **A4** which means that

The Commitment of the Establish the use cases pattern (*List of use cases corresponding to the business processes*) matches the Assumption of the E-commerce Site pattern *(There is a shopping use case for the E- commerce process).*

In circle 5: **C4** implies **C** which means that

The Commitment of the E-commerce Site pattern (*Website that provides the E-commerce process shopping*) matches the Commitment of the shopping website (*Website that provides the E-commerce process shopping*).

Where

A is the Assumption of the shopping website problem

A1 is the Assumption of the Establish the business objectives pattern

A2 is the Assumption of the Business process model pattern

A3 is the Assumption of the Establish the use cases pattern

A4 is the Assumption of the E-commerce Site pattern

C is the Commitment of the shopping website problem

C1 is the Commitment of the Establish the business objectives pattern

C2 is the Commitment of the Business process model pattern

C3 is the Commitment of the Establish the use cases pattern

C4 is the Commitment of the E-commerce Site pattern

Figure 5.10 shows in order to replace the shopping website pattern by a sequence of four basic patterns the designer needs only to check five conditions.

Step Two:

For the following two patterns, P4: E-commerce site and P5: Shopping need to be applied in the right context by using the Assumption and Commitment of each patterns listed in Table 5.2.

The framework is now used to give a concrete design for pattern P4: E-commerce.

Stage 1: there is an abstract pattern in the designer's pattern bank that can be used to solve this problem and it is P5: Shopping. Then the designer will use it and there is no need for **Stage 2**.

The relation is expressed as

P4 is refined by **P5**

In this case the abstract pattern P4: E-commerce site is refined by the concrete pattern P5: Shopping in a certain context. In this case the condition trivially holds and the matching of context is expressed as follows:

In circle 1: **A4** implies **A5** which means that

The Assumption of the Abstract pattern (**A4**) implies the Assumption of the Concrete pattern (**A5**).

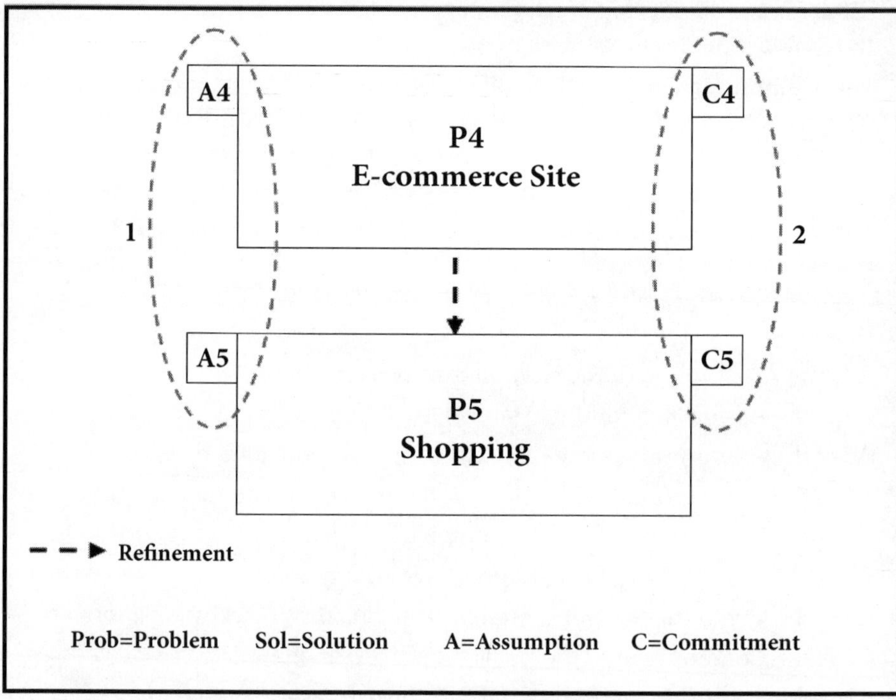

Figure 5.11: Illustrates the application of P4 and P5 in the etidy website

The Assumption of the E-commerce Site pattern (*There is a shopping use case for the E-commerce process*) matches the Assumption of the Shopping pattern (*There are objects to buy and there is a shopping use case*).

In circle 2: **C5** implies **C4** which means that

The Commitment of the Concrete pattern (**C5**) implies the Commitment of the Abstract pattern (**C4**).

The Commitment of the Shopping pattern (*A website for buying objects online*) matches the Commitment of the E-commerce site pattern (*Website that provides the E-commerce process shopping*).

Where

A4 is the Assumption of the E-commerce site pattern

A5 is the Assumption of the Shopping pattern

C4 is the Commitment of the E-commerce site pattern

C5 is the Commitment of the Shopping pattern

So the system designer needs to check those two conditions. In this case the two conditions trivially hold. So refinement holds between the patterns.

Step Three:

In this step a concrete design is given for the abstract pattern P4: E- commerce Site. This design will use the following four patterns, P5: Shopping, P6: View, P7:

Shopping Cart and P10: Purchase Process. Again the framework is used to check the application of the patterns in the right context.

The framework is now used to give a concrete design for pattern P5: Shopping.

Stage 1: there are no single concrete patterns in the designer's pattern bank that can be used to solve the problem of P5. Also there is no bigger concrete pattern that will provide a solution for this problem. Then the next stage in the framework is applied.

Stage 2: will have the following steps:

I. to decompose this problem into sub-problems and find patterns for these sub-problems (Divide). The shopping pattern problem is decomposed into three sub-problems: the View, Shopping Cart and Purchase Process. The decomposition is done using the sequential operator.

II. to compose the solutions of the sub-problems View, Shopping Cart and Purchase Process (Conquer). Since the sub-problems of those patterns are representing part of the solution for the problem of the shopping pattern problem the sequential composition of the solutions of three patterns will solve the shopping pattern problem.

These four patterns need to be applied in the right context. Again the Assumption and Commitment in Table 5.2 are used to check that the application of the patterns matches the context. The necessary conditions are illustrated in Figure 5.12.

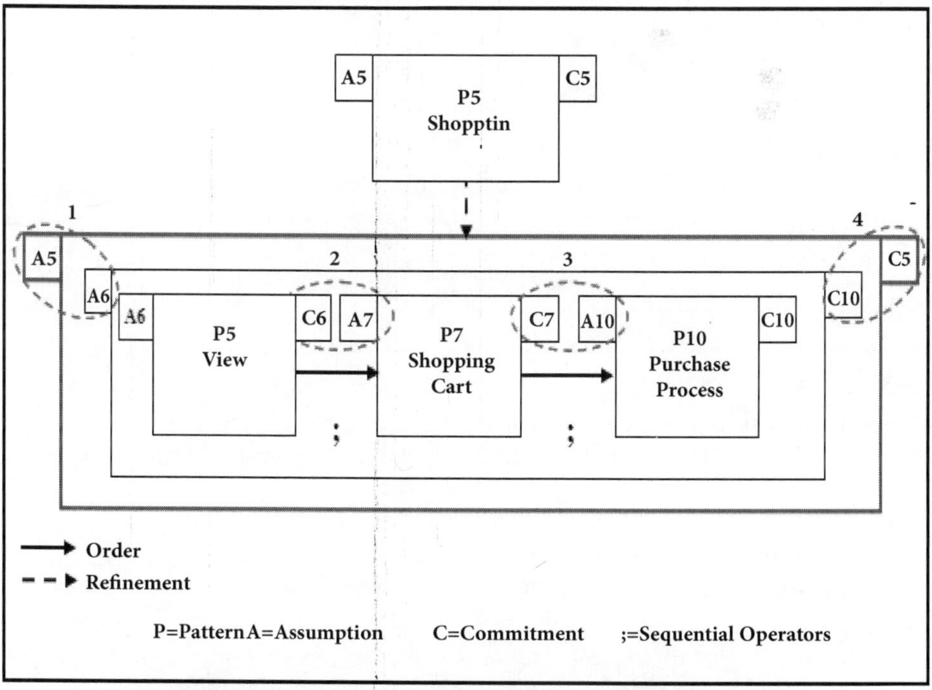

Figure 5.12: The patterns for the design of an E-commerce site

The operator used here is the sequential operator and the relation is expressed as

P5 is refined by **P6 ; P7 ; P10**

The system designer needs to check the four following conditions to make sure that the patterns are applied in the right context. In this case the four conditions trivially hold and the matching of context is expressed as follows:

In circle 1: **A5** implies **A6** which means that

The Assumption of the Shopping pattern (*There are objects to buy and there is a shopping use case*) matches the Assumption of the View pattern (*There is a set of objects*).

In circle 2: **C6** implies **A7** which means that

The Commitment of the View pattern (*Display the objects the user can buy*) matches the Assumption of the Shopping Cart pattern *(A collection of objects the user can buy).*

In circle 3: **C7** implies **A10** which means that

The Commitment of the Shopping Cart pattern (*List the objects the user wants to buy*) matches the Assumption of the Purchase Process pattern *(There are objects in the shopping cart).*

In circle 4: **C10** implies **C5** which means that

The Commitment of the Purchase Process pattern (*Buy the objects in the shopping cart*) matches the Commitment of the shopping pattern (*A website for buying objects online*).

Where

A5 is the Assumption of the Shopping pattern

A6 is the Assumption of the View pattern

A7 is the Assumption of the Shopping Cart pattern

A10 is the Assumption of the Purchase Process pattern

C5 is the Commitment of the Shopping pattern

C6 is the Commitment of the View pattern

C7 is the Commitment of the Shopping Cart pattern

C10 is the Commitment of the Purchase Process pattern

Figure 5.12 shows that the concrete design uses three basic patterns that need to be applied sequentially. It also shows the context in which those patterns are applied.

Step Four:

As show in Chapter 3 a concrete design can be given to the Shopping Cart problem using Pattern P8: Collector and P9: List Builder. This is repeated below for completeness.

Stage 1: there is no concrete pattern in the designer's pattern bank that can solve this problem and there is also no bigger concrete pattern that will provide a solution. Then the next stage in the framework is applied.

Stage 2: in this stage the Shopping Cart problem is decompose into two sub-problems and the patterns to solve these sub-problems are the Collector and List Builder. The composition of their solution here solved the Shopping Cart problem.

The Collector and List Builder patterns need to be applied in the right context. Table 5.2 lists the Assumption and Commitment of each patterns used. Figure 5.13 illustrates the relations between these patterns.

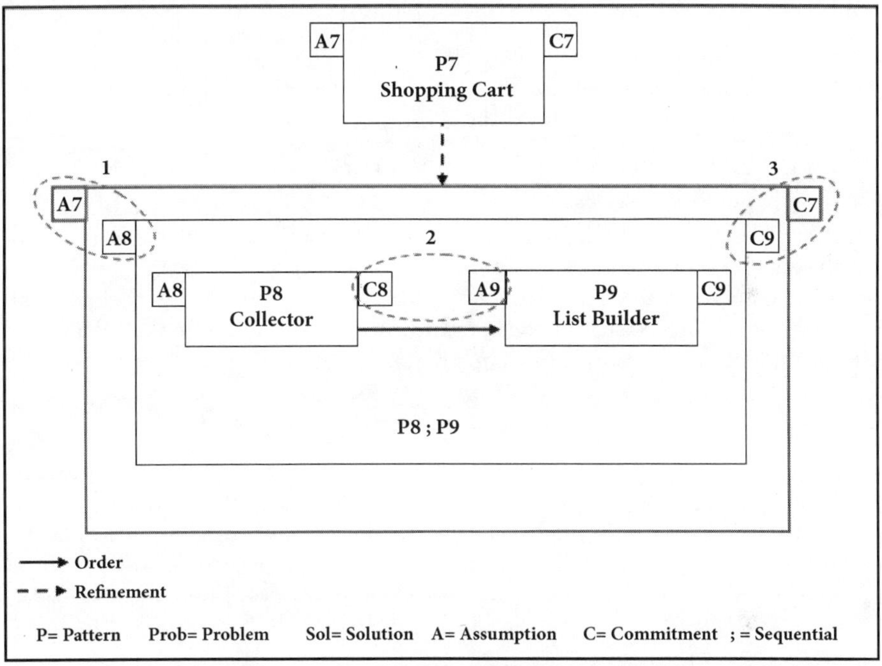

Figure 5.13: Illustrates the decomposition of the problem and composition of the solutions for the Shopping Cart pattern

The operator used here is the sequential operator and the relation is expressed as

P7 is refined by **P8 ; P9**

The system designer needs to check the three following conditions to make sure that the patterns are applied in the right context. In this case the three conditions trivially hold and the matching of context is expressed as follows:

In circle 1: **A7** implies **A8** which means that

The Assumption of the Shopping Cart pattern (*A collection of objects the user can buy*) matches the Assumption of the Collector pattern (*There are objects that the user can select*).

In circle 2: **C8** implies **A9** which means that

The Commitment of the Collector pattern (*Set of objects selected by the user*) matches the Assumption of the List Builder pattern *(There is a set of objects selected by the user).*

In circle 3: **C9** implies **C7** which means that

The Commitment of the List Builder pattern (*To list the objects in the set selected by the user in a particular order*) matches the Commitment of the shopping Cart pattern (*List the objects the user wants to buy*).

Where

A7 is the Assumption of the Shopping Cart pattern

A8 is the Assumption of the Collector pattern

A9 is the Assumption of the List Builder pattern

C7 is the Commitment of the Shopping Cart pattern

C8 is the Commitment of the Collector pattern

C9 is the Commitment of the List Builder pattern

Figure 5.13 shows that solving the shopping Cart problem needs more than one pattern and this is depending on the context. In this case the patterns are very basic showing the user what is inside the shopping cart. The establishment of the shopping cart is not done through one specific pattern but through the application of two patterns. The Assumption/ Commitment framework makes it easier for designer to decide which pattern to apply next in the design.

5.2.3 The Second Part of the Case Study

The website design analysed in the first part of the case study is modified so that the site can sell more than one product. The pattern map of the modified design is in Figure 5.15. Two extra patterns are needed for the design of the new website. The patterns used for the modified design are shown in Figure 5.14.

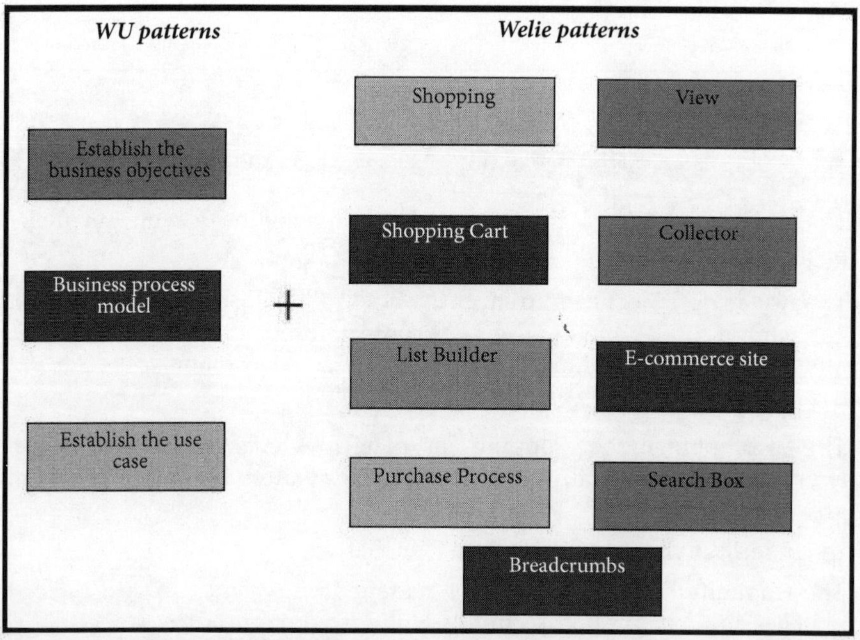

Figure 5.14: Illustrates the new addition of two patterns to be used in the etidy website

Figure 5.15 illustrates the new proposed patterns used in the etidy website.

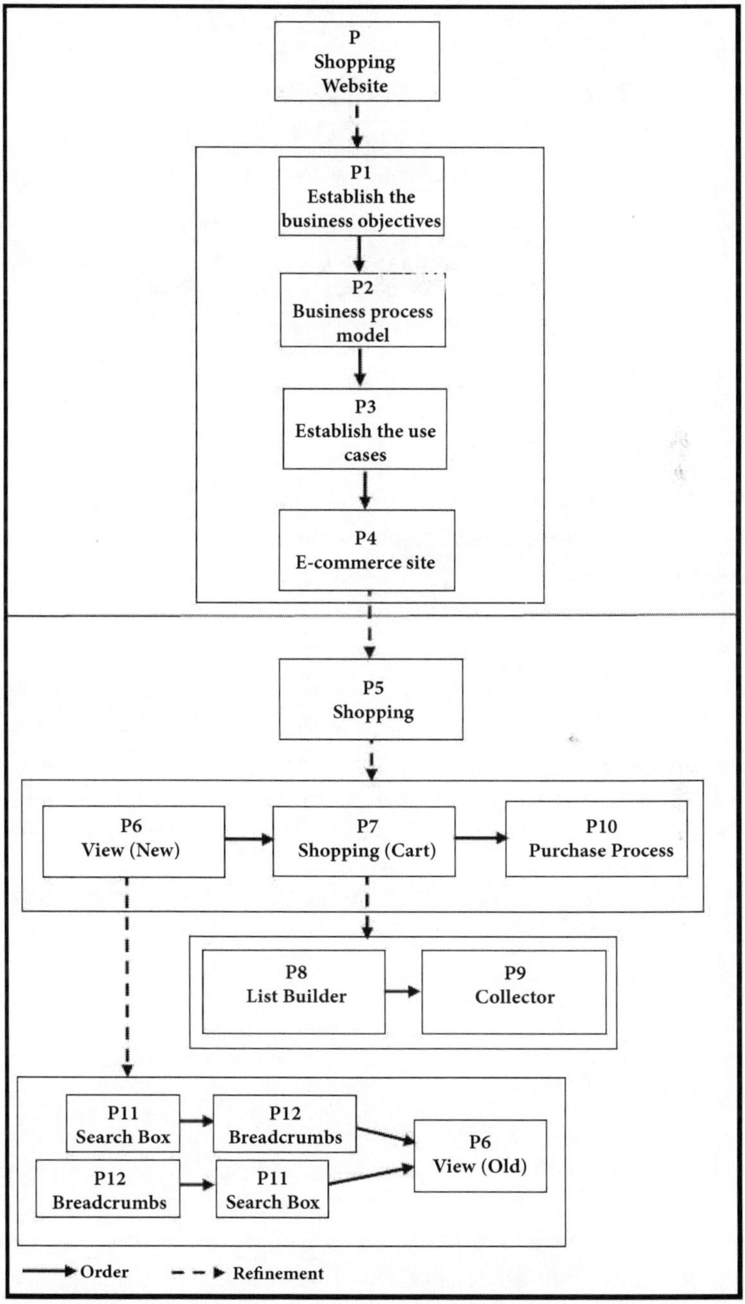

Figure 5.15: Illustrate the proposed patterns map used to build the new etidy website

The following tables summarise problem/solution and Assumption/ Commitment for each extra pattern used in the second part of the case study.

Table 5.3: The problem/solution of the extra patterns for the etidy website

The problem/solution of the new patterns			
Pattern name	**Source**	**Problem**	**Solution**
Pattern 11: Search Box	Welie	The users need to find an item or specific information.	Offer a search
Pattern 12: Breadcrumbs	Welie	The users need to know where they are in a hierarchical structure and navigate back to higher levels in the hierarchy	Show the hierarchical path from the top level to the current page and make each step clickable

These patterns do not affect the objects!

Table 5.4: The Assumption/Commitment of the extra patterns for the etidy website

The Assumption / Commitment of the new patterns			
Pattern name	**Source**	**Assumption**	**Commitment**
Pattern 11: Search Box	Welie	There are objects to buy.	There are objects to buy.
Pattern 12: Breadcrumbs	Welie	There are objects to buy.	There are objects to buy.

To support the selling of more than one product the designer of the website adds a search box and breadcrumbs to help the shopper in selecting the product to buy. The addition of these patterns means that P6: View is changed into P6′ View (New) to support this extra functionality. The designer needs to check that those extra patterns are applied in the right context. This is again checked using the framework.

Step Five:

In this step the pattern P6: View is replaced by P6′: View that provides a solution with the required extra functionality. The concrete design for P6′ uses the following patterns:

P6: View, P11: Search Box and P12: Breadcrumbs

Again the designer needs to check that the application of the patterns happens in the right context using the framework.

Stage 1: there are no single concrete patterns in the designer's pattern bank that can be used to solve this problem. Also there is no bigger concrete pattern that will provide a solution for this problem. Then the next stage in the framework is applied.

Stage 2: will have the following steps:

I. to decompose this problem into sub-problems and find patterns for these sub-problems (Divide). The View problem is decomposed into three sub-problems: the Search Box, Breadcrumbs and View. The decomposition is done using the sequential and the choice operators.

II. to compose the solutions of the sub-problems Search Box, Breadcrumbs and View (Conquer). Since the solutions to the sub- problems are representing part of the solution for the problem of the New View the composition of the solutions of Search Box, Breadcrumbs and View patterns will solve the New View problem.

These four patterns need to be applied in the right context. Figure 5.16 shows the relations that need to hold between the Assumption and Commitments of the patterns.

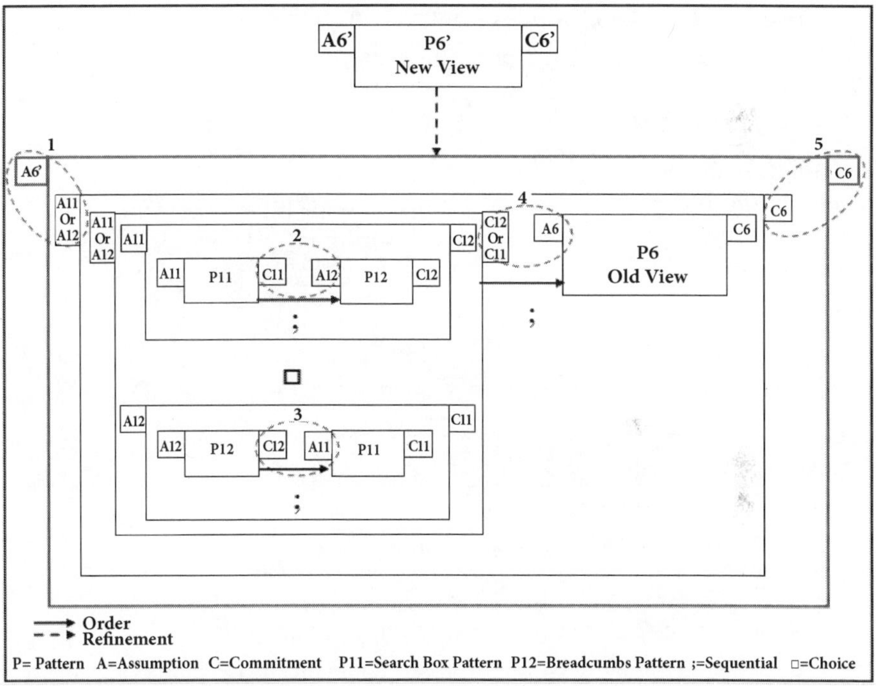

Figure 5.16: Illustrates the decomposition of the problem and composition of the solutions for the View pattern

The operator used here is the parallel operator and which is as explained in Chapter 4 is a combination of the sequential and the choice operator and the relation is expressed as

P6′ is refined by **(P11 | P12) ; P6** where

(P11 | P12) ; P6 = (P11 ; P12 ; P6) □ (P12 ; P11; P6)

Which means there is a choice in the application order of these patterns. So the system designer needs to check the five following conditions so that the patterns are applied in the right context. In this case the five conditions trivially hold and the matching of context is expressed as follows:

In circle 1, A6′ implies **(A11** or **A12)** which means that

The Assumption of the New View pattern (*There is a set of objects*) matches the Assumption of the Search Box pattern (*There are objects to buy*) or the Breadcrumbs pattern (*There are objects to buy*).

In circle 2, C11 implies **A12** which means that

The Commitment of the Search Box pattern (*There are objects to buy*) matches the Assumption of the Breadcrumbs pattern *(There are objects to buy).*

In circle 3, C12 implies **A11** which means that

The Commitment of the Breadcrumbs pattern (*There are objects to buy*) matches the Assumption of the Search Box pattern (*There are objects to buy*).

In circle 4, (C12 or **C11)** implies **A6** which means that

The Commitment of the Breadcrumbs pattern (*There are objects to buy*) or the Commitment of the Search Box pattern (*There are objects to buy*) matches the Assumption of the Old View pattern *(There is a set of objects).*

In circle 5, C6 implies **C6′** which means that

The Commitment of the Old View pattern (*Display the objects the user can buy*) matches the Commitment of the New View pattern (*Display the objects the user can buy*).

Where

A6 is the Assumption of the Old View pattern

A6′ is the Assumption of the New View pattern

A11 is the Assumption of the Search Box pattern

A12 is the Assumption of the Breadcrumbs pattern

C6 is the Commitment of the Old View pattern

C6′ is the Commitment of the New View pattern

C11 is the Commitment of the Search Box pattern

C12 is the Commitment of the Breadcrumbs pattern

Figure 5.16 shows that to build a website that sells more than one product the designer needs to modify only a part of the design.

To conclude, the case study examined the etidy shopping website and the aim was to illustrate the usability of the Assumption/Commitment framework in determining the best ways to apply patterns with the regard to the context before and after each single pattern application. It also makes the use of the patterns maps more precise by clarifying the arrows used in each stage of the map. The first part examined an existing website and a proposed design for it. In the second part the design was modified to build a website with extra functionality. The framework only needs to check the changed part of the design.

Figure 5.17 illustrates the use of the Assumption/Commitment framework in checking the application of the proposed design and the five steps involved in checking the design.

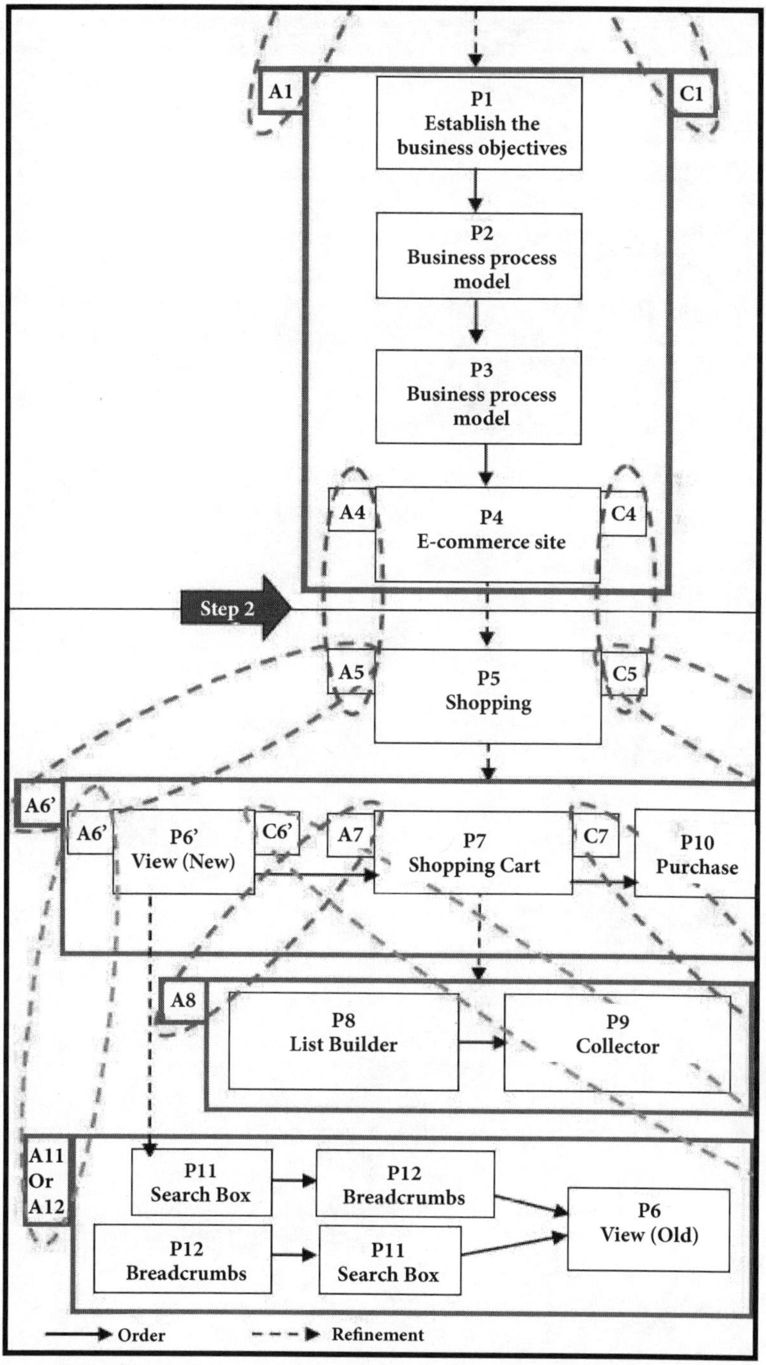

Figure 5.17: Illustrate the five steps used in checking the proposed patterns map for the etidy website

Figure 5.18: The Child Benefit website main page [22]

The main home page will take the user to the form page to be filled and it is below

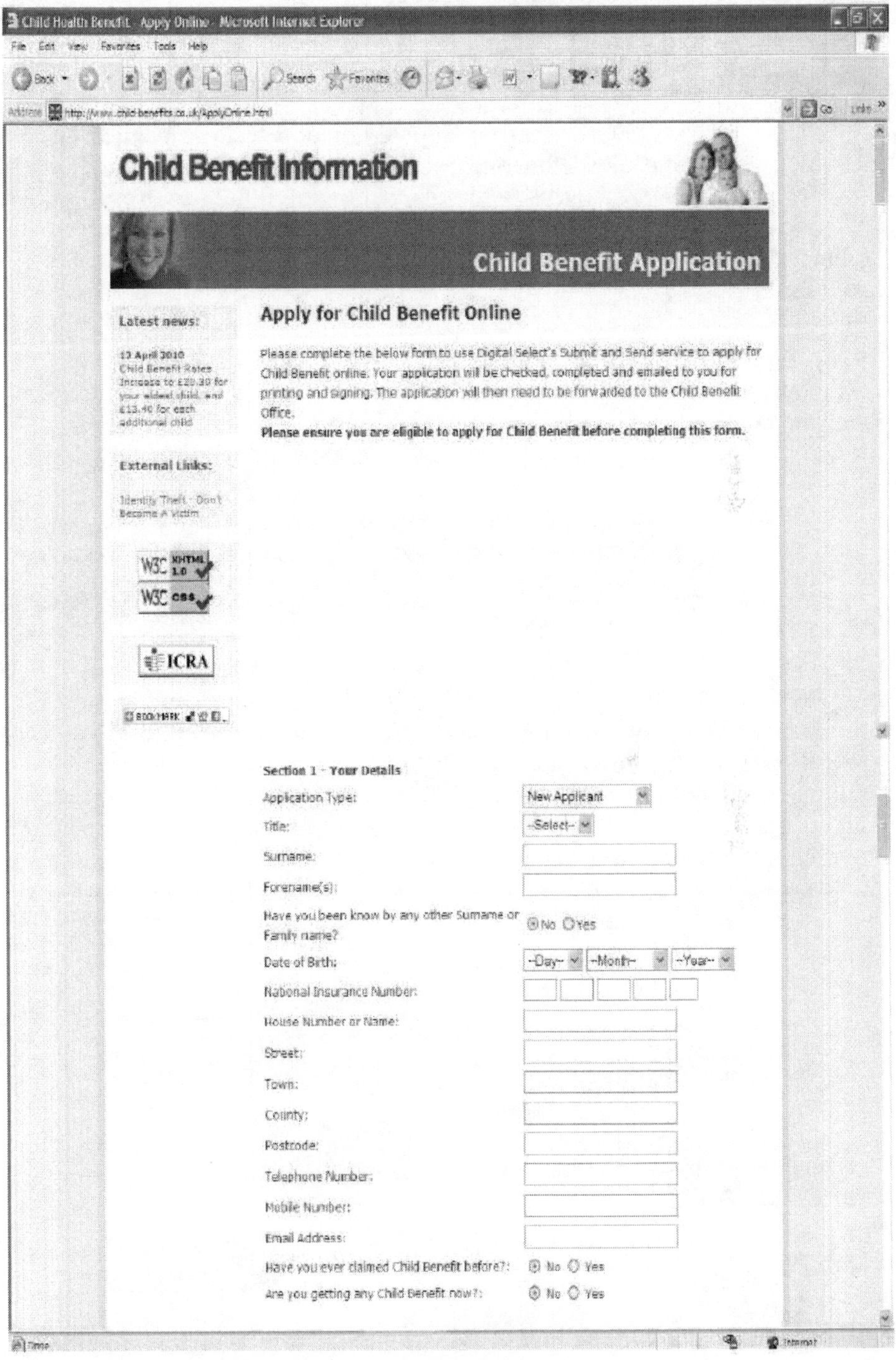

Figure 5.19: The Child Benefit website form Page 1[22]

5.3 E-GOVERNMENT WEBSITE CASE STUDY

5.3.1 Introduction

The case study will examine an existing E-government website for Child Benefit in the UK [22]. This website allows the user to fill an application form for Child Benefit. A closer examination of the website reveals that the designer used some patterns for the design of the website which can be found in many E-government websites like the city councils, Tax…etc. The selected patterns are User Interface patterns, taken from WU and Welie [44, 45, 88] and are sufficient to build a small E-government website. The examined website's main functionality is the gathering of data via a form (see Figures 5.18 and 5.19).

The purpose of this case study is to evaluate the usefulness of the framework Assumption/Commitment in detecting design errors.

The case study will be divided into two parts. In the first part the existing website will be examined by proposing a design. It turns out that this design is not right. This is determined by checking the design with the framework. In the second part the faulty design is modified and again checked by the framework.

5.3.2 The First Part of the Case Study

In this part the existing E-government website for Child Benefit in the UK will be examined and a design is proposed for this website.

In this first part a total of 8 basic patterns are picked from WU and Welie [44, 45, 88], the full patterns descriptions are in Appendix A and B. They are illustrated in Figure 5.20. The first four abstract patterns are picked to determine the type of the website to be built (see Figure 5.21). The rest of the patterns are picked to design the Child Benefit website (see Figure 5.22).

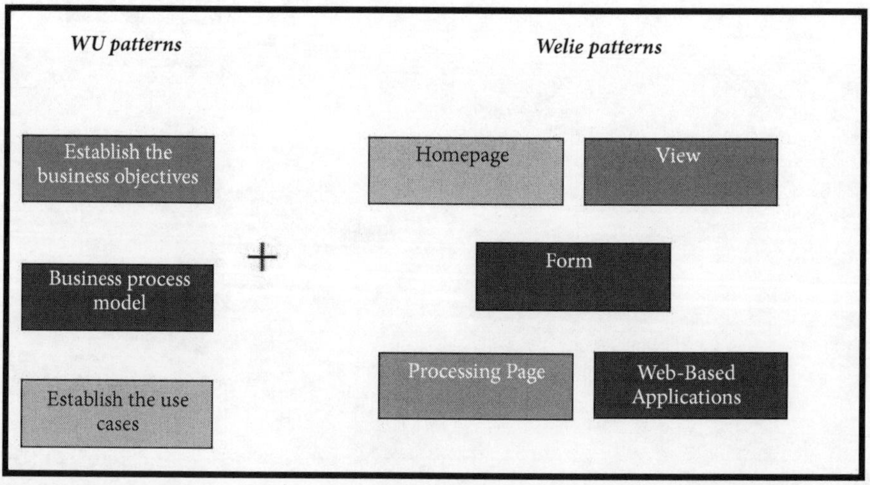

Figure 5.20: Illustrates the main patterns used in the E-government website for Child Benefit in the UK

Because the original design of the website is unknown a design in the form of a pattern map is proposed. This pattern map is illustrated in Figure 5.23. The proposed design is analysed using the Assumption/Commitment framework. In the analysis the application order of the patterns is checked, i.e., what is needed (Assumption) in order to apply a certain pattern and what is provided (Commitment) in order to apply the next pattern.

For the simplicity the pattern map will be divided into two sections:

a. Section One: ***The Site Type Design (Abstract Patterns)***

   In this section the first 3 patterns can be used as a start to design any type of business [45]. These patterns are applied according to the context. The 4th pattern determines the site type and in this case a web-based application site. The patterns in this section are *Abstract Patterns*. They are illustrated in Figure 5.21.

b. Section Two: ***The Site Concrete Design (Concrete Patterns)***

   In section two a concrete design of the site is given, i.e., a concrete design for the abstract pattern. Web-based Application is given. This is illustrated in Figure 5.22.

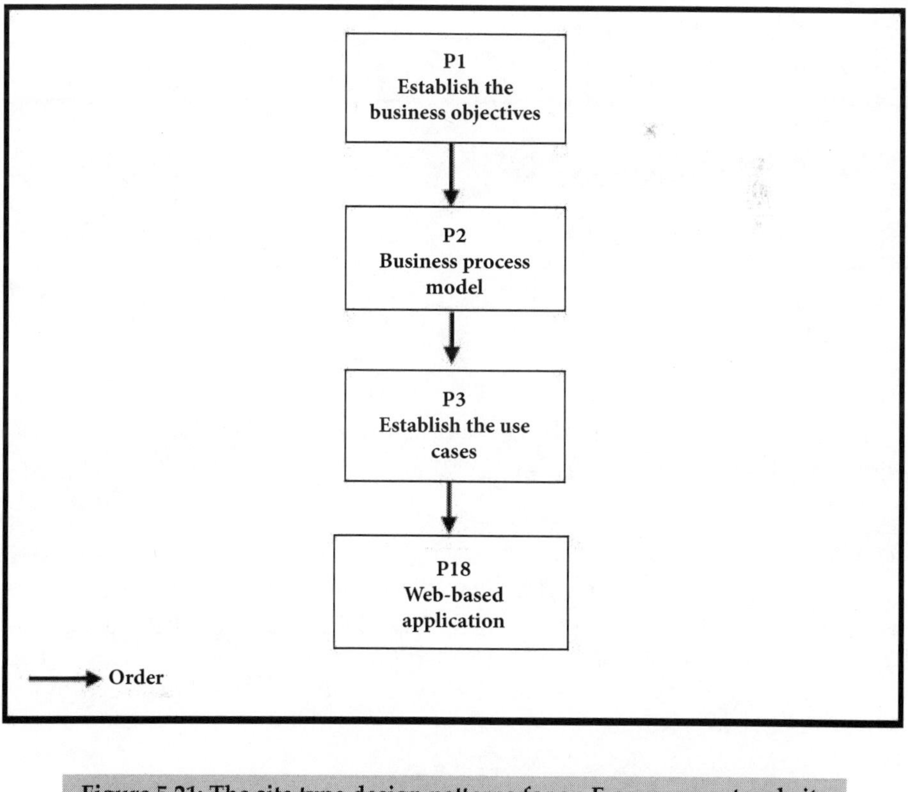

Figure 5.21: The site type design patterns for an E-government website

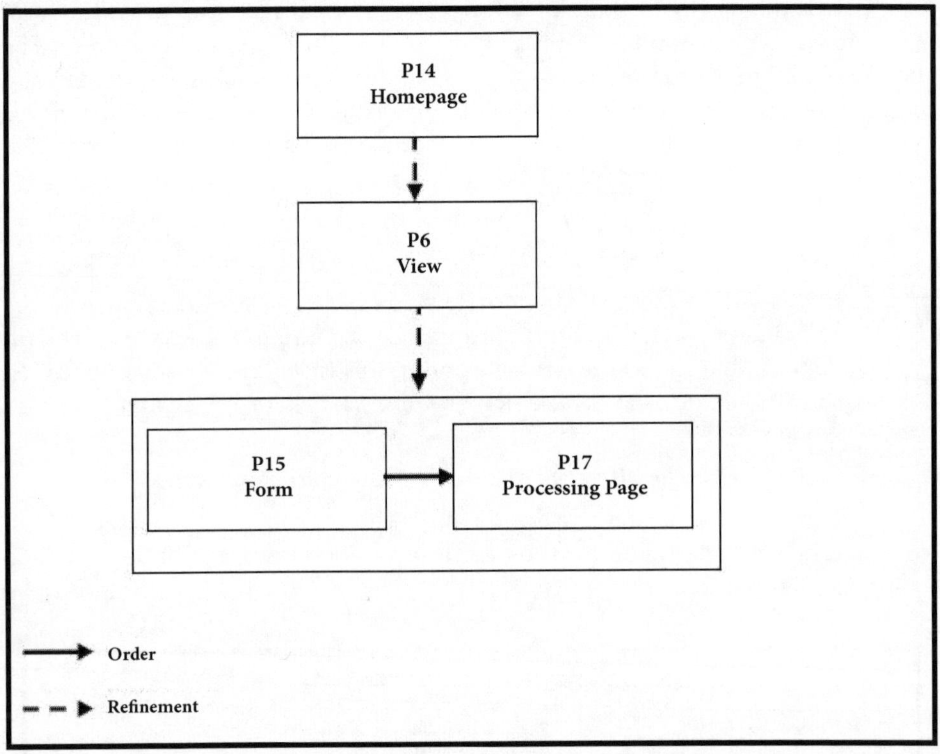

Figure 5.22: The Child Benefit website concrete design patterns

Figure 5.23 illustrates the proposed patterns used in the Child Benefit website.

The framework is used here to check the proposed design of a government site for Child Benefit. The steps of design are as follows:

Step Zero:

This step is defining the problem the designer wants to solve and in this case is creating an E-government website providing the child benefit application service (see Figure 5.23).

Step One:

The patterns used in Section One (see Figure 5.23), P1: Establish the business objectives, P2: Business process model, P3: Establish the use cases and P18: Web-based application, need to be applied in the right context and this is done via conditions imposed on the Assumption and Commitment of each patterns. The patterns are applied sequentially so the corresponding conditions need to hold.

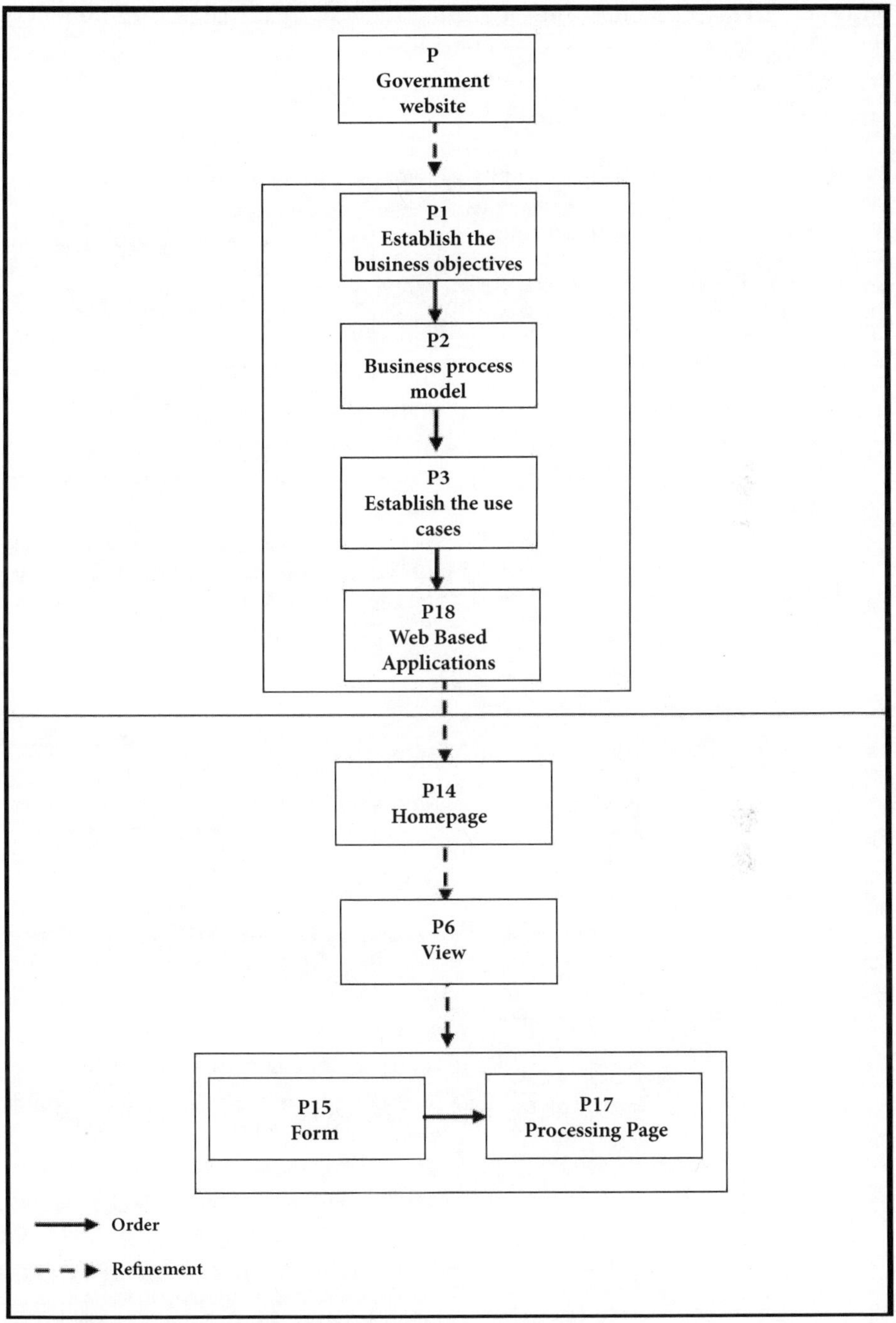

Figure 5.23: Illustrate the proposed patterns map used to build the Child Benefit website

The following tables summarise the problem/solution and Assumption/Commitment pair for each pattern used in the first part of the case study.

Table 5.5: The problem/solution of the used patterns in the Child Benefit website

The problem/solution of the used patterns			
Pattern name	**Source**	**Problem**	**Solution**
Pattern 1: Establish the business objectives	WU	To create a new website or modify an existing one	-Hold a workshop involving as many stakeholders as possible. -Make sure that potential users are represented by marketing personnel or the results of focus groups, surveys, etc. -Find a good facilitator. -Agree a mission statement. -Find measures for each objective.
Pattern 2: Business process model	WU	To organise the content in a way that supports several navigation structures simultaneously	-An understanding of the network of agents and commitments that make up the business must first be gained. -The conversations that take place at an appropriate level of abstraction must be specified, so that they become stereotypes for actual stories. -People must tell these stories. -Ensure that both 'before' and 'after' business process models are produced. -Eliminate conversations that do not correspond to business objectives (or discover the missed objective). -Ensure that every objective is supported by a conversation.
Pattern 3: Establish the use cases	WU	The site must serve at least one significant business purpose. For this reason we must look at all the use cases that we can predict users will want to execute.	-Extract the use cases from the conversations in the BUSINESS PROCESS MODEL (2). -Record their correspondences to the business objectives. -Write post-conditions for each use case. -Compare the vocabulary of the post-conditions to the type model. -Write use cases in stimulus– response form. -Convert the use cases into the user training manual and the test plan. -One stimulus/response pair from the use case should correspond to one step in the workflow if the site deals with workflows. If not, do not constrain the user's ability to perform steps in any particular sequence. -Ensure that you extract and document a business object type model from the use case goals.

The problem/solution of the used patterns			
Pattern name	**Source**	**Problem**	**Solution**
Pattern 18: Web-based Application	Welie	Users need to perform complex tasks on a website	Structure the site around 'views' and allow users to work inside views.
Pattern 14: Homepage	Welie	Users need to understand if they are at the right place, and if so, how they can move on to accomplish their task at your site	Create a home-page that introduces the site to users and that helps them to get on their way on the site
Pattern 6: View	Welie	Users need to manage a collection of objects	Create an overview of objects that together is meaningful to users
Pattern 15: Form	Welie	Users need to provide personal information and send it to a service provider	Offer users a form with the necessary elements
Pattern 17: Processing Page	Welie	Users need feedback that their action is being performed but may take a while to complete	Provide a feedback page with animation

Table 5.6: The Assumption/Commitment of the used patterns in the Child Benefit website

The Assumption/Commitments of the used patterns			
Pattern name	**Source**	**Assumption**	**Commitment**
Pattern 1: Establish the business objectives	WU	There are business objectives.	List of chosen business objectives.
Pattern 2: Business process model	WU	List of chosen business objectives.	List of business processes corresponding to the chosen business objectives.
Pattern 3: Establish the use cases	WU	List of chosen business processes.	List of use cases corresponding to the chosen business processes.

The Assumption/Commitments of the used patterns			
Pattern name	**Source**	**Assumption**	**Commitment**
Pattern 18: Web-based Application	Welie	There is a use case for any web-based application.	Website that provides web-based application for E-government child benefit form service.
Pattern 14: Homepage	Welie	There is a web-based application service.	A website that provides the service.
Pattern 6: View	Welie	There is a data collection service	A website that display the data collection service.
Pattern 15: Form	Welie	There is a data to be collected.	To collect the necessary data for the service.
Pattern 17: Processing Page	Welie	All the necessary data in the right format.	Provide the data collection service.

Again the framework is used to check this step of the design:

Stage 1: there are no single concrete patterns in the designer's pattern bank that can be applied to produce this website and solve this problem. Also there is no bigger concrete pattern will provide a solution for this website problem. Then the next stage in the framework is applied.

Stage 2: will have the following steps:

I. to decompose this problem into sub-problems and find patterns that provide solutions for these sub-problems (Divide). The government website problem is decomposed into four sub-problems in this context: the Establish the business objectives, Business process model, Establish the use cases and Web-based application. The decomposition is done using the sequential operator.

II. to compose the solutions of the sub-problems Establish the business objectives, Business process model, Establish the use cases and Web-based application (Conquer). Since the solutions of these sub-problems are representing part of the solution for the government website problem the sequential composition of these solutions will solve the government website problem.

The application of these four patterns will provide a solution provided the following conditions hold (see Figure 5.24).

The Assumption of the government website (*There are business objectives*) the Commitment of the government website (*Website that provide child benefit form service*).

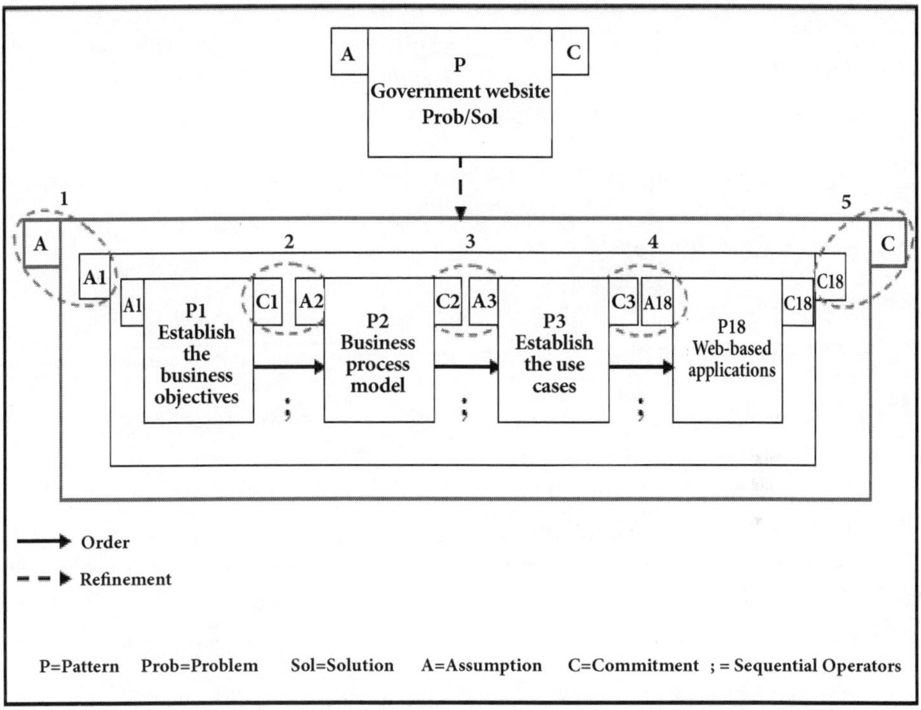

Figure 5.24: The basic patterns to start the design of an E-government site

In this case the five conditions trivially hold and the matching of context is expressed as follows:

In circle 1: **A** implies **A1** which means that

The Assumption of the government website (*There are business objectives*) matches the Assumption of the Establish the business objectives pattern (*There are business objectives*).

In circle 2: **C1** implies **A2** which means that

The Commitment of Establish the business objectives pattern (*List of chosen business objectives*) matches the Assumption of the Business process model pattern *(List of chosen business objectives).*

In circle 3: **C2** implies **A3** which means that

The Commitment of the Business process model pattern (*List of business processes corresponding to the business objectives*) matches the Assumption of the Establish the use cases pattern *(List of chosen business processes).*

In circle 4: **C3** implies **A18** which means that

The Commitment of the Establish the use cases pattern (*List of use cases corresponding to the business processes*) matches the Assumption of the Web-based application pattern *(There is a use case for any web-based application).*

In circle 5: **C18** implies **C** which means that

The Commitment of the Web-based application pattern (*Website that provides web-based application for E-government child benefit form service*) matches the Commitment of the government website (*Website that provide child benefit application form service*).

By applying those four patterns the website designer will determine the type of website to be built. In this case a Web-based Application. In the next step the designer designs a concrete web-based application.

Step Two:

The website designer again uses the framework to build a concrete web- based application.

This step is a refinement, i.e., the Homepage is a concrete design for Web-based application. The framework is used to check this refinement:

Stage 1: there is a concrete pattern that will provide a solution for web- based application and it is Homepage pattern.

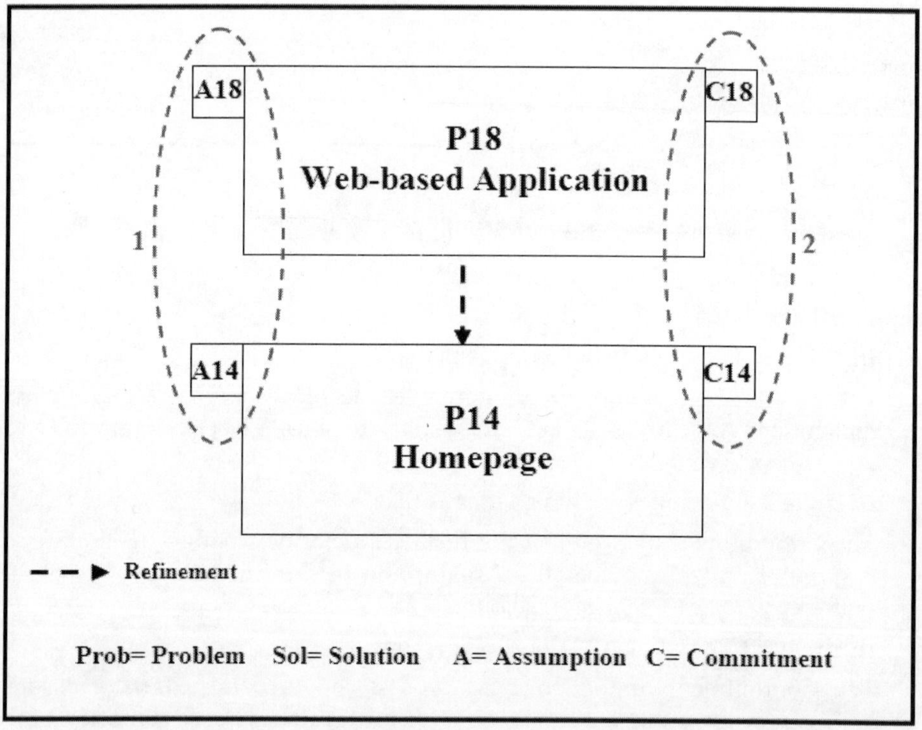

Figure 5.25: Illustrates the application of P18 and P14 in the Child Benefit website

In this case the abstract pattern P18: Web-based Application is refined by the concrete pattern P14: Homepage in a certain context. The following conditions should hold for this refinement:

In circle 1: **A18** implies **A14** which means that

The Assumption of the Abstract pattern (**A18**) implies the Assumption of the Concrete pattern (**A14**).

The Assumption of the Web-based Application pattern (*There is a use case for any web-based application*) matches the Assumption of the Homepage pattern (*There is a web-based application service*).

In circle 2: **C14** implies **C18** which means that

The Commitment of the Concrete pattern (**C14**) implies the Commitment of the Abstract pattern (**C18**).

The Commitment of the Homepage pattern (*A website that provides the service*) matches the Commitment of the Web-based Application pattern *(Website that provides web-based application for E-government child benefit form service).*

So the system designer needs to check those two conditions. In this case the two conditions trivially hold. So refinement holds between the patterns.

Step Three:

The website designer again uses the framework to build a concrete Homepage.

This step is a refinement, i.e., the View is a concrete design for Homepage. The framework is used to check this refinement:

Stage 1: there is a concrete pattern that will provide a solution for Homepage and it is View pattern.

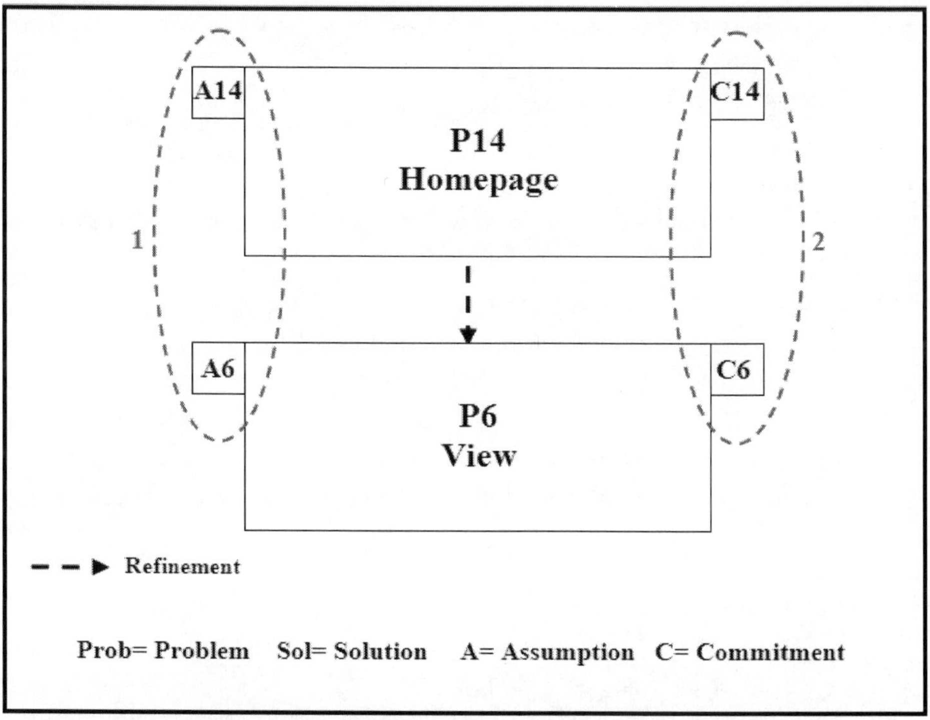

Figure 5.26: Illustrates the application of P14 and P6 in the Child Benefit website

In this case the abstract pattern P14: Homepage is refined by the concrete pattern P6: View in a certain context. The following conditions should hold for this refinement:

In circle 1: **A14** implies **A6** which means that

The Assumption of the Abstract pattern (**A14**) implies the Assumption of the Concrete pattern (**A6**).

The Assumption of the Homepage pattern (*There is a web-based application service*) matches the Assumption of the View pattern (*There is a data collection service*).

In circle 2: **C6** implies **C14** which means that

The Commitment of the Concrete pattern (**C6**) implies the Commitment of the Abstract pattern (**C14**).

The Commitment of the View pattern (*A website that displays the data collection service*) matches the Commitment of the Homepage pattern *(A website that provides the service).*

So the system designer needs to check those two conditions. In this case the two conditions trivially hold. So refinement holds between the patterns.

Step Four:

The following two patterns will be used to design the View pattern. P15: Form and P17: Processing Page and need to be applied in the right context.

To check this step the refinement is used again:

Stage 1: there are no single concrete patterns in the designer's pattern bank that can be applied to produce this government website and solve this problem. Also there is no bigger concrete pattern that will provide a solution for this problem. Then the next stage in the framework is applied.

Stage 2: will have the following steps:

I. to decompose this problem into sub-problems and find patterns for these sub-problems (Divide). The View pattern problem is decomposed into two sub-problems the Form and Processing Page. The decomposition is done using the sequential operator.

II. to compose the solutions of the sub-problems Form and Processing Page (Conquer). Since these solutions are representing part of the solution for the problem of the View pattern the sequential composition of the solutions of two patterns will solve the View pattern problem.

The sequence of the two patterns forms a design for the View pattern if the following conditions (see Figure 5.27) hold.

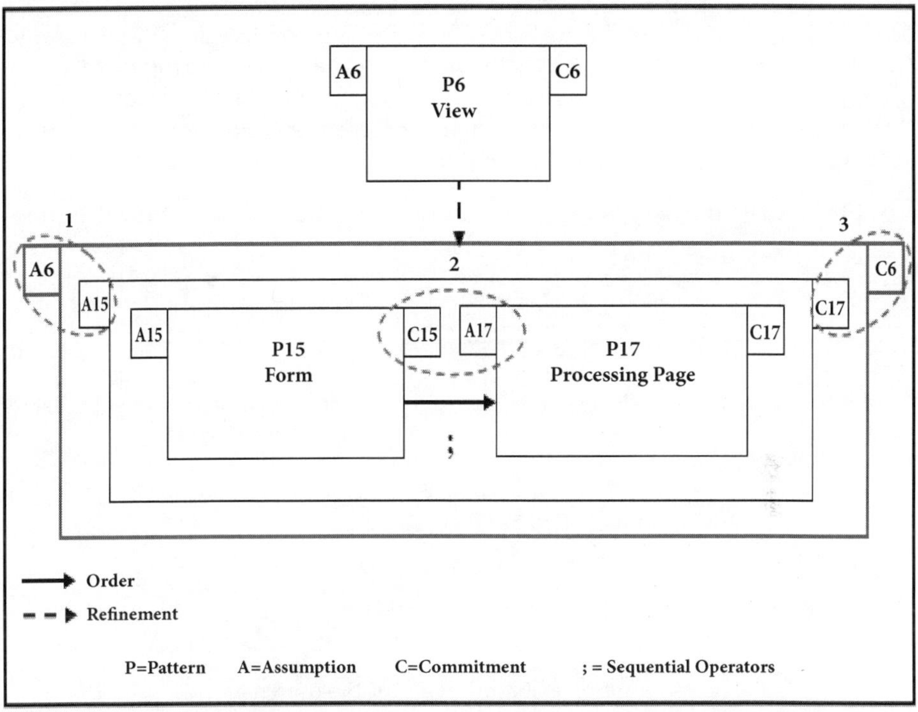

Figure 5.27: The patterns for the design of an E-government site

In this case the three conditions and the matching of context is expressed as follows:

In circle 1: **A6** implies **A15**

The Assumption of the View pattern (*There is a data collection service*) matches the Assumption of the Form pattern (*There is a data to be collected*).

In circle 2: **C15** implies **A17**

The Commitment of the Form pattern (*To collect the necessary data for the service)* should match the Assumption of the Processing Page pattern *(All the necessary data in the right format).* This condition dose not holds because the data collected by the form is not necessarily in the right format.

In circle 3: **C17** implies **C6**

The Commitment of the Processing Page pattern (*Provide the data collection service*) matches the Commitment of the View pattern (*A website that displays the data collection service).*

So the framework has detected a design error. In the second part a revised design is proposed. Again the framework is used to check this design.

5.3.3 The Second Part of the Case Study

The design proposed in the first part is modified to ensure that the needed data for the processing page is in the right format. For that the Constraint Input pattern will be used. The following tables list the problem/solution and Assumption/ Commitment pair of this pattern.

Table 5.7: The problem/solution of the added pattern to the Child Benefit website

The problem/solution of the used patterns			
Pattern name	**Source**	**Problem**	**Solution**
Pattern 16: Constraint Input	Welie	The user needs to supply the application with data but may be unfamiliar with which data is required or what syntax to use.	Only allow the user to enter data in the correct syntax.

Table 5.8: The Assumption/Commitment of the added pattern to the Child Benefit website

The Assumption / Commitments of the used patterns			
Pattern name	**Source**	**Assumption**	**Commitment**
Pattern 16: Constraint Input	Welie	There is service data.	There is service data in the right format

Step Four:

The new design for the pattern P 6: View uses the following patterns, P15: Form, P16: Constraint Input and P17: Processing Page.

The framework is again used to check this step:

Stage 1: there are no single concrete patterns in the designer's pattern bank that can be used to solve this problem. Also there is no bigger concrete pattern that will provide a solution for this problem. Then the next stage in the framework is applied.

Stage 2: will have the following steps:

I. to decompose this problem into sub-problems and find patterns for these sub-problems (Divide). The View problem is decomposed into four sub-problems: Form, Constraint Input and Processing Page patterns. The decomposition is done using the sequential operator.

II. to compose the solutions of the sub-problems Form, Constraint Input and Processing Page (Conquer). Since the solutions of the sub-problems of those patterns are representing part of the solution for the problem of the View the composition of the solutions will solve the View problem.

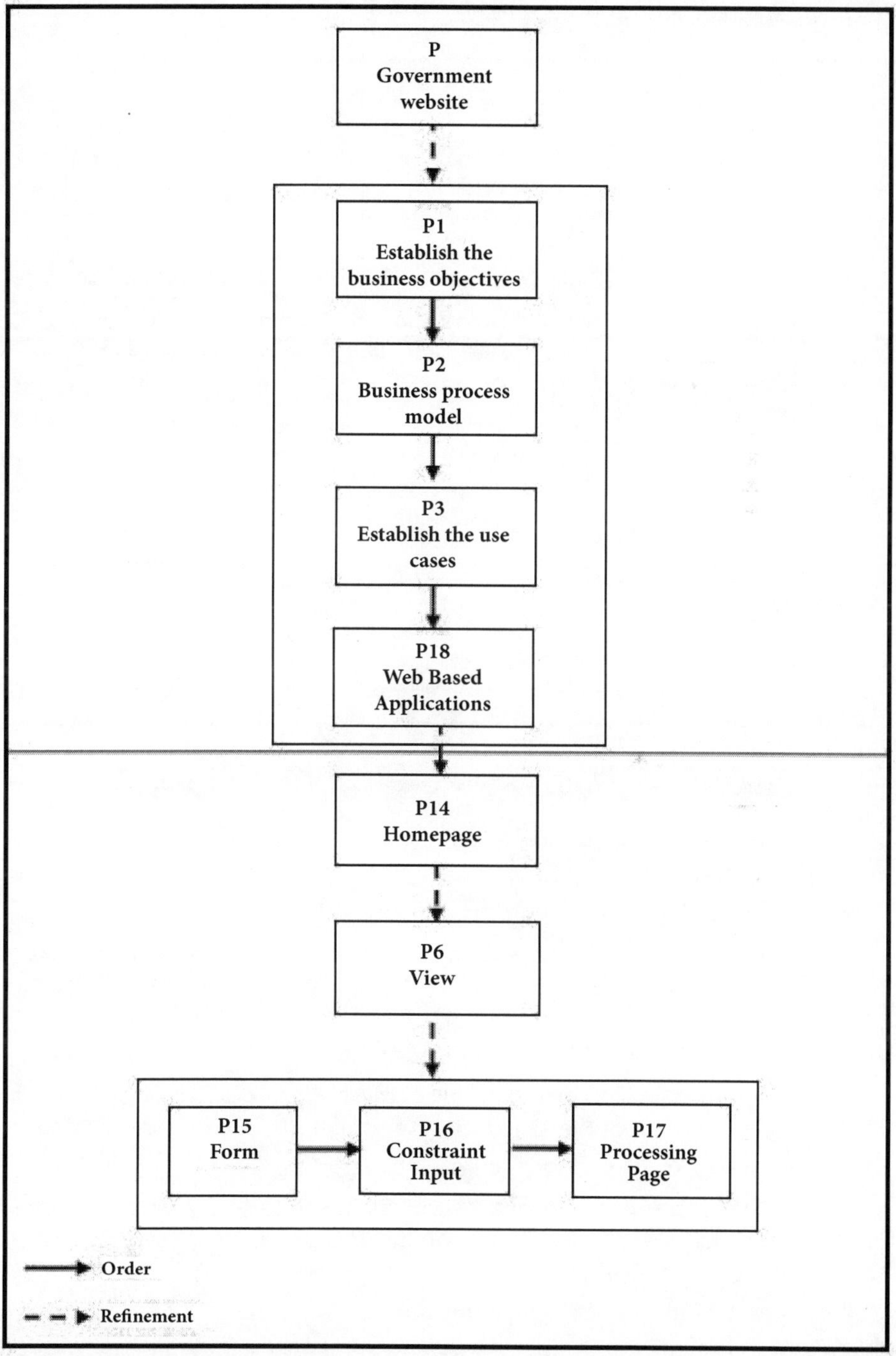

Figure 5.28: Illustrate the new proposed patterns of the design of the Child Benefit website

The following conditions need to hold (see Figure 5.29).

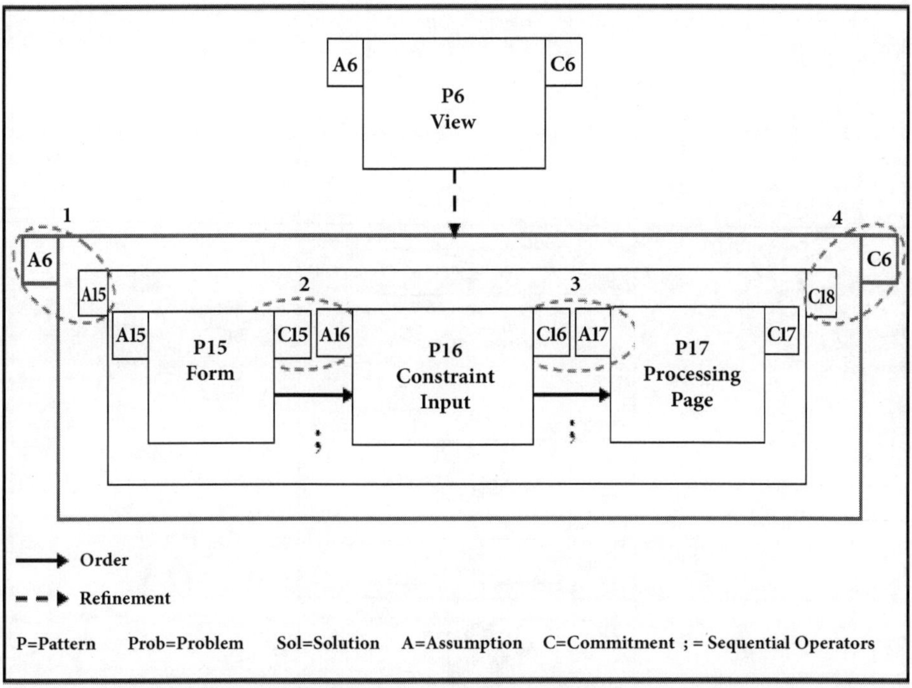

Figure 5.29: Illustrates the concrete design of the View pattern

In this case the four conditions trivially hold and the matching of context is expressed as follows:

In circle 1: **A6** implies **A15** which means that

The Assumption of the View pattern (*There is a data collection service*) matches the Assumption of the Form pattern (*There is a data to be collected*). The refinement rule met.

In circle 2: **C15** implies **A16** which means that

The Commitment of the Form pattern (*To collect the necessary data for the service)* matches the Assumption of the Constraint Input pattern *(There is service data).*

In circle 3: **C16** implies **A17** which means that

The Commitment of the Constraint Input pattern (*There is service data in the right format*) matches the Assumption of the Processing Page pattern *(All the necessary data in the right format).*

In circle 4: **C17** implies **C6** which means that

The Commitment of the Purchase Process pattern (*Provide the data collection service*) matches the Commitment of the View pattern (*A website that displays the data collection service*).

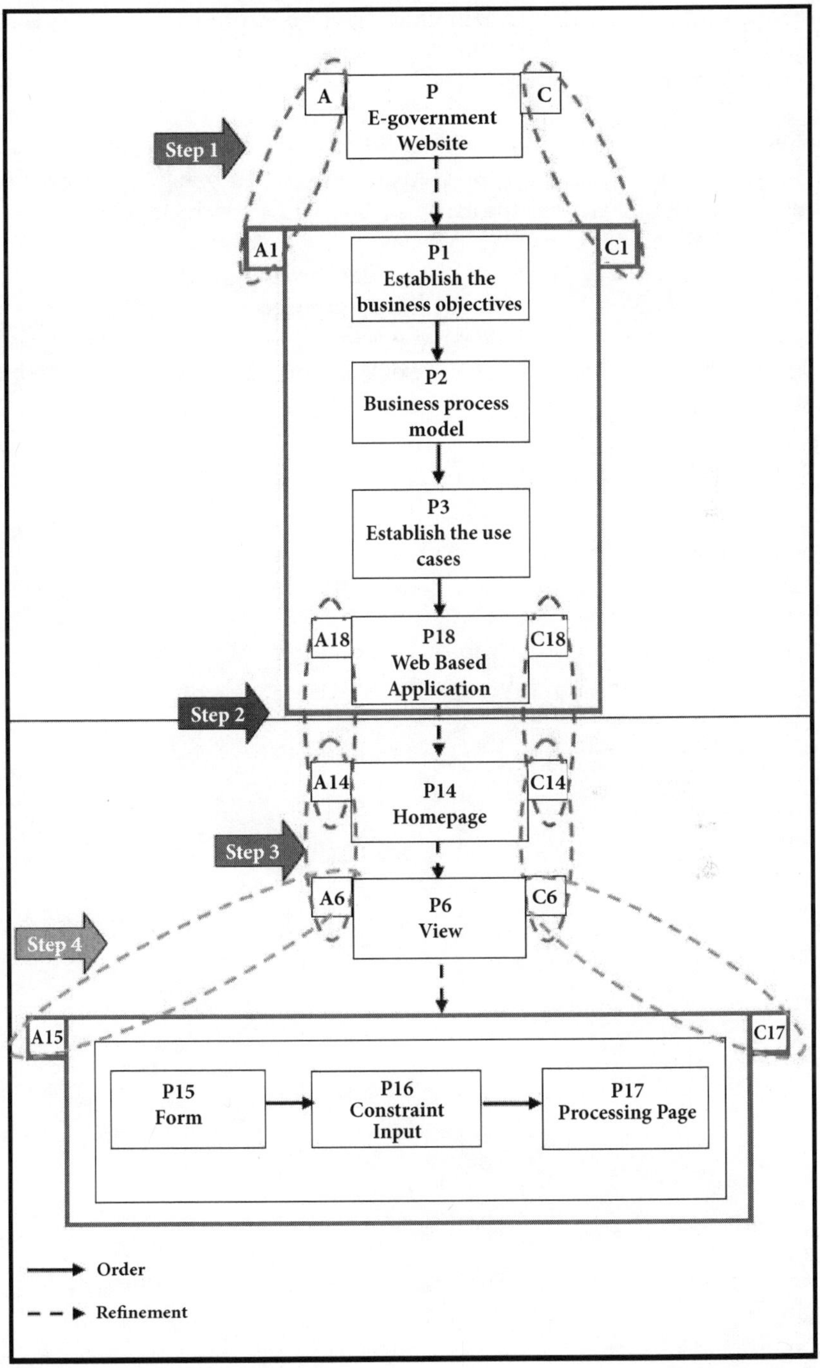

Figure 5.30: Illustrate the new proposed patterns map used in the design of the Child Benefit website

To conclude, the case study examined an E-government website specifically the Child Benefit website and the aim was to illustrate the usability of the Assumption/Commitment framework. The case study illustrated how the Assumption/Commitment constraint helped the designer in determining the best ways to apply patterns with the regard to the context before and after each single pattern application. It also make using the patterns map more precise and rigorous by translating what is the arrows indicating in each stage of the map and where the refinement or the order can be used. The first part examined the existing website and a design was proposed. Checking the design using the Assumption/ Commitment framework revealed that the proposed design was wrong. In the second part of the case study, the design was modified and checked again. Figure 5.30 illustrate all the steps in the design of the Child Benefit website used in the cases study.

5.4 SUMMARY

This chapter discussed the analysis of the design of two websites. The analysis used the Assumption/Commitment framework. The first case study shows that the framework can be used to modify an existing design while the second case study shows that the framework can detect and correct design errors. The two case studies also show that by distinguishing refinement from sequential application of patterns the design process is much more concise.

CHAPTER 6

Conclusions

6.1 Success Criteria Revisited

The book proposed a framework for pattern applicability, within which patterns' applicability can be analysed compositionally. This framework is therefore a part of the answer to the research questions of the book. This is because the framework facilitates the applicability of patterns, aids the designer in the construction of patterns sequences and describes the applicability relationships between patterns more rigorously. In Chapter 1 success criteria were formulated to measure the success of the book to answer the research questions. The success criteria determine whether the framework has key design elements. These key design elements are:

- The ability of the designer to apply patterns to solve a particular problem.
- The ability of the designer to detect design errors.
- The ability of the designer to modify an existing design to enhance the functionality of a system.

As shown in chapter 5 the framework gives the designer the ability to solve a particular problem via a series of steps involving the application of patterns. These steps are either the use or adaptation of existing patterns or the decomposition of the problem into sub-problems whose solutions when composed together will provide a solution to the problem.

The framework also enables the designer to detect design errors, i.e., the conditions on the Assumption and Commitment constraints when a particular pattern is applied do not hold. The second case study in Chapter 5 illustrates the detection of design errors.

The first case study in Chapter 5 shows how the designer can adapt an existing design in order to incorporate new functionality. This is done compositionally in the sense the designer only need to check the conditions on the part that is modified, i.e., there is no need to check the whole design again.

6.2 Comparison with Existing Related Work

Chapter 2 discusses pattern maps, a common feature of software pattern languages and there is strong anecdotal evidence that in Patterns Writers' workshops they are favoured by reviewers [73]. However, Kavanagh has clearly demonstrated problems with such an approach. She argues coherently that they present an overly static view of the relationships between patterns which, when applied, are actually dynamic. Simplistically, the overall process of building using a pattern language can be characterize like this: problem 1 is addressed by pattern A which, as a resulting context, creates problem 2 which can be addressed by Pattern B which creates a new context and so on. Remembering that, theoretically, a pattern can be implemented a million different ways depending on context, and that context is essentially the current state of the system being constructed, it is clear that pattern maps cannot give the necessary guidance for the order of application of patterns. In fact both Kavanagh [63] and Manns [66, 65, 64] before her have shown that the centre of gravity for the Patterns Movement has so far been the production of patterns (i.e., mining the expertise for the knowledge base that is required) rather than their consumption (i.e., their use). The point they make is easily illustrated by the fact that for all the PLoP conferences that have taken place across the world, only one - in 1997 [11] - was focussed on how patterns are used. The issues become clear when looking at pattern sequences and how they might be put together.

Some as Noble and Weir [71], as an example used in their map for *Small Memory Pattern Relationships* arrows to indicate that if a pattern at the plain end is used, the other pattern at the arrow end should also be considered to be used next. They also show specialisations (triangles) and conflicts (crosses on dotted arrows).

In the other hand another example from other roadmap styles is a pattern map for A Presentation Pattern Language by Reiβing [76]. He used different arrows on the pattern map to indicate whether one pattern 'may use' or 'does use' another. His map included the type of relationships between the patterns in the language. As in many other software pattern languages, Reiβing examples shows that the arrows on the pattern map effectively contain the rules of the language and the grammar.

Alexander uses solid lines in pattern maps to indicate the application of the next pattern. As discussed in Chapter 2 maps are confusing for the user of the maps. Taking any of Ian Graham's Web Usability (WU) pattern language maps it is not clear which pattern to apply next and it is in some cases very confusing to the designer or the user to figure out what some of the arrows point to.

Finally Welie and Veer also discussed the issue of structuring a collection of patterns into pattern languages in Interaction Design and they proposed that this language can be organized hierarchically, from high-level design problems to low-level design problems [87]. They also used solid arrows only to illustrate this organization.

None of the above mentioned representations of the relations between patterns in those maps was clearly specifying the type of relations and conditions on the context under which these relations should hold. Now the book framework will remove these ambiguities and confusion by introducing two types of arrows:

- Solid arrow indicating order
- Dashed arrow indicating refinement.

Furthermore maps contain context information in the form of Assumption and Commitment labels to visualise the conditions under which a relation between patterns hold.

6.3 CONTRIBUTION

The book made the following contributions:

- A framework is introduced within which context is characterised via Assumption and Commitment constraints. These constraints help the designer to choose the next pattern to be applied in the design of a system by imposing conditions on these constraints.
- The framework allows the designer to select "different" patterns application stages during the design. These two stages are:
- **Stage 1**: Use/Adapt Existing Patterns.

  In this stage the designer will have two choices. The first one to use a concrete pattern to solve the problem if there is any pattern that will solve the whole problem in any pattern bank. The second choice is used if the designer can't find any pattern in a particular pattern bank that solves the problem. The framework gives the designer the choice to search for a solution and the designer will have the following 2 options:

  a. To search for a concrete pattern that solves a bigger problem. Since also the context needs to match then the following conditions need to hold:

     A implies **Ap** (because of refinement)

     Cp implies **C** (because of refinement)

  b. Or to invent a new concrete pattern. This new pattern needs to be examined and used over and over again to become an accepted pattern.

If none of the above is appropriate or no solution is found using

Stage 1 then the system designer proceeds to **Stage 2**.

- **Stage 2**: Divide and Conquer

  In this stage the designer can use the Divide and Conquer principle which consists of two stages:

  Stage I: Decompose the Problem into Sub-problems (Divide).

  In this stage a problem is divided into sub-problems.

  Stage II: Compose the Solutions for the Sub-problems (Conquer).

  In this stage the composed solutions of these sub-problems will provide a solution to the overall problem.

- The framework uses the following operators for the Divide and Conquer steps: Sequential, Choice and Parallel. These operators play two roles:
- To decompose the problem into sub-problems:
- The operator in this case will be called decomposition operator (OPd).
- To compose the sub-solutions to form a solution:
- The operator in this case will be called composition operator (**OPc**).

In general the operator **OPd** for decomposition matches the one for composition **OPc.** An example where this is not the case is when the **OPd** is the Parallel operator and then the **OPc** could be in sequence. In this case the designer opted to provide a sequential solution for a parallel problem.

These operators provide a natural way of decomposing problems and composing solutions. Furthermore, within the framework, the designer is able to analyse the correct composition of the patterns used, hence incorrect designs can be eliminated. Not only that but these operators will also be used to indicate the order in which patterns are applied. As a result of that these operators will make the use of the pattern maps more precise and clearer.

- The book also provides rules that the designer can use to check whether a pattern is applicable or not. Rules for all three operators are given. Using these rules, a given design may be modified to incorporate new system requirements.
- The pattern maps have been enhanced to distinguish between the steps of the framework, i.e., refinement (dashed line) and sequential order (solid lines).
- The framework introduced in the book is type independent, i.e., it can be used and applied to any pattern bank and will allow the designer to analyse a design with the rules given in the book. Note in the book the framework was using design pattern banks.

6.4 LIMITATIONS

Whilst the framework is a solution to the research questions of the book, it forces the designer to follow strict rules in the choice of the application of the next pattern in a design process. This strictness might not be favoured by every system designer. The book has therefore made the checking of the conditions as light as possible by imposing no constraints on the language used to formulate the Assumption/ Commitment constraints. The system designer can still use the language as used in the description of the pattern itself.

The number of operators might look very restrictive but Sequential and Choice are the most primitive operators. With these two only one can define more complicated operators like the Parallel operator. One could even use them to define operations like those introduced by Kevlin Henney [54].

Finally, the book is analysing system design and the application of patterns and not doing any implementations. Furthermore only the application of design patterns was investigated. However there seem to be no restrictions of the framework on the application of other types of patterns.

6.5 FUTURE WORK

Further studies could develop a tool that automatically generates the conditions that need to hold in order to apply the next pattern based on the step the designer has chosen. This tool could be integrated in existing design tools like Rational.

The tool could also automatically verify the conditions under which patterns can be applied in a specific context. This tool will also have pattern banks facility for different types of patterns (architectural patterns, design patterns and idioms or coding patterns).

Even though the operators used in the framework are for the application of design pattern more derived operators can be obtained that cater for the application for other types of patterns.

Also these derived operators can be domain specific and for example the architectural patterns need more specific operators for decomposition and composition taking into account architectural constraints.

References

Alexander, C., Ishikawa, S., Silverstein, M., Jacobson, M., Fiksdahl King, I. & Angel, S. A. (1977). *A Pattern Language*. New York: Oxford University Press.

Alexander, C. (1979). *The Timeless Way of Building*. New York: Oxford University Press.

Alexander, C. (1996). *keynote Speech (OOPSLA)*. ACM Conference on Object-Oriented Programs, Systems, Languages and Applications. San Jose, California.

Alexander, C. (2001). *The Phenomenon of Life*. New York: Oxford University Press.

Alexander, C. (2002). *The Process of Creating Life*. Berkeley, California: The Centre for Environmental Structure.

Alexander, C. (2004). *A Vision of a Living World*. Berkeley, California: The Centre for Environmental Structure.

Alexander, C. (2004). *The Luminous Ground*. Berkeley, California: The Centre for Environmental Structure.

Ambler, S. (1998). *Process Patterns: Building Large-scale Systems Using Object Technology*. Cambridge: Cambridge University Press.

Ambler, S. (1999). *More Process Patterns: Delivering Large-Scale Systems Using Objects*. Cambridge: Cambridge University Press.

Anderson, F. (2006). *A Collection of History Patterns*. [Online]. Available from World Wide Web: http://hillside.net/plop/plop98/final_submissions/[Accessed 6/12/06].

An International Conference on Using Patterns (UP). (1997). Austin, Texas.

Appleton, B. (2007). *Patterns and Software: Essential Concepts and Terminology*. [Online]. Available from World Wide Web: http://www.cmcrossroads.com/bradapp/docs/patterns-intro.html [Accessed 20/01/07].

Beck, K. & Cunningham, W. (1987). *Using Pattern Languages for Object-Oriented Programs*. [Online]. Available from World Wide Web: http://c2.com/doc/oopsla87.html[Accessed 19/12/07].

Booch, G., Rumbaugh, J. & Jacobson, I. (1997). *Unified Modelling Language User Guide*. Addison-Wesley.

Brown, P. J., Bovey, J. D. & Chen, X. (1997). *Context-Aware Applications: From the Laboratory to the Marketplace*.

Brooks, F. J. (1998). *The Man-Month: and other Essays in Software Engineering*. Addison Wesley, Reading, MA.

Buschmann, F. (1999). *Patterns @ Work*. In Proceedings of Object Technology Conference, Oxford, England.

Buschmann, F., Meunier, R., Rohnert , H., Sommerlad, P. & Staln, M. (1996). *Pattern-oriented Software Architecture – A System of Patterns*. J. Wiley and Sons Ltd.

Buschmann, F., Henney, K. & Schmidt, D. C. (2007). *Pattern- Oriented Software Architecture Volume 4: A Pattern Language for Distributed Computing*. John Wiley & Sons; Volume 4 edition.

Cassell. (1997). *The Cassell English Concise Dictionary*. London: Orion.

Cheesman, J. & Daniels, J. (2000). *UML Components: A Simple Process for Specifying Component-Based Software*. Wokingham, England: Addison-Wesley.

Child Benefit Information. (2010). [Online]. Available from World Wide Web: http://www.child-benefit.org.uk/index.html [Accessed 10/01/10].

Coplien, J.O. & Schmidt, D.C. (1995). *Pattern Languages of Program Design*. Reading, MA.: Addison-Wesley.

Coplien, J. O. (1996). *Software Patterns*. New York: SIGS Publications.

Coplien, J. O. (1998). *C++ Idioms*. In EuroPLoP 1998 Conference Proceedings, Irsee, Germany: UVK.

Coplein, J. O. (1998). *The Patterns Handbook: Techniques, Strategies, and Applications*, chapter Software Design Patterns: Common Questions and Answers, pages 311–320. Cambridge University Press, New York, January.

Coplien, J.O. & Harrison, N. (2004). *Organisational Patterns*. Addison- Wesley.

Coplien, J. O. & Harrison, N. (2004). *Organisational Patterns: Beyond Agility to Effectiveness*. In OOPSLA '04 Conference Proceedings, Vancouver, British Columbia, Canada.

Coplien, J. O. & Harrison, N. (2004). *Organisational Patterns of Agile Software Development,* Upper Saddle River, NJ: Pearson Prentice Hall.

Coplien, J. O. (2008). *Fault-Tolerant Telecommunication System- Pattern: Riding Over Transients.* [Online]. Available from World Wide Web: http://users.rcn.com/jcoplien/Patterns/PLoP95_ telecom.html [Accessed 19/2/08].

Cunningham, W. (1995). *The CHECKS Pattern Language of Information Integrity.* In J. O. Coplien and D. C. Schmidt (eds.) Pattern Languages of Program Design. Reading, MA: Addison- Wesley. pp.145.

DeLano, D. (1998). *Patterns Mining*. In L. Rising (ed.) The Patterns Handbook. Cambridge: Cambridge University Press. pp.87.

De Roever, W., Hooman, J. & De Boer, F. (2001). *Concurrency Verification: Introduction to Compositional and Non- Compositional Methods.* Cambridge University Press.

Dey, A. K. (1998). *Context-aware Computing: The CyberDesk Project.,* In the Proceedings of the AAAI 1998 Spring Symposium on Intelligent Environments (AAAI Technical Report SS-98-02), pp. 51-54, Palo Alto, CA, AAAI Press. March

23-25, http://www.cc.gatech.edu/fce/cyberdesk/pubs/AAAI98/AAAI98.html

Dey, A.K., Abowd, G.D. & Wood, A. (1999). *CyberDesk: A Framework for Providing Self-Integrating Context-Aware Services*. Knowledge-Based Systems, 11.

Dijkstra, E. W. (1975). *Guarded Commands, Non-determinacy and Formal Derivation of Programs.* Communications of the ACM. Volume 18, Issue 8: 453–457.

Doug, Lea. (2007). *Christopher Alexander: An Introduction for Object-Oriented Designers.* [Online]. Available from World Wide Web: http://gee.cs.oswego.edu/dl/ca/ca/ca.html[Accessed 02/1/07].

Etidy. (2006). *The Home of the Necklace Hanger.* [Online]. Available from World Wide Web: http://etidy.co.uk/ [Accessed 20/01/10].

Fact-Archive. (2008). [Online]. Available from World Wide Web: http://www.fact-archive.com/encyclopedia/Context[Accessed 20/09/08].

Fowler, M.(1997). *Analysis Patterns: Reusable Object Models*. Addison-Wesley.

Gabriel, R. P. (1996). *Patterns of Software: Tales from the Software Community*. New York: Oxford University Press.

Gamma, E. Helm, R., Johnson, R. & Vlissides, J. (1995). *Design Patterns: Elements of Reusable Object-Oriented Software*. Reading, MA. Addison-Wesley.

Glass, R.L., Ramesh, V. and Vessey, I. (2004). *An Analysis of Research in Computing Disciplines*. Communications of the ACM, June, 47, 6.

Graham, I. (2002). *A Pattern Language for Web Usability*. London: Pearson Education.

Graham, I. (2007). *A Pattern Language for Web Usability.* [Online]. Available from World Wide Web: http://www.trireme.com/WU/browse.htm [Accessed 22/02/07].

Gregg, D. G., Kulkarni, U. R. and Vinzé, A. S. (2001). *Understanding the Philosophical Underpinnings of Software Engineering Research in Information Systems.* Information Systems Frontiers, 3(2), pp. 169-183.

Guha, R. (1991). *Contexts: A formalization and Some Applications*. PhD book, Stanford University.

Harrison, N. (1996). *Organisational Patterns for Teams*. In J. M. Vlissides, J. O. Coplien and N. L. Kerth (eds.) *Pattern Languages of Program Design 2*. Reading, MA.; Harlow: Addison-Wesley. pp.345.

Harrison, N. (1998). *Potential Pattern Pitfalls, or How to Jump on the Patterns Bandwagon Without the Wheels Coming Off.* In L. Rising (ed.) The Patterns Handbook. Cambridge, Cambridge University Press.

Harrison, N. (1998). *Patterns for Logging Diagnostic Messages.* In R. C. Martin, D. Riehle and F. Buschmann (eds.) Pattern Languages of Program Design 3. Reading, MA: Addison-Wesley. pp.277.

Harrison, N. & Coplien, J. (2001). *Pattern Sequences.* [Online]. Available from World Wide Web: http://c2.com/cgibin/wiki?PatternSequences [Accessed 01/08/04].

Harrison, N., Foote, B. and Rohnert, H. (2000). *Pattern Languages of Program Design 4*. Reading, MA: Addison Wesley.

Hay, D. C. (1995). *Data Model Patterns*, New York: Dorset House Publishing.

Henney, K. (2005). *Context Encapsulation-three Stories, A language, and some Sequences.* Proceedings of the 10th European Conference on Pattern Languages of Programs (EuroPLoP 2005), Irsee, Germany, July 2005. Universitätsverlag Konstanz (UKV): Konstanz.

Hevner, A. R. and March, S. T. (2003). *The Information System Research Cycle*. IEEE Computer, 36 (11), November, pp.111-113.

Hillside. (2006). *A Pattern Definition*. [Online]. Available from World Wide Web: http://hillside.net/patterns/definition.html [Accessed 24/09/06].

Hillside. (2007). *Patterns Library.* [Online]. Available from World Wide Web: http://hillside.net/patterns [Accessed 24/03/07].

Hillside. (2006). *Proto Pattern Page.* [Online]. Available from World Wide Web: http://c2.com/cgi/wiki?ProtoPattern[Accessed 5/12/06].

Hillside. (2007). *Patterns Catalog.* [Online]. Available from World Wide Web: http://hillside.net/patterns/onlinepatterncatalog.htm [Accessed 20/05/07].

Hillside. (2007). *Pattern Languages of Programs Conferences.* [Online]. Available from World Wide Web: http://hillside.net/conferences/plop.htm [Accessed 24/09/07].

Hillside. (2007). *European Conference on Pattern Languages of Programs*. [Online]. Available from World Wide Web: http://hillside.net/conferences/europlop.htm [Accessed 20/08/07].

Jackson, M. (2001). *Problem Frames*. Addison Wesley.

Kavanagh, M. J. (2005). *Foci and Centres in the Design and Use of Pattern Languages.* PhD book, De Montfort University, Leicester.

Manns, M. L. (1999). *Mining for Patterns*. OT'99 Conference. Oxford, England, 29-31 March.

Manns, M. L. (1999). *Introducing Patterns into an Organization*. Conference on Object-Oriented Programming, Systems, Languages and Applications. Denver, CO, 1-5 Nov.

Manns, M. L. (2002). *An Investigation into Factors Affecting the Adoption and Diffusion of Software Patterns in Industry*. PhD book, De Montfort University, Leicester.

McCarthy, J. (1993). *Notes on Formalisation Context*. In Proc. IJCAI-93, pp 555-560, Chambery, France.

Manolescu, D., Völter, M., Noble, J. (2006). *Pattern Languages of Program Design 5*. Reading, MA: Addison Wesley.

Martin, R. C., Riehle, D. and Buschmann, F. (1998). *Pattern Languages of Program Design 3*. Reading, MA.: Addison-Wesley.

Meszaros, G. & Doble, J. (1998). *A Pattern Language for Pattern Writing*. In R. Martin, D. Riehle and F. Buschmann (eds.) Pattern Languages of Program Design 3. Reading, MA: Addison-Wesley. pp. 529-574.

Noble, J. & Weir, C. (2001). *Small Memory Software: Patterns for Systems with Limited Memory.* Harlow: Addison-Wesley.

O'Callaghan, A. (1999). *So You Think You Know about Patterns?* Application Development Advisor. 2(6), July/August 1999.

O'Callaghan, A. (2009). *Personal communication with the author* 19/08/09.

Olson, D. (2006). *Patterns Article - Train Hard Fight Easy.* [Online]. Available from World Wide Web: http://c2.com/cgibin/wiki?TrainHardFightEas [Accessed 7/12/06].

Porter, R., Coplien, J. & Winn, T. (2005). *Sequences as a Basis for Pattern Language Composition,* Science of Computer Programming, v.56 n.1-2, p.231-249, April.

Reißing, R. (1998). *A Presentation Pattern Language.* In EuroPLoP '98 Conference Proceedings, Irsee, Germany: UVK.

Riehle, D. & Züllighoven, H. (1996). *Understanding and Using Patterns in Software Development.* In: Karl Lieberherr/Roberto Zicari (eds.): Theory and Practice of Object Systems, Special Issue Patterns. Vol. 2, No. 1, 3-13.

Rising, L. (1998). *Design Patterns: Elements of Reusable Architectures*. In Rising (Ed.). The Patterns Handbook. UK: Cambridge University Press.

Ryan, N., Pascoe, J. & Morse, D. (1997). *Enhanced Reality Fieldwork: the Context-Aware Archaeological Assistant.* Gaffney, V., van Leusen, M., Exxon, S. (eds.) Computer Applications in Archaeology.

Salingaros, N. A. (2000). *The Structure of Pattern Languages* .Architectural Research Quarterly 4: pp.149-161.

Schilit, B. & Theimer, M. (1994). *Disseminating Active Map Information to Mobile Hosts.* IEEE Network, 8(5) 22- 32.

Schmidt, D., Fayad, M. & Johnson, R. (1996). *Special Issue on Software Patterns.* Communications of the ACM, Vol. 39, No. 10. New York: ACM Press.

Schümmer, T. (2003). *GAMA: A Pattern Language for Computer Supported Dynamic Collaboration*. In EuroPLoP 2003 Conference Proceedings 2003 Irsee, Germany.

Theodorakis, M., Analyti, A., Constantopoulos, P. and Spyratos, N. (1998). *Context in Information Bases*. In Proceedings of the 3rd International Conference on Cooperative Information Systems (CoopIS'98), New York City.

The Open Group. (2008). [Online]. Available from World Wide Web: https://www.opengroup.org/togaf/ [Accessed 20/09/08].

Tidwell, J. (2005). *Designing Interfaces: Patterns for Effective Interaction Design.* O'Reilly Media.

Van Welie, M. & van der Veer, G. (2003). *Pattern Languages in Interaction Design: Structure and Organization*. Proceedings of Interact '03, Zürich, Switserland, M. Rauterberg, Wesson, Ed(s). IOS Press, Amsterdam, The Netherlands, pp. 527-534, 2003.

Van Welie, M. (2010). *Patterns in Interaction Design*. [Online]. Available from World Wide Web: http://www.welie.com/ [Accessed 01/01/10].

Vlissides, J. M., Coplien, J. O. and Kerth, N. L. (1996). *Pattern Languages of Program Design 2*. Reading, MA: Harlow: Addison- Wesley.

Vlissides, J. (1998). *Pattern Hatching: Design Patterns Applied*. Reading, MA: Addison-Wesley.

Webster, M. (2007). *Merriam-Webster's Collegiate Dictionary* [Online]. Available from World Wide Web: http://www.merriam- webster.com/dictionary/context [Accessed 24/09/07].

Zdun, U. (2007). *Systematic Pattern Selection Using Pattern Language Grammars and Design Space Analysis*, Software: Practice & Experience, Vol. 37, No. 9, p. 983-1016, Wiley, 2. July.

Appendices

Appendix A

Appendix A: WU Patterns

These patterns are taking from the web usability WU website [45] and it is used in Chapter 3, 4 and 5(No changes were made to the contents). The link is **http://www.trireme.com/WU/structure.htm**

Pattern 1: Establish the business objectives ***

You are about to create a new website or modify an existing one. The organization has a strategy, but there are possibly several stakeholders with conflicting requirements. If you do not know what they are or how to resolve these conflicts, you will almost certainly produce a site that is unfit for use. However...

Many people think that writing down a few use cases for the site is coextensive with understanding the requirements. Jackson (1998) has amply demonstrated that this is not so and that specification and requirements are quite different things. Furthermore, business objectives are not the same as requirements. For example, the statements 'we must double our DVD sales' and 'the site must make the DVDs more prominent than books' are quite different, though related of course.

When you decide to use TIMEBOXES_(4) to control iterative development you can only negotiate sensibly on evolving requirements if you have consensus on the things that will not change during the project.

Therefore

Hold a workshop involving as many stakeholders as possible. Make sure that potential users are represented by marketing personnel or the results of focus groups, surveys, etc. Find a good facilitator. Agree a mission statement. Find measures for each objective. Agree a numerical rank ordering of the priorities.

Each mission statement is now linked to several measurable and prioritized business objectives. We can now begin to construct a BUSINESS PROCESS MODEL (2) within the workshop and manage the project beyond it using TIMEBOXES (4).

Discussion - forces - known uses

This pattern is one of several in this language whose applicability is far wider than web design and could – no should – be adopted usefully on non-web projects. We include it because it is as fundamental to the success of web projects as to others and because it is, in our experience, one of the patterns most often ignored by web developers– to the ultimate detriment of their projects. It is a process pattern.

Business objectives allow teams to validate their use case and business process models. How should they be discovered? Historically, system requirements were captured from users during a series of interviews. Systems analysts would interview individual users or, sometimes, small groups of users, on an aspect of the required system. The results of these interviews would be collected into a systems analysis report, which would then be circulated for comments. Based on the comments received, a revision would be issued for further comments, and so on. Such reports were usually very large and often quite unreadable. It is difficult to believe that anyone ever both read and understood them all. One suspects that they were often signed in default of a full understanding, rather than provoke a fruitless confrontation. Other significant defects of this approach include the following.

- Often different stakeholders and groups will present contradictory opinions, which lead to contradictory requirements specifications. These may be uncovered later during use case modelling but are usually not noticed until the site has gone live.
- The approach is inclined to inculcate an 'us and them' attitude in the business and the developers. The business people ask for features and state requirements. The developers go away and produce something. What is produced rarely matches the – perhaps unarticulated – requirements exactly. Squabbling and finger-pointing follow inexorably.

A facilitated joint requirements workshop can be run to address these problems directly. Such a workshop will:

- ensure that all participants hear the contributions of others at first hand, which eases the problem of arriving at compromises where these are necessary;
- help developers gain a first-hand appreciation of the real goals of the business, as opposed to a mediated set of requirement statements;
- develop a shared ownership of the project between and among developers and the business;
- reduce the elapsed time needed to establish the requirements;
- establish the tempo of a rapid development process.

A workshop will focus on a particular process-oriented business area and its mission. Agree and write the mission statement for the site on a flip chart page and place where everyone can see it – and possibly amend it as discussion proceeds. Next, the facilitator asks participants call out and discuss the specific objectives of this site. These are written on a flip chart. Experience has taught that there are usually about 13 objectives, either due to the fact that people run out of ideas after that much discussion, that 13 objectives comfortably fills two flip chart pages or, as a more remote possibility, reflecting some obscure law of nature yet to be articulated by rational Man. No activity should be allowed to produce a deliverable without it being tested. This principle is applied to the objectives by seeking a measure for each objective. For example, if our business is running an hotel and an objective is to provide a high quality service then the measure might be a star rating system as provided by many tourist boards or motoring organizations. Of course, there are cases where a precise measure is elusive. Discussing the measures is an important tool for clarifying, elucidating and completing the objectives shared and understood by the group. The discussion of measures helps a group think more clearly about the objectives and often leads to the discovery of additional ones or the modification of those already captured. Setting aside plenty of time for the discussion of the measures is seldom a waste of time.

The minimum requirement is that it must be possible to prioritize all the objectives. A formal preference grid can be elicited by asking that each pair of objectives be ranked against each other. In workshops, this is too time consuming and a quicker, more subjective technique is needed. One way to come quickly to the priorities is to allow participants to place votes against each objective. We usually permit each person a number of votes corresponding to about 66% of the number of objectives; e.g. 9 votes for 13 objectives. A good way to perform the voting is to give each eligible participant a number of small, sticky, coloured paper disks, of the sort that are sold in strips by most stationers. Then the rules of voting are explained: 'You may place all your stickers on one objective or distribute them across several, evenly or unevenly according to the importance you place on the objectives. You need not use all your votes; but you are not allowed to give – or sell – unused votes to other participants.' Then everyone must come up to the flip charts all at once. No hanging back to see what others do is permitted. This helps inject a dynamic atmosphere into the proceedings and stops people waiting to see what the boss does before voting.

Two rounds of voting should be done, under different interpretations, and the results added to reach a final priority score for each objective. Of course, two colours are then needed for the sticky disks. An example of two possible interpretations that can be combined is:

1. Vote from your point of view as an individual.
2. Vote from a corporate viewpoint.

Another pair might be:

1. Vote from the supplier's viewpoint.
2. Vote from the customer's viewpoint.

The results often generate further useful discussion. Also one should allow for re-prioritization at this point, if surprising results have emerged. This is often due to overlap between objectives that is highlighted by the priorities given.

An objective that cannot be measured and/or prioritized must be rejected or, at least, consigned to a slightly modified mission statement. The priorities are a key tool for project management since they determine what must be implemented first from the point of view of the business sponsor. Technical dependencies must also be allowed for, of course. Often a discussion around these issues elicits new objectives, clarifies existing ones or leads to their recombination or even placement in the overall mission statement. Issues that cannot be resolved are recorded with the names of the people responsible for resolving them. Specific assumptions and exclusions should also be recorded.

Priorities will be used to resolve conflicts later. They should be numerical. The DSDM (Stapleton, 1997) MoSCoW ratings system will not usually work for this – every stakeholder insists that his pet objective is a Must Have.

Known uses

Detailed guidelines for organizing and running workshops can be found in Graham (2001). The technique has been used successfully on hundreds of projects around the world over ten years or so. About ten of these were web design projects.

Pattern 2: Business process model **

You have ESTABLISHED THE BUSINESS OBJECTIVES (1) and prioritized them in the first sessions of a joint requirements workshop.

You now need to understand the requirements and the business processes involved, both as they are now and after the site goes live. You realize that this is different from merely specifying the use cases for the site's potential users, since many people involved (such as warehouse staff or credit card authorizers) may never even see the site. However, you must understand their needs and activities as well as those of users.

Therefore

Understand first the network of agents and commitments that make up the business. Specify the conversations that take place at an appropriate level of abstraction, so that they are stereotypes for actual stories. Get people to tell these stories. Ensure that you produce both 'before' and 'after' business process models. Eliminate conversations that do not correspond to business objectives (or discover the missed objective). Ensure every objective is supported by a conversation.

Now that you understand the before and after business models it is necessary to specify the site, so we must first ESTABLISH THE USE CASES (3) at the system boundary and divide them into groups to be delivered in individual TIMEBOXES (4).

Discussion - forces - known uses

This is another process pattern of sweeping generality but too often ignored by web developers.

The commonest misconception in computing is that understanding a client's requirements is the same as specifying a system that will meet those requirements. On such a premise one can then blithely state that use case analysis is the only requirements modelling technique needed. Jackson (1998) pours scorn on this idea, arguing that use cases are useful for specifying systems but that they cannot describe requirements fully. Use cases connect actors, which represent users adopting rôles, to systems. Requirements, on the other hand, may be those of people and organizations that never get anywhere near the system boundary.

A requirements document must be written in a language whose designations concern things in the world in which the system is embedded (including of course that system). Specifications need only describe the interfaces of the system and therefore depend on different designations. The specification describes the interface of phenomena shared between the world and the system; use cases may be used to express these. The requirements model is a description over these and other phenomena in the world; it depends on both the specification and the world. He also states that 'the customer is usually interested in effects that are felt some distance from the machine'.

Ignoring the non-user interactions can lead to us missing important re- engineering opportunities. The model above depicts a rule-based order processing and auto-pricing system, whose aim was to take orders from customers electronically and price them automatically using various, often complex, pricing engines via the corporate object request broker (ORB). The problem was that some orders were too complex or too large to admit of automatic handling. These had to be looked at by a salesman who would of course have an interface with the 'system'. So far, so good: a rule engine would screen 'illegal' or 'handle manually' orders. The salesman would then apply his various spreadsheet and other routines to such orders. But a further problem existed; some orders were so complicated as to be beyond the skills of the salesman, who did not have expertise in financial mathematics. For these orders, the salesman had to go across the office and talk to a specialist trader. She did have the requisite PhD in Financial Engineering. We also modelled non-use- case conversations (depicted in yellow) and, as a result, when our domain expert looked at the simulation we had built, she realized immediately that if we gave the trader a screen we could radically improve the workflow, and thereby customer service. Even this relatively minor excursion away from the system boundary thus had a big cash impact. In many web applications the importance of going beyond the boundary will be greater still. Jackson's argument implies that we need a specific technique for modelling business processes distinct from, but compatible with, use case models of specifications.

The alternative is to fall back on a veritable 'Russian doll' of nested models described in terms of 'business use cases' (Jacobson et al., 1995): an approach that is not only clumsy but fails to address the above arguments.

Once the objectives are clearly stated with defined measures and priorities we can construct our first object model: an object model of the business area that we are dealing with. To do this we must understand what a business (process) actually is. Most vendors of business process modelling tools and techniques find it very difficult to answer the question: 'what is a business process?' Typically, they might answer that a business is a set of processes connected by data flows, with timings for each process and (possibly) allocations of process responsibility to functional units. In other words, data flow diagrams enhanced with timings or perhaps UML (Unified Modelling Language) activity diagrams are all that is needed. What all these approaches have in common is that they lack an adequate theory of what a business process is. The theory behind this pattern is rooted in the science of Semiotics, and the work of Winograd and

Flores (1986) on workflow systems. Rather than taking use cases as a starting point, we extract them from a process model.

Both requirements engineering and business process re-engineering must start with a model of the communications and contracts among the participants in the business and the other stakeholders, customers, suppliers and so on.

Consider some business or enterprise. It could be an entire small company, a division or department of a larger one or even a sole trader. A business process (or business area) is a network of communicating agents. Flores (1997) refers to this as a network of commitments. An agent is any entity in the world that can communicate; so it could represent a customer, regulator, employee, organizational unit, computer system or even a mechanical device of a certain type, such as a clock. Agents are autonomous and flexible. They respond to appropriate stimuli and they can be proactive and exhibit a social aspect; i.e. communicate. Typically agents exhibit some level of intelligence, human agents certainly so but mechanical agents insofar as they can initiate and respond to communication. This now begs the question of what it means for two agents to communicate. Agents need not be site users; i.e. actors. Agents – like actors – are to be thought of as adopting a rôle. This 'business' must communicate with the outside world to exist at all and, if it does so, it must use some convention of signs and signals thereto. We can call these signals between agents semiotic acts. They are carried by some material substratum. They involve a number of semiotic levels from data flows up to implicit social relationships . For example, the substrate may consist of filled-in forms and the social context might be that one assumes that no practical jokes are to be played. If the substratum is verbal (or written) natural language then we can speak instead of speech acts or conversations. These are the speech acts of Austin (1962) and Searle (1969). Flores (1997) argues that business conversations have a constant recurrent structure based on only five primitive speech acts: assert, assess, declare, offer/promise and request. Semiotic acts (or conversations as we wall call them from now on) can be represented by messages, which are directed from the initiator (source) of the communication to its recipient (target). By *abus de langage* we can identify semiotic acts, or conversations, with their representation as messages although strictly they are different; the same semiotic act may be represented by many different messages. This defines equivalence classes of messages and we can think of our actual message as a generic representative of its class; many contracts may express the same relationship so we choose one to represent its equivalence class.

A typical conversation is represented below where a typical external customer agent places an order with some business. This message includes the definition of the reply: {order accepted | out of stock | etc.}. We, quite legitimately, use the UML use case symbol to represent the conversation, but overload the UML actor symbol to represent agents. Data flow in both directions along message links (via the request and hand-over stages discussed below). This is why we have chosen to terminate message links at the recipient end with a filled circle rather than an arrowhead. The line segment is directed from the initiator of the communication, not from the origin of the data.

We now begin to see that agents can be modelled as objects that pass messages to each other. Clearly agents can also be classified into different types as well.

We think of a business process as a network of related conversations between agents, represented by messages. It is inconceivable in most businesses that the message initiator does not wish to change the state of the world in some way as a result of the communication. This desired state of the world is the goal of the conversation and every conversation (or message) has a goal or post-condition, even if it is often unstated: the contract representing the conditions of satisfaction of the conversation.

A goal is achieved by the performance of a task. The innovation here is twofold. The tasks we perform can often be reduced to a few stereotypes: typical tasks that act as pattern matching templates against which real tasks can be evaluated and from which real tasks (or use cases) can be generated. This prevents an explosion in the number of use cases.

In business, only serious, goal-oriented conversations are relevant and therefore we can argue that each conversation has a sixfold structure as follows:

1. A triggering event: a world event that triggers the interaction.
2. A goal: a world state desired by the initiator of the conversation.
3. An offer or request, which contains the data necessary for the recipient to evaluate the offer or request.
4. A negotiation, whereby the recipient determines whether the goals are shared and the conditions of acceptance, leading to either a contract being agreed or the offer rejected. The contract formalizes the goal and provides formal conditions for knowing when the goal has been achieved satisfactorily.
5. A task that must be performed by the recipient of a request to achieve the goal and satisfy the contract. This is what is normally thought of as a use case when one of the agents is an actor.
6. A handover of the product of the task and any associated data, which checks that the conditions of satisfaction of the goals have been met.

This structure accords generally with that of a conversation for action in the terminology of Winograd and Flores (Flores, 1997; Winograd and Flores, 1986). Note also that there is a symmetry of offers and requests, so that we can replace every offer with an equivalent request by swapping the initiator with the recipient. Flores presents the theory in terms of a customer (our initiator) and a performer (our recipient) who executes the primitive speech acts – shown in italics in what follows. The customer assesses her concerns and asserts a request to the performer (dually the performer makes an offer). A process of negotiation then ensues, aimed at defining a contract that can be promised by the performer and accepted by the customer. This, and other stages in the conversation, may involve recursion whereby subsidiary conversations are engaged in. At the end of negotiation the contract defines the conditions of customer satisfaction, and then some task must be executed to fulfil their promise. Finally, the results of this work are declared complete and handed over to the customer who should declare satisfaction.

Consider the concrete example of buying a house. An initiator might say 'would you like to buy my house?' and the recipient would need to know, and would negotiate on, the price. This negotiation could well involve (recursively) subsidiary conversations between the recipient and a mortgage provider and a building surveyor. If everything is agreed then a contract will be agreed and signed (literally in this case). Now there is work to do; in England it is called conveyancing. The work involves searching local government records and land registry documents along with many other – all fairly straightforward – tasks. So this is the place where we might rely on a standard task script, as exemplified for example by the words (or flowcharts) in a book on conveyancing. Finally, when this task completes satisfactorily we can hand over the keys and the contract is said to be completed.

Of course, in business process re-engineering, we are eager to capture not just the messages that cross the business boundary, such as order placement, but to model the communications among our customers, suppliers, competitors, etc. This provides the opportunity to offer new services to these players, perhaps taking over their internal operations – for a fee of course.

Having analysed the business process in terms of conversations, we now focus on the task performance segment of the conversation: the use case if actors are involved. Before doing so let us remind ourselves of the model sequence. We started with a mission grid leading to several processes. Each process has several objectives. Also, there is now a network of conversations (messages). We should now ask two critically important questions:

- Does every message support the achievement of at least one objective?
- Is every objective supported by at least one message?

If the answer to either question is 'no', then the model must be amended. Either we have missed some conversations or we are modelling conversations that do not contribute to the achievement of any stated business objective. Of course, it is possible that we have missed an important objective and, in that case, the users should be consulted to see if the statement of objectives needs to be modified. If not, we have a clear re-engineering opportunity: just stop doing the work that supports no objective.

Known uses

This technique has been used successfully on hundreds of projects known to us around the world over ten years or so. About ten of these were web design projects.

UML provides another notation for business process modelling: the activity diagram. Our agent conversation diagrams offer a convenient alternative to activity diagrams which makes all implementation assumptions very explicit and, more importantly, in a way more readily understandable by users; the activity notation is quite hard to remember, understand and explain. Of course, there may be occasions when activity diagrams are helpful. Martin and Odell (1998) give the following criteria for deciding whether or not to use this kind of representation. Consider using activity charts if:

- an object has complex, significant state (use state charts);
- there is complex interaction between a few objects which trigger state changes in each other – as often found in real-time control systems;
- object behaviour is event driven and single threaded and objects have only one state variable (note that business processes are notoriously multi-threaded);
- the user culture supports their use – as in the telecoms sector.

Avoid them if:

- there are several threads (as in a typical business process);
- there is complex interaction between large numbers of objects;
- objects have several significant state variables.

Pattern 3: Establish the use cases

Aka: establish the use case and object models; understand users' tasks first;task-centred information architecture.

You have constructed a Business Process Model (2) consisting of agents and conversations. This was linked to the prioritized business objectives established earlier in the workshop: Establish The Business Objectives (1).

The site must serve at least one significant business purpose. For this reason we must look at all the use cases that we can predict users will want to execute.

Therefore

Extract the use cases from the conversations in the Business Process Model (2). Record their correspondences to the business objectives. Write post-conditions for each use case. Compare the vocabulary of the post-conditions to the type model. Write use cases in stimulus–response form. Convert the use cases into the user training manual and the test plan. Develop Context-Sensitive Help (17) from them. One stimulus/response pair from the use case should correspond to one step in the workflow if the site deals with workflows. If not, do not constrain the user's ability to perform steps in any particular sequence. Ensure that you extract and document a business object type model from the use case goals.

You must now Classify Your Site (11). One reason is to establish whether it must enforce workflows. Use a SITE MAP (12) and for workflow sites Context-Sensitive Help (17) to help the user complete use cases accordingly to the constraints set by the organization and the needs of the user. Use the use cases as the basis to Automate Testing (6).

Discussion - forces - known uses

This is another process pattern of sweeping generality often ignored by web developers.

It is widely believed that establishing users' tasks and responsibilities is a prerequisite for building any useful computer system. The vulgar term for this is use case analysis. Other people talk of task analysis or usage- centred design. Sometimes we need to organize these tasks into a workflow ... BUT ... task-centric interfaces constrain the freedom of users and inhibit their creative use of sites. How do we balance these forces?

During the construction of the business process model, we got people to tell stories and produce storyboards. Now we focus on the stories that concern people interacting directly with the site: users, maintenance staff, content managers, and so on.

How will users for example, react to our forcing them to complete Mandatory Fields (71); will they regard them as intrusive attacks on their privacy or an unnecessary waste of their valuable time and phone bill? How will they cope with a disabled Back Button (35) should we decide to disable it? More generally, how do we assure the user of a successful completion to her tasks in terms of navigating to required content or completing a workflow transaction?

An answer to these questions is only possible if you really understand who your users are and how they might interact with the site. The most common way to gain such understanding is to identify the actors (users adopting a rôle) that use the sites and the tasks they wish to carry out: the use cases. This is not a tutorial on UML or object-oriented analysis but we will pause to give a brief description of the technique. For a fuller tutorial see any of (Graham, 2001; Cockburn, 2000; Fowler, 1997) there is an extensive tutorial based on Graham's work at www.trireme.com.

Use case modelling

The technique starts with the 'business use cases' discovered using Business Process Model (2). We now focus on the system boundary and the actors that will use the site. For each of these we enumerate and document the use cases. There are several possible styles of doing this.

Many people fill in templates, often based on those of Cockburn. Richard Dué (private communication) recommends using a stimulus– response format. We think that a use case is best specified by writing pre- and post-conditions using a minimalist template having roughly the following form.

1. Name and description
2. Actor(s)
3. Component use cases (if any)
4. Pre-conditions
5. Post-condition (goal)
6. Recoverable exception use cases
7. Fatal exception use cases
8. Comments

Note that we include non-functional requirements in the goal, so that it is possible to state: 'the user has submitted a valid order and received confirmation in less than n seconds'. As an example consider a web- based postal lending library.

There will be a use case named Borrow whose goal might be written: The MEMBER has been *identified* and a loan recorded for a BOOK. The same book has been *dispatched* to the member within 8 hours and the book is no longer *in stock*.

This example shows that the use case goals provide the vocabulary for discussing the problem domain. Nouns (caps) suggest object types and verbs (in italics) suggest associations and operations. Nothing is said about how the goal is accomplished at this stage. We must now go on to specify an object model that provides and ontology for the site.

Object modelling

This is not the place for an exegesis on object modelling even though it is an essential prerequisite to using the further patterns in this language. The technique summarized above has its origins in Catalysis (D'Souza and Wills, 1999) and is summarized in (Graham, 2001). For a tutorial on building use case and object models specifically in the context of web design see (Cato, 2001).

Cato seems to regard building the use cases and building the object model as separate patterns. We think these activities are too inextricably linked to do this. Thus the first alternative name given above for this pattern.

Establishing as many use cases as possible lets you think rationally about subsequent design decisions that you will make. If the priorities are carried over from the business process model, they will turn into a valuable tool for managing projects using TIMEBOXES (4). They also form a sound and invaluable basis for the testing patterns that we will meet later.

Known uses

Use case modelling is a well-established technique for systems development and is part of most mainstream methods for object-oriented and component based development. This applies equally to object modelling using UML as a notation.

*Pattern 23: Breadcrumbs ***

You are trying to provide users with a Sense Of Location (15) and, in particular, a clear Canonical Location (21).

How can users see where they are relative to the site's home page, which probably offers more navigation options then other pages?

Therefore

Do not rely solely on breadcrumbs for navigation unless you are very short of space. Breadcrumbs should be complimented by a Navigation Bar (25) and/or other navigational devices. Some navigation however may only be available from the home page, but breadcrumbs need to go on every page.

Put breadcrumbs near the navigation bar and always at the top of the page. Make it clear that they a secondary form of navigation, perhaps by using a lighter or smaller fount. Highlight or embolden the current location. Separate them with a > symbol or other pointer-like device.

Clarify their function by saying 'you are here'. Don't use them in place of a well chosen page name.

Next Display The Options (79) and use Navigation Bar (25) in parallel with this pattern. Put the Site Logo At Top Left (24).

Contributors and sources

Krug (2000), Nielsen (2000).

Discussion - forces - known uses

The site shown above uses breadcrumbs and a search box as its sole navigation. This works well for a site consisting mostly of articles and reviews and the site is well worth a visit if you are interested in usability.

Breadcrumbs provide a depth-oriented navigation bar. They show you how the current page is related to the home page.

Pattern 24: Site logo at top left **

You have developed a Site Map (12) but users visit sites other than yours. Channel switching between different site layouts causes cognitive dissonance and extra work. Therefore you Follow Standards (36). Users need to know that they can always Go Back To A Safe Place (34) and may not be able to rely on the Back Button (35) to do this. A prominent logo will also support a user's Sense Of Location (15).

How do I know which site I am currently on? How do I know what will happen when I click on the site logo. How can I always get back to the site's home page?

Therefore

Follow the standard. Place you logo at the top left of every page. Clicking on the logo always takes you home. No time is spent looking around for the home button. Spend time thinking up a good tag line.

Fit the logo into the Navigation Bar (25), within the home page's Three-Region Layout (26). Avoid making the user a Prisoner of War (37).

Discussion - forces - known uses

Since most sites place their logo at the top left of every page and use it as a link to their home page, users come to expect this. It is guaranteed to be visible when a page loads and even when a user arrives from a search engine she will know whose site she is on. Therefore follow the standard. The logo on the home page can be larger than on other pages and may have a tag line. The tag line needs to be chosen carefully because it must differentiate and characterize you enterprise without naming it. Among the best ones we've seen we'll mention BabyCenter who use the phrase 'cradle and all', which seems to sum up what they sell very well. The trouble is that thinking up such a phrase is very difficult.

Pattern 25: Navigation bar **

You have created a SITE MAP (12) and want to make it accessible to the user.

How can the number of clicks the user needs to make to get from one section (or major section) of the site to another be reduced? How can we ensure that the user knows her location relative to the site and relative to the web as a whole?

Therefore

As in Figure 25.1, use colour to indicate current location and where the user has been already. Try to Follow Standards (36) when doing this.

Avoid using pull down menus for navigation. The user has to perform an extra action to see what the options are, and the links don't change colour when visited in these lists. Provide a bar on the home page – and possibly on other pages – that allows the user to jump to any section of the site or at least the top three levels. Place it above the fold. Consider the use of the tab metaphor if there a less than about 7 categories.

Next include Breadcrumbs (23) and make sure that the are No Frames On Public Sites (27). Embed the navigation bar in a THREE-REGION LAYOUT (26). For large suites consider using Structured Menus (19).

Contributors and sources

Paul Dyson, Dave Sissons, Krug (2000), Nielsen (2000), Veen (2001)

Discussion - forces - known uses

A navigation bar lists either the top level structure of the site or the use cases it offers. Many sites list the high level services down the left hand side and the use cases across the top.

Highlight the current location in the navigation bar by changing its colour, emboldening it or using an image or character that looks clearly like a pointer. Preferably do at least two of these things.

Reinforce the idea that your navigation bars are to do with navigation by using a unique colour background for navigation throughout the site.

Items that should go on the bar for all sites include:

- the site logo (which takes you home consistently);
- about the organization or company;
- privacy policy;
- contact information.

For workflow or sales sites you should include:

- registration and log-in;
- checkout;
- shopping basket;
- account information.

Other possibilities include:

- downloadable items;
- site map;
- communities;
- frequently asked questions;
- news and press releases;
- jobs.

Structural links, which point to other parts of the site, should be displayed consistently on each page to reinforce user understanding of the navigation scheme. However, this takes up a lot of space and sometimes a compromise solution is needed. The service navigation bar, usually displayed left, shows the breadth of the site but occupies a lot of valuable screen space. Therefore, consider placing it only on the home page – only a click away via the site logo, which is on every page.

Index card tabs are a commonly-used metaphor on navigation bars, with Amazon sites being the best known example as shown in the sensitizing image of this pattern. Notice how colour is used to connect the current navigation options to current tab. This works a lot better when there a only a few options. As Amazon's product range has been extended the usability of the sites seems to have degraded slightly. Also, at a glance the All Products combo box on the German site doesn't seem to do anything but duplicate the tabs – or does it restrict the search somehow? Here is something that could well confuse users – and confusing people is bad. Amazon supplement this navigation with a vertical bar on the left that contains deeper navigation options. Notice how the different placement of the combo box makes its function much clearer.

Browsers change the link colours for sites that have already been visited. This is helpful information and should not be overridden or hidden in any way. Nielsen's studies indicated that the standard link colours should be retained to maximize usability. If we Follow Standards (36) then anything clickable will be underlined.

Figure 25.1 Show users clearly their current location and where they've been already. [Refer to book]

Pattern 76: Content is linked to navigation *

You are concerned with providing a Sense Of Location In Workflow (75) through a sound navigation scheme, but your development budget is limited.

Can I base the navigation scheme on a standard product and so save development time?

Therefore

Link navigation to a model of users' domain knowledge. One page implements one workflow step. Avoid shell architecture. This pattern is terminal within this language.

Contributors and sources

Richard Dué, Detlef Vollmann, Spool et al. (1999)

Discussion - forces - known uses

The study by Spool et al. (1999) showed that when users visited shell sites they found it very hard to hard to use for searching for the information they needed. Shell sites are those where a fixed organization and navigation scheme is defined and content is then plugged into it.

Just as form and content are intertwine in art and nature so on the web. The way you navigate depends deeply on the material you are navigating and therefore the navigation scheme should reflect the exigencies of the content as well as the use cases. Consider, for example, the different ways that bibliographical, leisure and commercial sites are approached. A tourist does arrive at a travel site with a conception of library-style organization that he might have used in his day job – a librarian.

On workflow sites it is clear that the workflow itself should guide at least some of the navigation.

Appendix B

Appendix B: Welie Patterns

These patterns are taking from Welie website [88] *and it is used in Chapter 3 and 5 (No changes were made to the contents). The link is* ***http://www.welie.com/***

E-Commerce Site pattern

http://www.welie.com/patterns/showPattern.php?patternID=commerce

Problem

User want to shop for a product.

Solution

Create a 'virtual' store where visitors can browse, choose and pay for all their selections in one go.

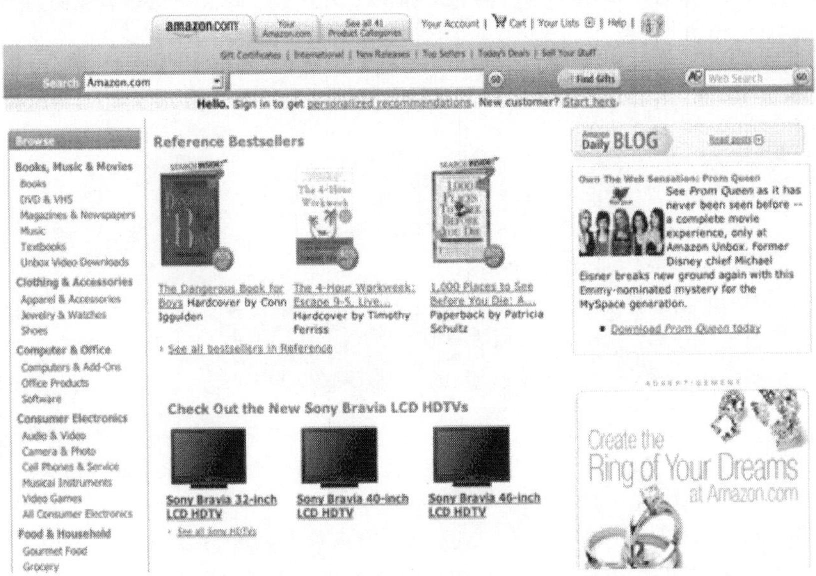

From www.amazon.com

Use when

When visitors can buy products or services online. The number of products can be bought is not very important, this pattern applies very every basic online shopping site.

How

The basic e-commerce site is based around the same idea as a normal shop; you search for the products and put them in you cart until you decide to actually buy them. The main real difference is that people cannot 'touch' the products before buying them. So for successful commerce sites it is really important to make users 'feel good' about buying the product. You need to make sure they know EXACTLY what it is they are buying. use pictures or animations to show all relevant aspects of the products. Sometimes, a 3D model that people can manipulate can be a nice way to reach that 'touching the product' feeling online.

An e-commerce site is based around the following components:

- ❖ A database with product description
- ❖ Client profiles for personalization and purchase processes
- ❖ Some sort of Shopping cart mechanism

The home-page | When users visit an e-commerce site, it must be clear that products can be bought. This can be achieved by showing a Shopping Cart, an icon for accessing the cart or a mini-cart, on the home-page. Also list some categories of products that you sell. Use a pay-off to give a reason why visitors should buy at your site and not any other site.

An E-commerce site is based on the following principle; personal, effective, and efficient. When people shop online, the following issues are very important to take into account:

- ❖ People must be able to **find** a product they like
- ❖ People must be able to **buy** selected products
- ❖ Care about the privacy of customers
- ❖ Offer good services after the actual purchase: e.g. being able to track the order or return purchased products
- ❖ Give people to shop at your site!

The Shopping Experience | The first part in the shopping experience is getting people to buy something. If you are trying to sell something, you need to put the products under the users' nose as much as you can without overdoing it. Show what you have, what is popular/hot/new/ etc. For example using various Hotlist. When they see products, make sure they resemble the real thing as much as possible and let them 'virtually' touch/use the product. Also allow for Product Comparison in order to help people **choose**

When you allow for Login, visitors can be recognized for even better suggestions. The site can offer recommendations based on previous purchases or wish-lists.

Once people have found a product they want to buy, use the Shopping Cart for dealing with the purchase process. Make sure your design is clear and effective. You must show additional cost such as shipping costs at all times and be flexible with things such as delivery addresses.

The second part of the shopping experience is about actually getting the product you ordered and making sure the customers is happy with the purchase. Offer the possibility to track the order and offer information about what to do when something has gone wrong e.g. the wrong product was delivered or the product was damaged.

The third part concerns the creation of extra value so that people keep on using the site and buy more products. Using personalization in the form of recommendations is a nice way to suggest relevant products to returning customers. Other possibilities are 'wish lists' or 'favorite readings' that people can share with other visitors of the site.

Why

The basic ideas behind an e-commerce site is to mimic a normal shop. The essentials are simple but getting the details right can be hard and have a big impact on your success.

More Examples

This example from Esprit shows an interesting approach. User can shop for clothes and once the arrive at a product they can see the item in different colors, see the material from close-by (the zoom button) and how it looks on a person (fitting button). Just as you would in a shop. It also shows in the bottom of the screen how many items you have in your cart and the total amount.

Shopping pattern

http://www.welie.com/patterns/showPattern.php?patternID=shoppi ng

Problem

Users want to look for products of interest and potentially purchase them

Solution

Create an online shopping experience that matches off-line shopping experiences

Use when

You are building a web site where you sell products, typically an E- commerce Site but it can also be a site with paid content. The sort of products that you are trying to sell may vary a lot, ranging from books, electronics, to holiday and clothes. Some products can be delivered directly by downloading it and others will have to be delivered 'later' by some logistical process. No matter what product you are trying to sell, there are well known aspects to shopping that apply to all products and to all ways of shopping.

How

Shopping involves several fundamental activities that apply to both online and offline shopping activities. These activities needs to be supported for each type of product and domain. How to do that best is largely domain dependent, but some basic ideas can be defined:

- **Discovering**. People need to know what they can buy in the store, as far as they don't already know it. Even if they have been in the store before they need to be informed of new products that are for sale. Even if there are no new products to sell, there may be products that should be brought under the users attention because of other reasons e.g. because they are discounted, very popular etc. Use Hotlist.
- **Browsing.** Most people like to browse through the store for seeing what they have and whether something attracts their attention. Browsing is

made easier when products are categorized in ways that customers expect them to be. The categories allow them to browse in a specific manner that is a bit more directed than no structure at all. Use structured navigation such as a Double Tab Navigation with Breadcrumbs so that people are fully aware of where they are and where they can go to.

- **Comparing**. Often people do not know exactly which product they want. They may have several options that they want to compare using a Product Comparison or Product Configurator.
- **Trying**. When people try a product they want to make sure it is the right product for them. Trying is all about 'seeing' certain aspects of the product. In many cases it is even possible to 'interact' with the product by 'virtually touching it', seeing close-ups, table of contents or a preview of a part of the object. Sometimes it may also be possible to try the real thing with some limitations on the use of it. In other words, create a Virtual Product Display.
- **Asking Opinions**. Many shops have shop assistants that help customers to find the right product for them. Online this is difficult to achieve but one could create Product Advisor or collect recommendations/ratings/ comments of other people that bought the product.
- **Choosing**. Choosing is not the same as buying. Customers may choose several products and before they actually start buying, discard several of them at the last minute. Give them a place to keep products they may want to buy such as a Shopping Cart or wish list
- **Recommending**. Many times when people shop they do not find anything for themselves but they find something that might interest a friend or relative. In that case they want to recommend it to others or letting others know about the existence of the product. Use Send-a- Friend Link or list of recommended products.

Besides finding a product people like, there are other factors that give people greater satisfaction with their purchase:

- Having struck a bargain
- The cheapest price
- A unique product
- The product comes with exceptional service
- The product is more durable
- The product is quickly delivered

Why

People know the off-line shopping experience very well. The essentials of shopping should be taken into account for online shopping as well since they have little to do with the medium itself. The goal is to find the appropriate way to sell particular products in the web while paying attention to all aspects of the shopping experience.

More Examples

The Gore-tex product advisor that helps people find the right product for them:

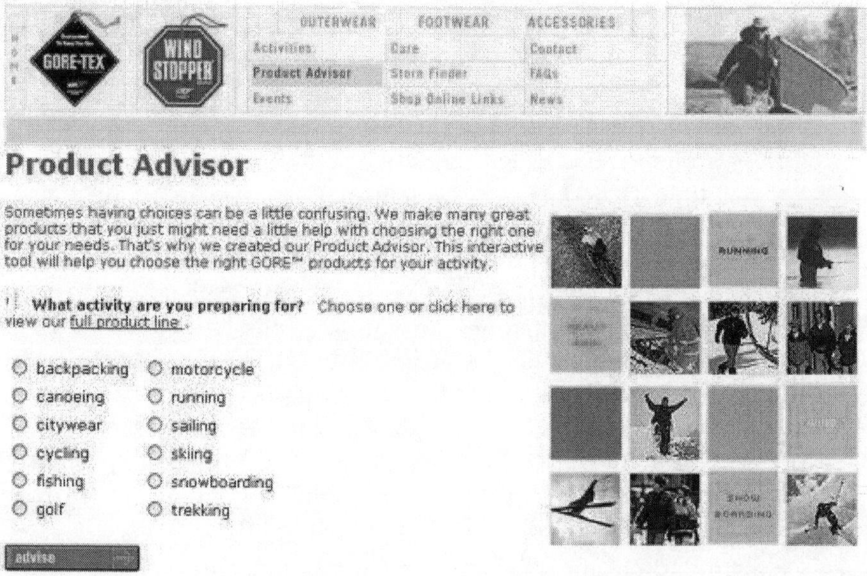

The 3D phone demo at Nokia allows people to 'touch' and 'play' with the phone without physically holding it:

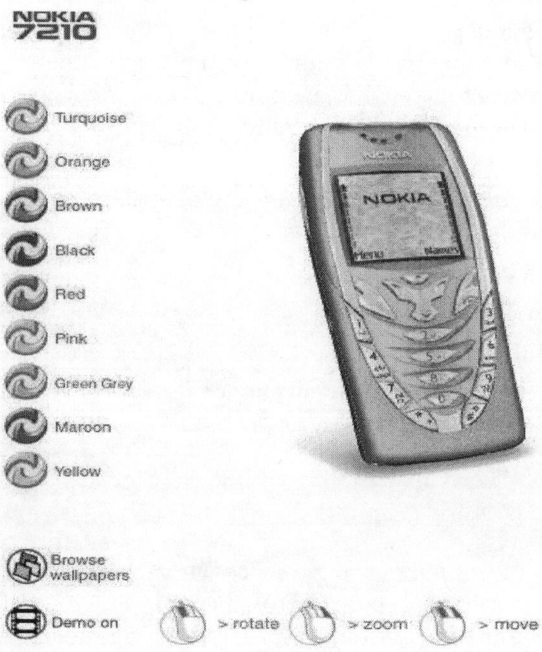

Purchase Process pattern

http://www.welie.com/patterns/showPattern.php?patternID=purchase- process

Problem

Users want to purchase an already selected product

Solution

Present users with the purchase steps

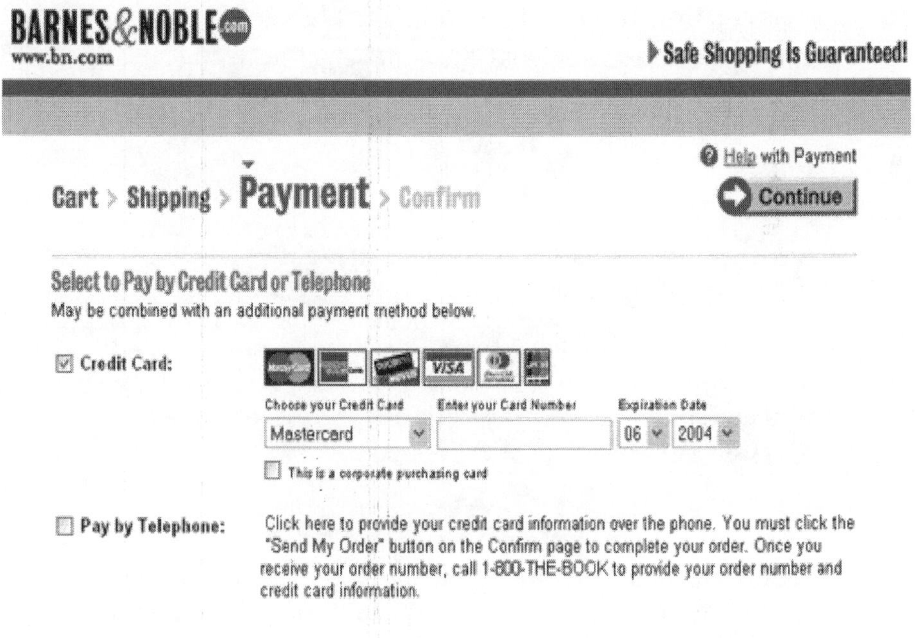

From www.bn.com

Use when

The site allows purchasing of goods, typically a E-commerce Site but it can also a site that happens to sell products as well such as a Museum Site. A purchase can also be part of larger tasks such as a Booking.

How

In order to purchase the products in the cart they need to select the checkout action. The checkout is a five step Purchase Process with the following tasks:

- Identify they client
- Select shipping address and special options
- Select payment method
- See overview of the entire order
- Confirm and place order

❖ Receive confirmation by email

The users can abort the checkout procedure at any step. When users retry the checkout later, they start again at the first task. Consider a Wizard to guide the user through these tasks while minimizing the number of web pages used. However, a wizard is not always needed for just a purchase. Often sites ask for details that are not strictly necessary to process the order. In many cases, all of the order information may easily fit on one page and hence eliminating the need for a wizard.

Minimize navigation and non-relevant page elements

Since purchasing is a task that requires quite some focus, the standard page layout during the purchase process has to be simplified. Sub- navigation and contextual elements should not be shown. All distracting elements should be removed.

User Login

Many sites require users to Login as the first step of the process. While this is convenient for returning customers because all their personal data can be re-used, it is not very nice for new users. New customers should be allowed to purchase items without creating an account. At the end of a purchase, users can be asked to Registration. Registration can then be made very simple because all the basic data has already been captured during the purchase process, only the username and password still needs to be selected.

Confirmation by email

It is important to 'give' the users something that is easily accessible after the browser has been closed. An email with the information about the purchase is like a 'receipt' for users. It should contain an order number, list of items in the order, all amount, shipping address, payment information, date of placing order. It should also contain help for users how to track they order, cancel it, or request assistance.

Why

First time customers or infrequent customers are best helped with a Wizard that allows the to complete the purchase in small steps. Returning customers usually use the same shipping address and same credit-card. Therefore the process can be more efficiently done in only one overview screen with a 'purchase' button.

More Examples

At Amazon, the wizard is not shown for frequent customers who's data has been stored already. All information is shown in one screen while still allowing users to change parameters:

Shopping Cart pattern

http://www.welie.com/patterns/showPattern.php?patternID=shopping- cart

Problem

Users want to buy a product

Solution

Introduce a shopping cart where users can put their products in before they actually purchase them.

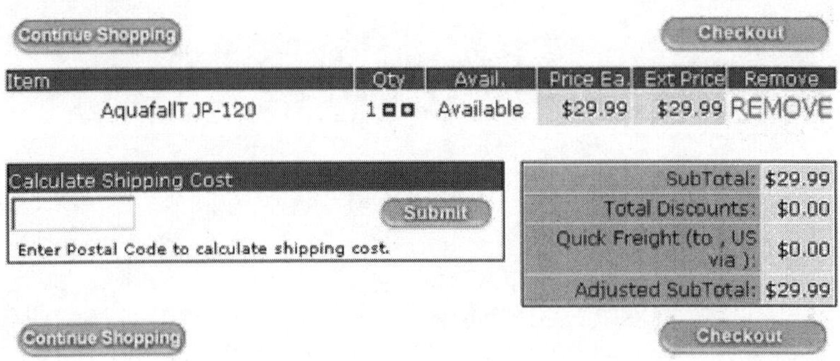

From www.waterpikstore.com

Use when

A site where users can browse through products and buy them. Users are not very frequent buyers and are possibly novices. For returning customers, consider a One-Click Shopping system. Users may buy more than one product. Users may want to select products now but pay later. Users may decide to purchase somewhere else at any time

How

When users view a product description, they can choose to add it to their shopping cart. After adding an item to their cart, the users are shown the current contents of the cart. Users can inspect their cart contents at any time using a link that is available on every page. A persistent mini-cart could also be shown directly on the content pages. Basically the cart is a Collector that is used to collect products.

The description of the cart contents typically includes the name of the items, the quantity, availability and prices. Users can remove items from their cart if they wish and change quantities. The description of the goods is a link to the product details. Users always see the total costs of a purchase, so including shipping costs if applicable. The users must also be informed of the payment options such as which credit cards are accepted. From the cart page, the users can continue shopping or proceed with the checkout procedure. The items stay in the cart for a certain period of time, e.g. 90 days.

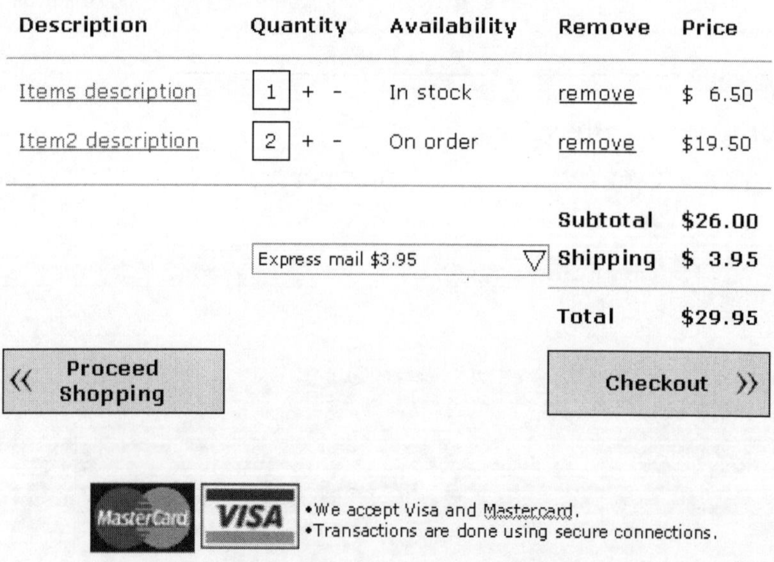

View wireframe

Why

The shopping cart is a very well known and international metaphor. This pattern allows users to gather all products first and pay for them all at once and whenever they want. By showing the total costs including shipping the users know exactly what they will have to pay when they decide to purchase. The checkout procedure using a Wizard helps users to accomplish the actual purchase with all possible assistance.

More Examples

At amazon.com users can browse through many products and add them to their shopping cart without any commitments. They can view the contents of their cart with one click and proceed with the actual purchase whenever they want. The option to view the contents of the cart is available on every page.

Barnes and Noble show a mini-cart on every page so that users can always see a brief overview of their cart contents.

At www.gap.com, shoppers find this "mini-cart" on every page. In fact, they call it a "bag" and shop a small image of the bags you get when shopping in a Gap store:

An inspection of the "bag" shows the following overview:

At www.guess.com, they combined the number of items and the cart icon, well a bag in this case...

Collector pattern

http://www.welie.com/patterns/showPattern.php?patternID=favourites

Problem

Users need to temporarily gather a set of items for later use

Solution

Allow users to build their list of items by selecting the items as they are viewing them. Place a link to the collected items list on every page in the site.

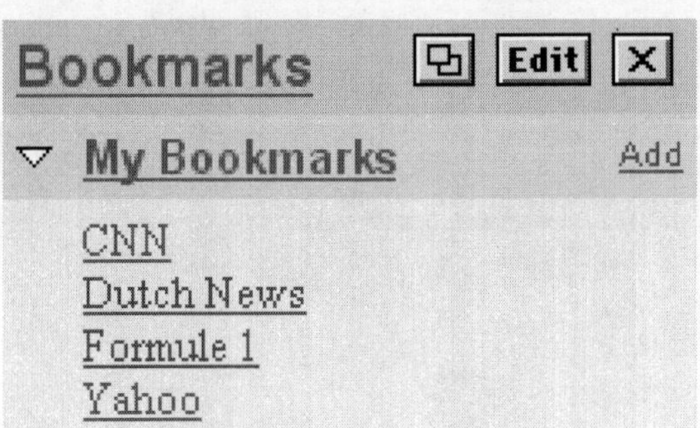

From www.yahoo.com

Use when

In many sites users encounter 'objects' that they will later again read, view, or use in general. For example, in a E-commerce Site users view products which they will put in their Shopping Cart so that they may purchase them or throw them out of the cart again. A 'wish list' is another temporary storage for products. For other type of sites such as News Site users may gather articles based on headlines and read the collected articles afterwards. Often a 'favorites/bookmarks' list is part of a Personalized 'My' Site. Collecting items can also be used for a Product Comparison or any other situation where the task consists of 'collect and take action on the collection'.

Users must be able to quickly access their 'collection' and independently of the task at had. Users must be able to add items as they find them and they must be able to manipulate their gathered items.

How

Place a link 'add/save to list/cart/clippings/...' on pages with items of interest. Typically such a link is present on a Article Page or Product Page. Provide some subtle feedback that the item has been added to the set of items. For example, by showing the number of items in the set being updated. Alternatively, show the updated list of items.

The set of items is accessible from any location in the site. It is hence usually part of the Meta Navigation. Selecting the list shows the set either on a new page or in an overlaid section. The list itself is just a very basic View. Although the set of items is only intended to gather few items, users need some basic functionality for deleting all or some items. Provide functionality in the area of the list itself, for instance using simplified List Builder_pattern.

Why

Temporarily collecting items is something we do all the time in our daily life. The collector provides a simple mechanism that allows for a small number of items to be gathered for later use. By making it accessible on every page it truly becomes a handy 'cart' to put stuff in.

More Examples

The International Herald Tribune site makes different use of a favourites list. Here users can click on the icon next to an article to "clip" the article. By going to the "clippings" section in the top bar, users can manage their selected articles.

Use when

Users have several items to manage. They may be confronted directly with a long list or they may need to build up a new list. The list of items is typically ordered and could be quite long. Users want to have a complete overview of the list but the space to display it is limited. Users need to perform operations on them and see the results. Certain operations can be done on many items at the same time while other operations can only be done on one item at a time.

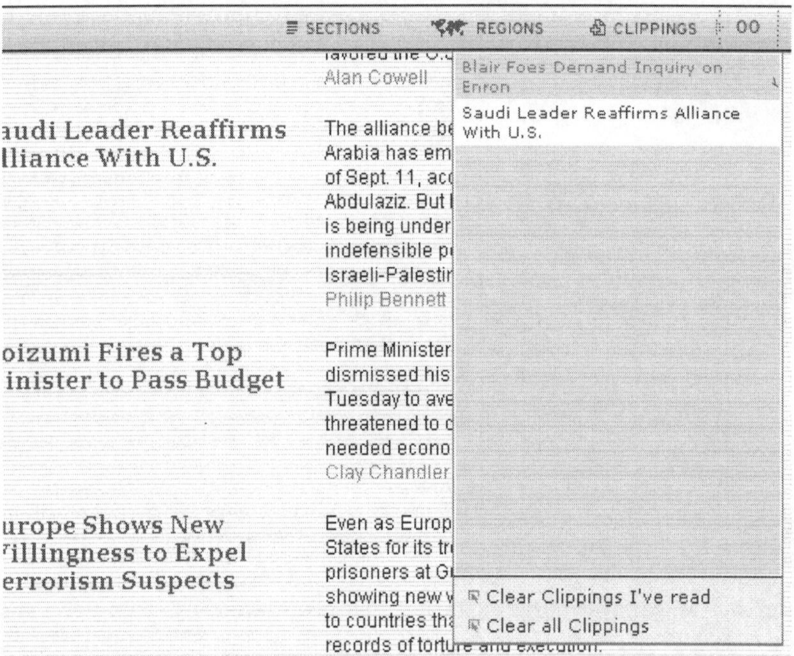

At CNet, articles can be 'saved' and are directly accessible again in a pull down list

List Builder pattern

http://www.welie.com/patterns/showPattern.php?patternID=list-builder

Problem

The users need to build up and manage a list of items

Solution

Present the total list and provide editing functionality next to it.

From www.bol.com

How

The users first see the total of items in the list. If the list is empty it says so, for example "no items added" or "empty". If **all** operations can be performed at the same time, use a **type A** solution, otherwise use a **type B** solution. If type A is chosen, provide the editing functionality below the list. If the list is likely to become longer than 10 items the functionality should be placed above the list. Type B solutions are typical when the functionality contains an "Edit..." function where some properties of the item can be changed.

Type A		Type B		
ColumnLabel		**ColumnLabel**		
☐ ItemName1		ItemName1	**Function1**	**Function2**
☐ ItemName2		ItemName2	**Function1**	**Function2**
☐ ItemName3		ItemName3	**Function1**	**Function2**
Function1	**Function2**			

When an item is added to the list, the view on the list shows the added item by highlighting it, as feedback to the users that the operation has been performed correctly. If necessary the list should "scroll" to the position of the new item in the list.

Why

By showing the overview first the users always know what the current status is. Editing functionality is then seen as "operations" on the current list.

More Examples

This example from the Hotmail service shows a type A solution.

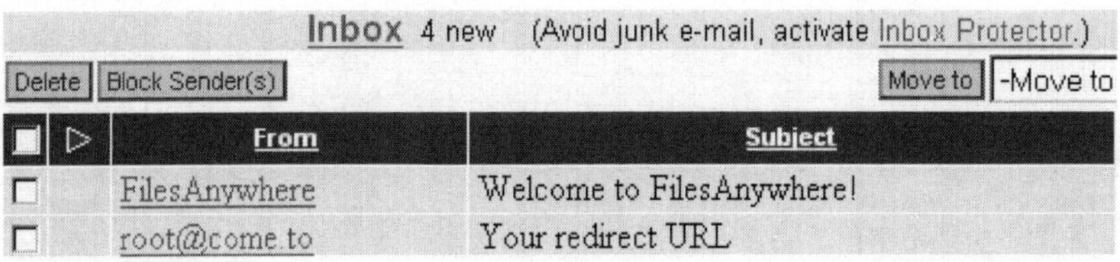

View pattern

http://www.welie.com/patterns/showPattern.php?patternID=view

Problem

Users need to manage a collection of objects

Solution

Create an overview of objects that together is meaningful to users

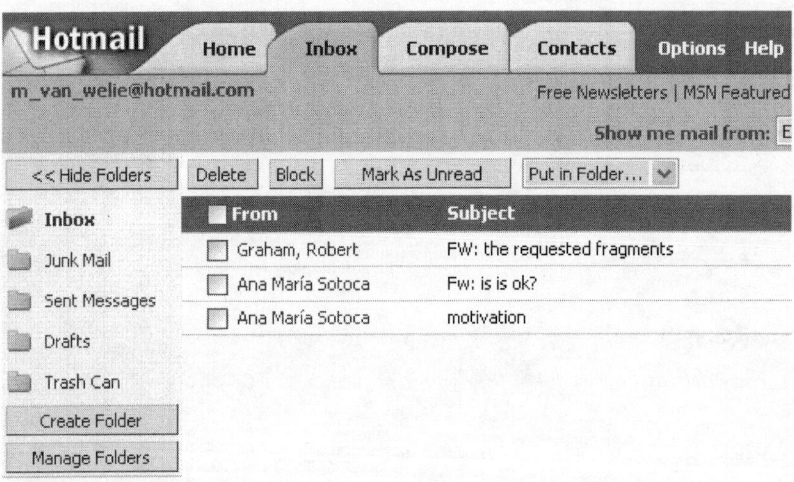

From www.hotmail.com

Use when

Typically used in a Web-based Application in which 'Views' are the main elements. Users need to manage objects such as emails, bank accounts, stocks, orders and so on.

How

A view usually is an overview of a set of objects, e.g. email messages, orders, appointments, products, image, . When views are editable, they may take the form of a List Builder or a list of thumbnails or a custom- designed overview. Views usually contain 'abbreviated' description of the objects themselves. These descriptions are usually clickable which results in a detailed view of the object. Closing the detailed view takes users back to the view itself. Views are typically placed in the Center Stage of the page. When views are very large, some form of Paging or Stepping can be used. Switching from one view to another is done using the Main Navigation.

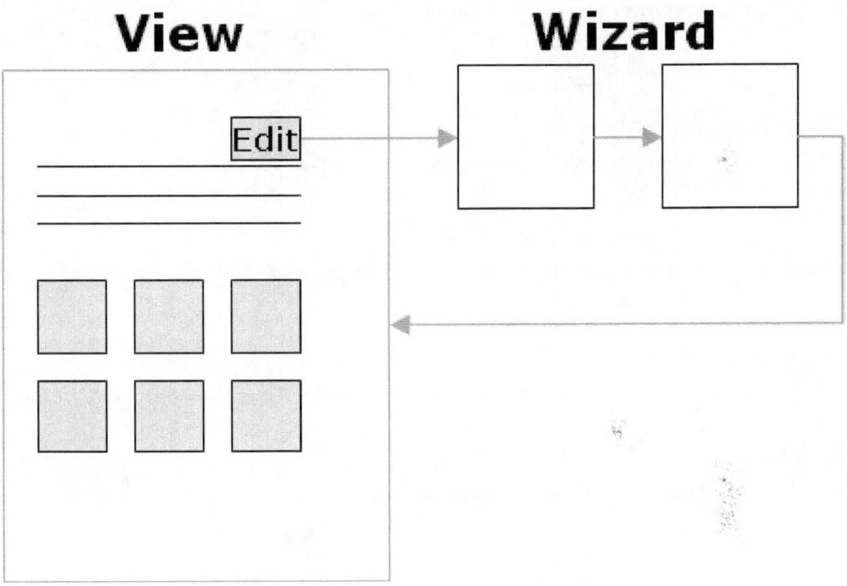

Typical behavior with forms consists of 'view-edit-return'. The user selects an item in the view and edits the detailed description using a Form and/or a Wizard. Once the editing is completed, the users is presented with the view again.

Why

A view is sort of a 'safe place' from which all kinds of 'management' functionality can be used. It gives users the overview they need and it is obvious how users can access the management functionality.

More Examples

At www.vodafone.nl can manage a collection of MMS-es. An overview is given from which users can 'copy', 'move', 'view', or 'delete' MMS-es.

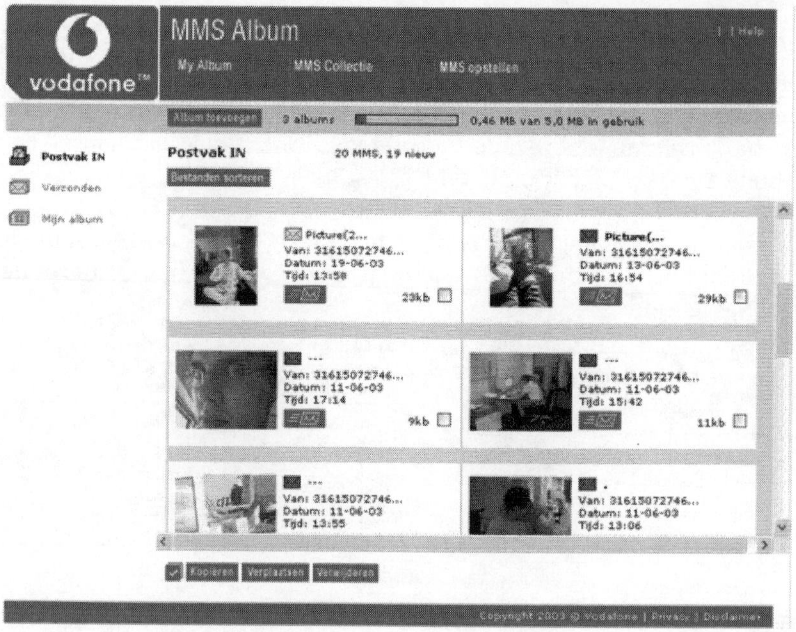

Search Box pattern

http://www.welie.com/patterns/showPattern.php?patternID=search

Problem

The users need to find an item or specific information.

Solution

Offer a search

From www.tucows.com

Use when

Any web site that already has primary navigation. User may want to search for an item in a category. User might want to further specify a query

How

* The search interface

Offer search functionality consisting of a search label, a keyword field, a filter if applicable and a "go" button. Pressing the return key has the same function as selecting the "go" button. Also provide Search Tips and examples in a separate page. A link to that page is placed next to the search functionality. The edit box for the search term is large enough to accommodate 3 typical user queries (typically around 20 characters). If the number of filters is more than 2, use a combobox for filter-selection, otherwise a radiobutton.

Search -- editbox -- **for/in** -- filter -- **Go button**

or just... -- editbox -- **Go button**

* Presenting search results

The search results are presented on a new page with clear label containing at least "Searchresults" or similar. The search function is repeated in the top-part of the page with the entered keywords, so that the users know what the keywords were.

The number of "hits" is reported and the list of search results is organized; sorted or rated with the best matches at the top. When there are more than 10 results use a Paging mechanism. Each search result shows a link to the item itself and a snippet of text to explain the item. Preferably that would a summary or abstract but can also be the first lines of text of the resulting item. The structure of a "result" typically shows:

1. Page Title
2. Description
3. Categorisation
4. URL, Size, Date

* Keyword matching

If more than one search term is used the search engine must handle them as follows: if no special separators are used (not including the space), the search is interpreted as an OR function, the results that match both terms are listed first. If special separators are used the search engine must be able to handle more than one convention. For example, sometimes the "AND/OR" separators are used but using a "+" or a "-", include and exclude, must also be handled correctly. The engine must also be able to handle spelling mistakes of at least one character.

Why

By using this setup the whole search becomes a sentence that reads like the search query.

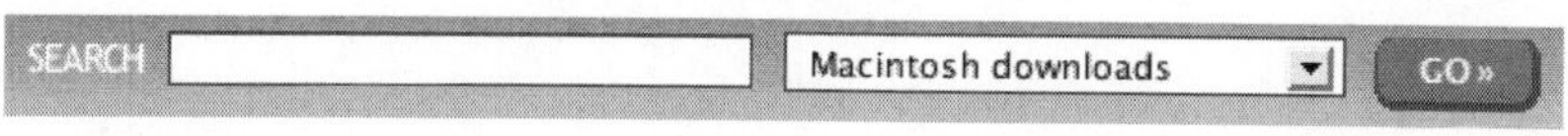

More Examples

In this example from tucows, the designers actually were able to make the search read like a sentence. Users can "download software package X for Win2000"....

Breadcrumbs pattern

http://www.welie.com/patterns/showPattern.php?patternID=crumbs

Problem

The users need to know where they are in a hierarchical structure and navigate back to higher levels in the hierarchy

Solution

Show the hierarchical path from the top level to the current page and make each step clickable

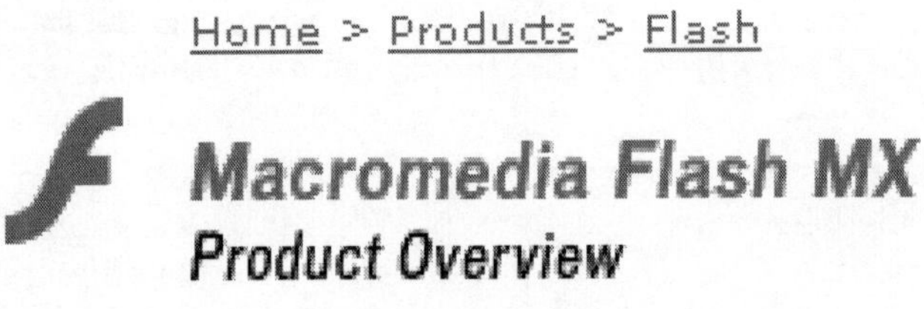

From www.macromedia.com

Use when

Sites with a large hierarchical information structure, typically more than 3 levels deep. Such sites are medium to large sized and include E- commerce Site, catalogs, Portal Site, Corporate Site etc. The site has got some type of Main Navigation that allows users to traverse the hierarchy. Users may want to jump several steps back instead of following the hierarchy. Users may be unfamiliar with the hierarchical structure of the information.

How

The path shows the location of the current page in the total information structure. Each level of the hierarchy is labeled and functions as a link to that level. The current page is marked in order to give the users feedback about where they are now and should not be a link. Don't use the current page name in the breadcrumb as the only way to show section title, add a title anyway.

Home > NextLevel > NextLevel > **Current page**

The path shows that a top-down path is traversed by using appropriate separators such as > or \ that suggest a downward motion. If the path becomes too long to fit in the designated place, some of the steps can be replaced by an ellipsis e.g. "...". The path is placed in a separate "bar" that preferably spans the entire width of the content area. It is placed close to the content area, preferably above the content area but below the page header.

Why

The bread crumbs show the users where they are and how the information is structured. Because users see the way the hierarchy is structured they can learn it more easily. By making each label a link, the users can quickly browse up the hierarchy. They take up minimal space on the page and leave most of the space for the real content. Breadcrumbs are not for primary navigation and should always be used together with a form of Main Navigation. Usability testing has shown that breadcrumbs are never cause trouble and that at least some people use them. So it is nearly always good to use them.

The name breadcrumb refers to the fairy-tale of Hansel and Gretel where a breadcrumb trail is used to mark the places Hansel has been. If the analogy were correct a breadcrumb should show the **history** of the users' actions rather than the **position** in the hierarchy. So the name breadcrumb is actually wrong...

More Examples

This example is taken from Sun's web site and shows the use of bread crumbs in product pages. The path from the top level is visible and the users can go to any of the other higher level product categories.

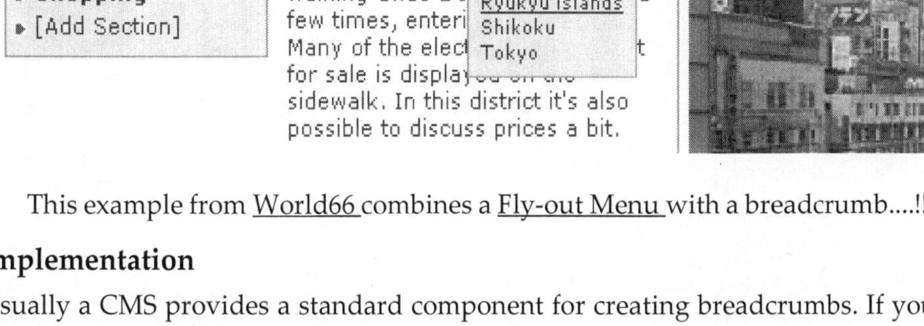

This example from World66 combines a Fly-out Menu with a breadcrumb....!!!

Implementation

Usually a CMS provides a standard component for creating breadcrumbs. If you are not using a CMS but you have a database driven site, you can easily write some custom code for it.

Form pattern

http://www.welie.com/patterns/showPattern.php?patternID=forms

Problem

Users need to provide personal information and send it to a service provider

Solution

Offer users a form with the necessary elements

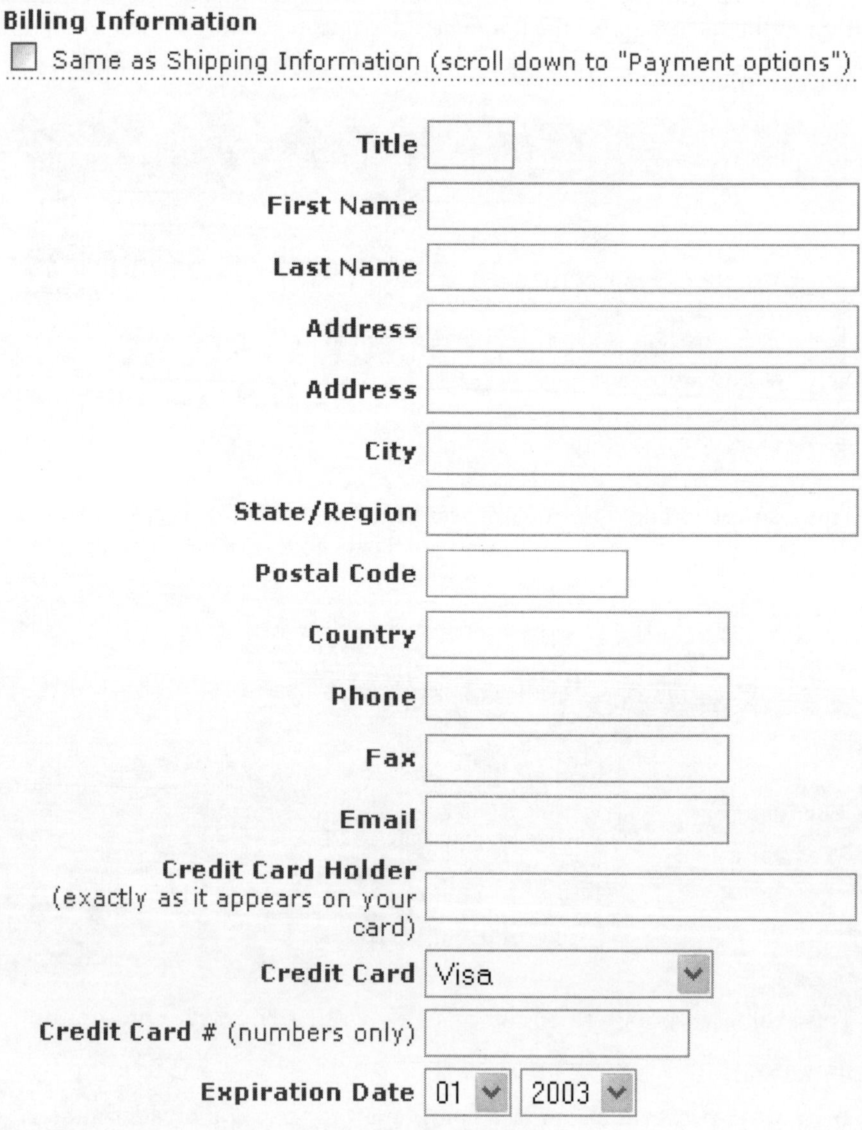

From www.iht.com

Use when

Users need to provide information. In many occasions, there can be a need for users to give information via a site. For example, when Booking a flight, using an Advanced Search, when doing a Registration on a site, doing some online tax calculations, or simply to Login. Giving particular information must be part of a user task or at least provide benefit for the end users.

How

A form is essentially a collection of labels and input fields on a single page. When designing forms, the following issues must be taken into account.

Wording. Make sure that users understand what you are asking from them. Realize that there are internationalization issues here, e.g. "state" is only for US, "title" can be easily misinterpreted. Give examples to re- enforce the meaning of the field. Put examples below or at the right of the input field. Use prompts sparely, adding more text also increases the chance that people won't read it. So keep any form of introduction text short, no more than a couple of lines.

Grouping and ordering. Place elements in a logical ordering and group fields that together describe an entity, e.g. name and address could form "personal information".

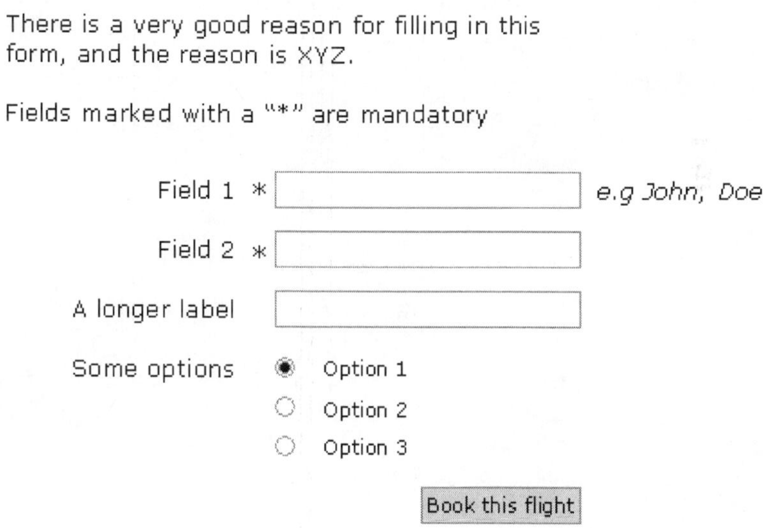

Basic Form *Wireframe*

Layout of label and input elements. Use grids, put the label left of the element or above it there are sever space limitations. Right align the label with the field so that label and field are always closely together. Both the labels and input elements must be aligned using Grid-based Layout. Design in one column only, avoid having multiple input elements on the same line. Only do that if an entity is sensibly split up in part for which you need separate input elements. The length of text input fields must be determined by the information that needs to be supplied. However, keep in mind that this can vary because of internationalization issues as well. A surname in the US is usually quite short (one or two words), but in Spain they use much longer surnames (three to six words is not uncommon).

Mandatory and optional fields. In general making a distinction between mandatory and optional fields is a bad idea. Users should never have to fill in anything that is not required for the task at hand. However, there are certainly exceptions where optional fields make sense. In such cases it is important that it is clear to the user how filling in these fields will benefit them. For example, so that recommendations can be improved or so that the service can be improved (supporting multiple shipping addresses). If you have mandatory fields AND optional fields, mark the mandatory fields with an asterisk "*". If the users submits the form but not all mandatory fields have been filled in, show a popup that says which fields (still) need to be filled in. Also add a privacy statement....?

Using the right input element It is important to use the right input element for a certain field. This depends on the number of options, single/multiple choice, and the sort of information that is required. For selecting elements from fixed sets use:

Single Choice from a fixed set: (e.g. number of guests,)

- less than 5 options: radio buttons
- 5-10 options: a list box
- more than 10 options, listbox or editbox or a special control

Multiple Choice from a fixed set: checkboxes

Alternatively, use edit boxes and check afterwards if the input has been interpreted correctly. For example www.ns.nl

Good defaults In order to speed up data entry, it is often good to use appropriate default values. However, do not use default values for sensitive fields such as "gender".

Preventing input errors Consider Constraint Input to make sure users cannot provide invalid input. Otherwise, validate the data and give an Input Error Message. Be aware that validation is not always 100 percent waterproof, e.g. it is simply not possible to verify that an email address is valid by checking it syntactically.

Keyboard navigation Filling in forms is tedious and it goes much faster if you can use the keyboard to go from one field to the other. Make sure that the TAB key can be used to do this and that the ENTER key is a shortcut for "confirm", submit, save etc. When the page is loaded the cursor should be already in the first field and it should have the focus so that users can start typing straight away. Using the tab key users go to the next item in the form, i.e. the element to the right or below the current element.

Why

Filling in forms is error-prone and things must be made as clear as possible for users. Using the right labels, widgets and defaults all contribute to the successful completion of the form.

More Examples

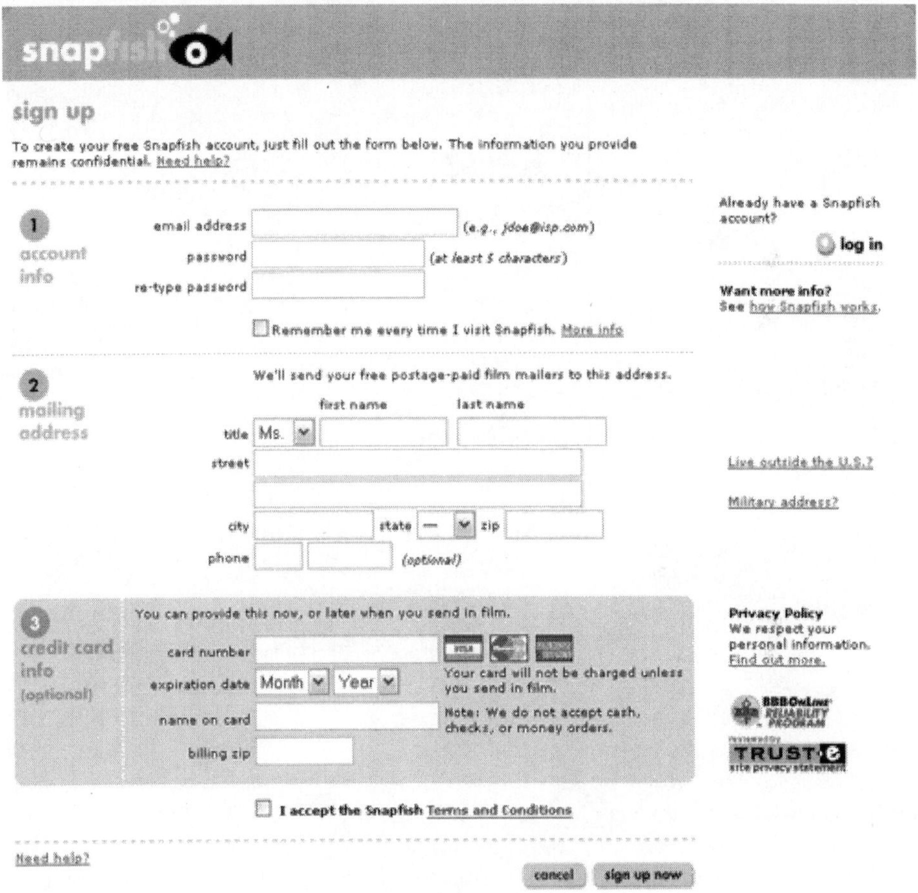

Constraint Input pattern

http://www.welie.com/patterns/showPattern.php?patternID=format

Problem

The user needs to supply the application with data but may be unfamiliar with which data is required or what syntax to use.

Solution

Only allow the user to enter data in the correct syntax.

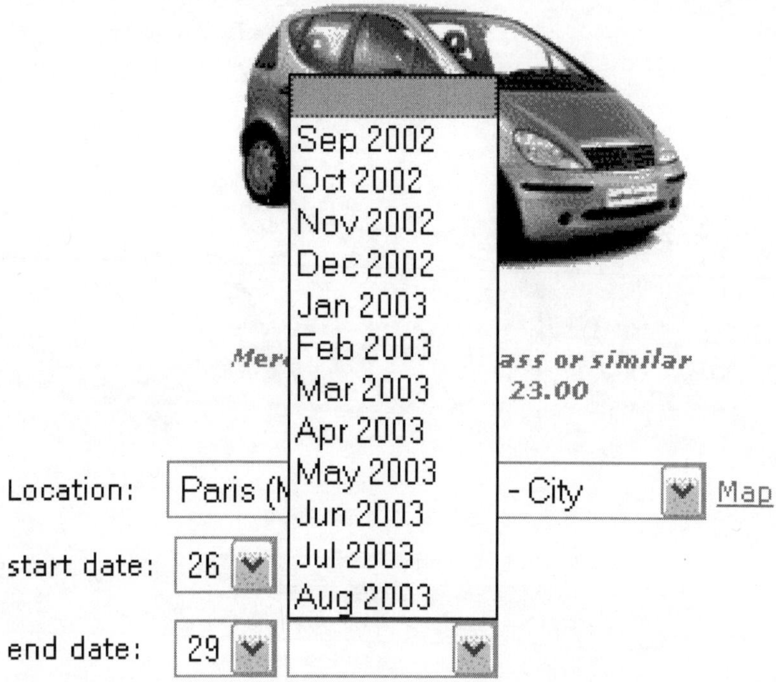

From www.easycar.com

Use when

Any system where structured data must be entered. Data such as dates, room numbers, social security numbers or serial numbers are usually structured. The exact syntax used for such data may vary per country or product. When the data is entered using an unexpected syntax, the data cannot be used by the application. The user may be familiar with the data but may not know the exact required syntax. The user strives for entry speed but also wants it to be entered correctly. Cultural conventions determine what the user expects the syntax to be. For example, dd/mm/yy is usual in Europe while mm/dd/yy is used in the United States.

How

Present the user with fields for each data element of the structure. Label each field with the name of the data unit if there can be doubt about the semantics of the field. The field does not allow incorrect data to be entered. Avoid fields where users can type free text. Additionally, explain the syntax with an example or a description of the format.

Provide sound defaults for required fields, fields that are not required should be avoided or otherwise marked as optional. When optional fields are used, the consequences for the user must be explained.

Why

The main idea is avoid entering incorrect data by not making it possible to enter wrong data. By showing the required format the chances of errors are reduced because the user is given complete knowledge. However, because the user now has to give multiple data inputs instead of one, more time is needed to enter the data. The solution reduces the number or errors and increases satisfaction but the performance time may go down.

More Examples

This snapshot is from the date selection at Expedia.com. Entering the date is spit up in three input areas. Each of the input fields allows only valid entries. Entering an invalid date becomes impossible.

Processing Page pattern

http://www.welie.com/patterns/showPattern.php?patternID=processing- page

Problem

Users need feedback that their action is being performed but may take a while to complete

Solution

Provide a feedback page with animation

From www.british-airways.co.uk

Use when

You are designing a site where slow back-end systems are connected to. Some requests to the back-end system may take 5 to 30 seconds to complete and the users need some feedback telling them that their request is being performed and that they'll have to wait a bit. Only use this pattern when it is not possible to speed up the back-end processing time. Typically, a Travel Site using this when flight-availability is being looked-up. It also occurs frequently in a Web-based Application

How

Provide information about the reason for the slow response so that users can have understanding of the problem. Also add an animation or real progress feedback so that users get a sense of continuity or progress.

Why

Although it would be best to provide real progress feedback, this is often not technically possible in a web environment. Providing this type of feedback is the least that should be done for users who need to wait.

More Examples

Homepage pattern

http://www.welie.com/patterns/showPattern.php?patternID=homepage

Problem

Users need to understand if they are at the right place, and if so, how they can move on to accomplish their task at your site

Solution

Create a home-page that introduces the site to users and that helps them to get on their way on the site

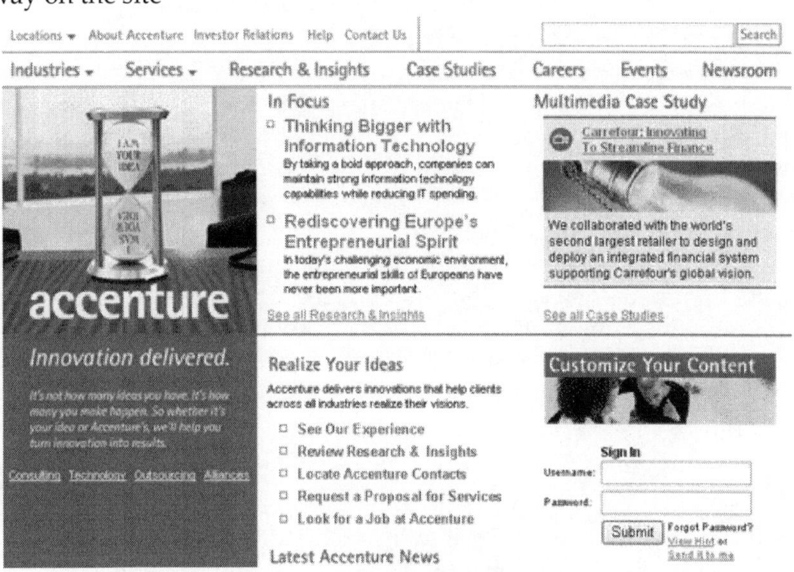

From www.accenture.com

Use when

Every website has a home-page. It is like the front door of your house. For most users, it will be the starting point for navigating through your site. Typically, the home-page will be your most requested page of the entire site.

How

The home-page is an important page, it is the front door of your site. Users that found your site intentionally need feedback to confirm that they are in the right place. For other users that don't know you very well, you need to make clear who is behind the site and what there is to find. The home-page is often packed with stuff, but although it is ok to indicate what the site is about, putting a lot of stuff on the page is not always good. When links are buried in a Christmas tree of page elements, users will not notice it. The home-page must balance navigation, branding, content, and promotion elements. Be careful not to make your page too full, users can only notice a couple of things at a time.

On a more conceptual level, the home-page has three functions:

Introduction The site must be introduced, both its purpose and identity. Users must know almost immediately what the site is for and who is behind it. This can be done in several ways. For example using a tag-line or pay-off. A tag-line is a short "one-liner" that makes it clear what the site or company is about. Identity can also be established using photography or by showing the company's logo, If identity cannot be established well visually, you can always add a short explanation. Animation can also be used to literally show who you are and what you do. For very well known brands, the introduction can be very short, just a logo and nothing else, e.g. nike. For unknown brands or sites with a highly specialistic purpose, a textual introduction is best. Another aspect of establishing an identity is having an About Us reachable from the Meta Navigation.

Entrance . Users seldom find what they need on the home-page. Therefore, the site's Main Navigation must be clearly shown. On the home-page so that users know where to get started. Besides the usual menu bar, you can also use special home-page navigation such as a Doormat Navigation. Other important elements include a Search Box, Login if needed and so on. For international site a Language Selector or a Country Selector. Next to the navigation, a home-page often also reveals so content from somewhere within the site. This can help to make users understand what the site is about and in some cases even **Announcement** On most sites, things happen and the site changes. The home-page is to place to communicate what is new, what is going on, new promotions and so on. Use a News Box for general news, or special news blocks for things like Case Study.

Which exact elements are part of the home-page highly depends on the site. It will be different for every single site out there. Other less important issues in home-page design include having a proper title defined, and a nice simple/ guessable URL.

The home-page is a special page. It is therefore quite normal that it has a slightly different layout than the other pages of the site. Nonetheless, some level of consistency should be retained so that the home-page and other pages clearly "belong" to the same site!

Why

The home-page is all about making a first impression.

More Examples

This example from www.nike.com is a good example of a very "empty" page. The Nike brand is so strong that they don't need to spend much words to establish identity. The navigation is very clear and users easily find their way.

Web-based Application pattern

http://welie.com/patterns/showPattern.php?patternID=application

Problem

Users need to perform complex tasks on a web site

Solution

Structure the site around 'views' and allow users to work inside views

Use when

Users have several items to manage. They may be confronted directly with a long list or they may need to build up a new list. The list of items is typically ordered and could be quite long. Users want to have a complete overview of the list but the space to display it is limited. Users need to perform operations on them and see the results. Certain operations can be done on many items at the same time while other operations can only be done on one item at a time.

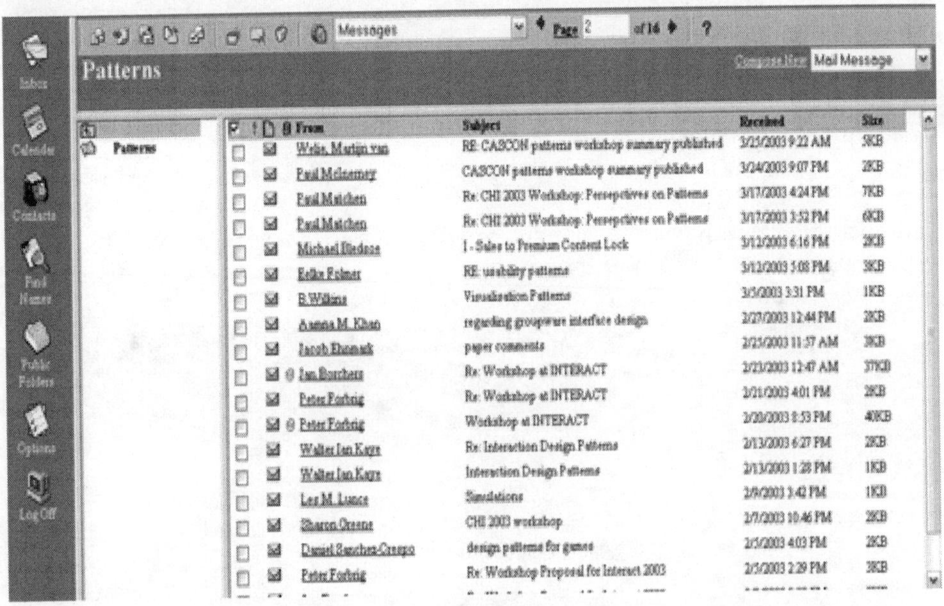

Microsoft Outlook Web Access

Use when

The site is for 'doing' things rather than finding information. Users can perform complex tasks such as reading and writing emails, placing orders, managing a bank-account. In most cases there are 'objects' involved that belong to the users which the users need to create, change, delete or update. A web-based application is an application that could just as well be a normal application. It now just runs in a web browser.

How

Web-based applications are based on Views for showing the objects and Form for changing them. The view provides a "safe" place where the users always return to after doing something using a Form or Wizard. The views are usually lists or tables that allow the display of information to be controlled. For example, using a Table Sorter or Table Filter. When tables are being used, consider Alternating Row Colors for making them better scannable. In applications such as a Content Management System, Tree controls are also widely used.

Web-based applications are often personal and therefore require users to Login. The information shown and the functionality that is accessible will depend on the user's identity or 'role'. That also means that not every users will see the same views or data per view. In some cases, users can use a demo account to see what the application looks like before commencing Registration.

Since web-based applications can be quite complex there is often help information or a Frequently Asked Questions (FAQ) as part of Meta Navigation. Other elements in the meta navigation are often 'logout', 'home', 'feedback' and so on.

A web-based application usually has a simple navigation mechanism that allows users to switch between views. A simple horizontal/vertical menu or Double Tab Navigation will usually suffice. The views are labeled based on the objects rather than the actions. The actions will be present in the view itself. However, in practice, some actions such as "compose email" are so important that they will be part of the navigation as well.

Why

Views contain the objects of interest and the view should therefore also be label according to the objects rather than the actions. Structuring the web-based application mainly on views makes it easy for users to understand what they can do and how to interact with it.

More Examples

This is an example of a Dutch online banking application. A simple horizontal menu with Fly-out Menu is used. The main actions are done using Form such as this one:

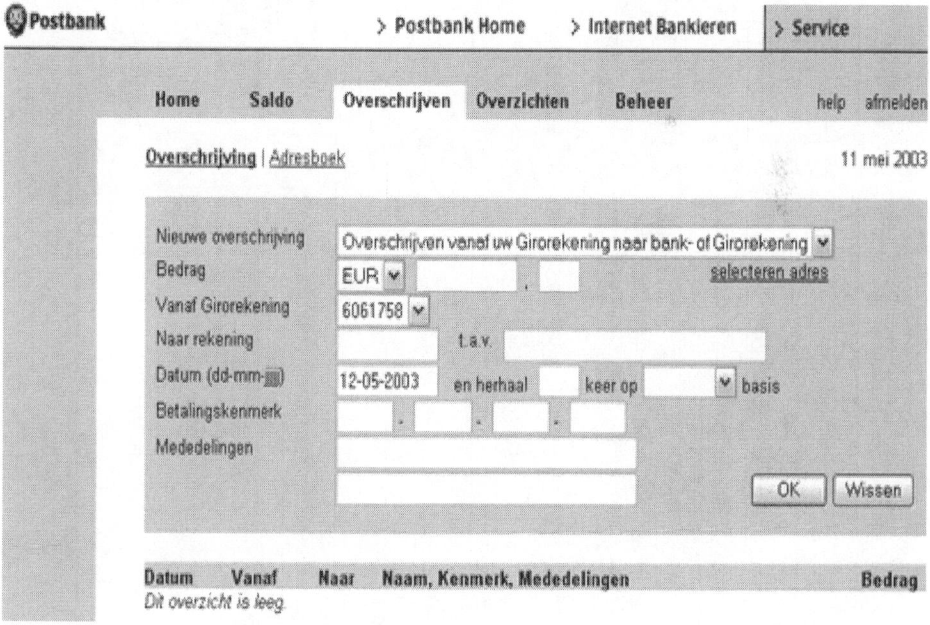

This example is from OpenCMS, an open source CMS. It uses many types of views that each show a different aspect of the website:

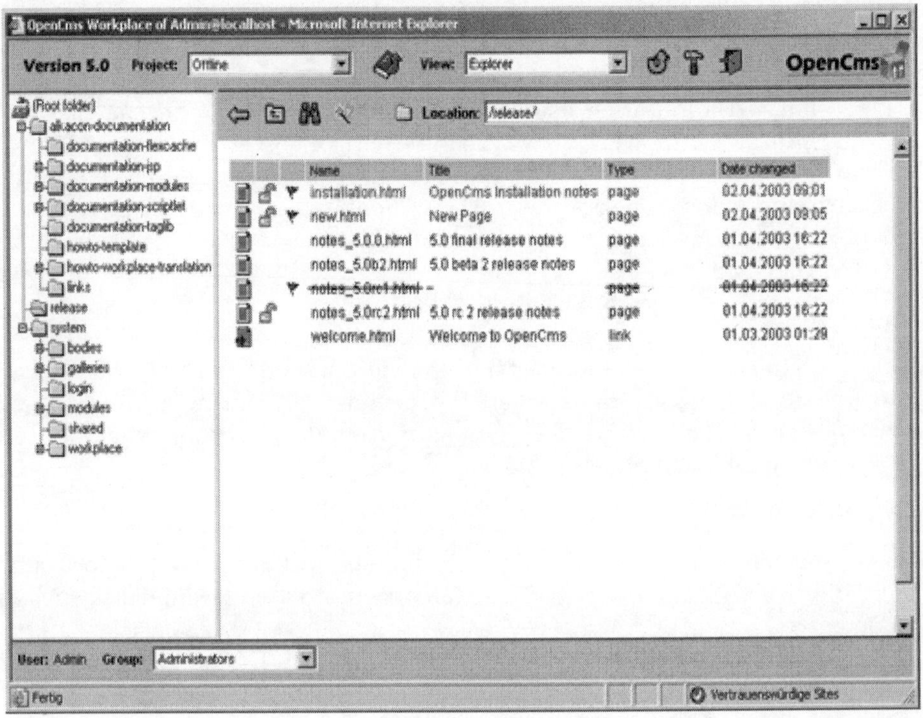
OpenCms Workplace of Admin@localhost - Microsoft Internet Explorer
Version 5.0
Project: Offline
View: Explorer
OpenCms
(Root folder)
alk.acon-documentation
documentation-flexcache
documentation-jsp
documentation-modules
documentation-scriptlet
documentation-taglib
howto-template
howto-workplace-translation
links
release
system
bodies
galleries
login
modules
shared
workplace
Location: /release/
Name
Title
Type
Date changed
installation.html
OpenCms Installation notes
page
02.04.2003 09:01
new.html
New Page
page
02.04.2003 09:05
notes_5.0.0.html
5.0 final release notes
page
01.04.2003 16:22
notes_5.0b2.html
5.0 beta 2 release notes
page
01.04.2003 16:22
notes_5.0rc1.html
page
01.04.2003 16:22
notes_5.0rc2.html
5.0 rc 2 release notes
page
01.04.2003 16:22
welcome.html
Welcome to OpenCms
link
01.03.2003 01:29
User: Admin
Group: Administrators
Fertig
Vertrauenswürdige Sites

Index